REPRODUCTION, KIN AND CLIMATE CRISIS

Making Bushfire Babies

Celia Roberts, Mary Lou Rasmussen,
Louisa Allen and Rebecca Williamson

D1613193

BRISTOL
UNIVERSITY
PRESS

First published in Great Britain in 2023 by

Bristol University Press
University of Bristol
1–9 Old Park Hill
Bristol
BS2 8BB
UK
t: +44 (0)117 374 6645
e: bup-info@bristol.ac.uk

Details of international sales and distribution partners are available at bristoluniversitypress.co.uk

British Library Cataloguing in Publication Data
A catalogue record for this book is available from the British Library

ISBN 978-1-5292-2684-3 hardcover
ISBN 978-1-5292-2685-0 paperback
ISBN 978-1-5292-2686-7 ePub
ISBN 978-1-5292-2687-4 ePdf

The right of Celia Roberts, Mary Lou Rasmussen, Louisa Allen and Rebecca Williamson to be
identified as authors of this work has been asserted by them in accordance with the Copyright,
Designs and Patents Act 1988.

Cover design: Lyn Davies Design
Front cover image: Getty/Andrew Merry
Bristol University Press uses environmentally responsible print partners.
Printed and bound in Great Britain by CPI Group (UK) Ltd, Croydon, CR0 4YY

FSC
www.fsc.org
MIX
Paper | Supporting
responsible forestry
FSC® C013604

Contents

List of Figures and Table

Figures

Table

Notes on the Figures

We wish to acknowledge that, though many of the figures included in this book are of a low resolution, they are integral to the authors' content. The decision to publish these figures was made on the understanding that these are the best versions available. For those reading in digital formats, it will be possible to zoom in on any image to achieve greater clarity.

We also wish to acknowledge that the text describing some of the images included in this book refers to colours in the images, despite the images being printed in black and white in the print version of this book. The decision to retain these colour descriptions was made in order to provide greater visual clarity to readers. The images are available in full colour in the electronic version of this book; furthermore, a PDF containing all the colour images in their original form can be viewed at: https://bristoluniv ersitypress.co.uk/reproduction-kin-and-climate-crisis.

Notes on the Authors

Louisa Allen is Professor in the Faculty of Education and Social Work at the University of Auckland. She specializes in research in the areas of sexualities, reproduction, gender and schooling. These areas are examined through the lenses of queer, feminist poststructural and feminist new materialist frameworks. She is interested in the use of innovative research methodologies such as sensory methods to engage hard-to-reach populations and know the world differently. Currently she is Editor-in-Chief with Mary Lou Rasmussen of the *Palgrave Encyclopedia of Sexuality Education*, and her latest book is entitled *Breathing Life into Sexuality Education* (2021, Palgrave).

Mary Lou Rasmussen is Professor in the Research School of Social Sciences at the Australian National University. Their research focuses on building transdisciplinary understandings of reproduction, sexuality and gender across diverse lifeworlds. Rasmussen is associate editor of the journal *Sex Education*. She is also Editor-in-Chief, with Louisa Allen, of the *Encyclopedia of Sexuality Education* (Palgrave) and has co-authored *Becoming Subjects: A Study of Sexualities and Secondary Schooling* (Routledge, 2006), *Progressive Sexuality Education: The Conceits of Secularism* (Routledge, 2016) and *Faiths, Freedoms and Futures: Teenage Australians on Religion, Sexuality and Diversity* (Bloomsbury, 2021).

Celia Roberts is Professor in the School of Sociology at the Australian National University. Working in feminist technoscience studies and social studies of health, biomedicine and sexuality, she is the author of several books, including *Messengers of Sex: Hormones, Biomedicine Feminism* (Cambridge University Press, 2007), *Puberty in Crisis: The Sociology of Early Sexual Development* (Cambridge University Press, 2017) and, with Adrian Mackenzie and Maggie Mort, *Living Data: Making Sense of Health Biosensing* (Bristol University Press, 2019).

Rebecca Williamson is Research Officer in the School of Sociology at the Australian National University and a research associate at the Social Policy Research Centre at the University of New South Wales. She specializes in ethnography and qualitative research. Her research interests and published work encompass the topics of maternal health and embodiment, spatialities of care, and migration and urban diversity. She has been involved in several projects examining the impact of the Australian bushfires and the COVID-19 pandemic on vulnerable populations and community wellbeing.

Acknowledgements

Three of us live and work on Ngunnawal and Ngambri Country, Australia, and the other in Aotearoa-New Zealand. Some of the research documented here took place on Ngunnawal and Ngambri country, and some on lands of the Yuin Nation. We pay our respects to the elders of these lands, and of Australia's First Nations more broadly, acknowledging that sovereignty was never ceded and that reconciliation is ongoing and unfinished business. This book describes the devastation of vast tracts of land and argues that this has close ties to the unlawful and violent colonization of this country. It also pays tribute to the enduring knowledges of First Nations people, particularly in relation to the significance of fire-related practices in caring for country. These knowledges are essential to our collective ongoing survival.

We would like to acknowledge the generosity of our participants who gave us their time and energy during a very difficult period. We hope they feel we have listened carefully and treated their stories with the respect and care they deserve. We learnt so much from our conversations with them.

We would also like to thank our colleagues in the Mother and Child 2020 project at the Australian National University (ANU), especially Professor Christopher Nolan, for including us in their study of the impact of bushfires on pregnant women and babies. We have benefited enormously from participating in discussions about the biomedical, psychological and maternity care elements of that research.

The research in this book was funded by a Cross-College grant provided by the Research School of the Social Sciences, ANU. We are grateful to the College of Health and Medicine, and particularly our colleagues, Professor Paul Dugdale and Professor Sotiris Vardoulakis, who agreed to be named on our bid and helped us shape our research and understand our findings.

In 2022, Celia and Mary Lou spent time at Silverwattle, a beautiful Quaker retreat centre on Lake George (Weereewa) near Canberra. We would like to thank our hosts for a peaceful and convivial time, which made the framing of the book's themes so much easier.

Finally, we like to thank our colleagues, families and friends for their support and encouragement during this project. It was so important to discuss our ideas with colleagues around the world and we thank them for their feedback and responses. Special thanks to Professor Catherine Waldby, who read each chapter draft and provided exceptionally helpful feedback.

Interleave 1

Flying to Canberra, December 2019: Louisa's story

In early December I set out from Aotearoa-New Zealand for a conference in Canberra, where Mary Lou and I were to present a paper entitled 'Crisis, sexuality education, reproduction and kinship'. My journey involved a stopover in Sydney, where the smoke was inescapable. I remember my shock as the plane landed and there was no difference between the colour of the sky and the tarmac – both were grey. This didn't look anything like an overcast day; this shade of grey spoke of something being terribly wrong. As I peered from the plane window, I also noticed that ground staff working on the tarmac were wearing masks, which at this pre-COVID-19 time was a highly unusual occurrence. After landing and hearing the usual announcements about disembarking, there was an additional notice reassuring passengers that the smell of smoke, which had now penetrated the plane, was not something burning onboard, but caused by the fires outside. I didn't feel reassured; I remember thinking this is just awful, this beautiful city is being smothered in smoke, how in the world are people living in this? In the course of transferring to the flight for Canberra, I had to exit the international terminal building. The first blast of air as the sliding glass doors opened was a shock, even though I'd registered that the smoke was everywhere. My first gulp was like standing by a bonfire on Guy Fawkes Night without the ability to retreat from the stronger fumes. The combined heat and smoke made my eyes water and I rushed to get back into the air-conditioned and comparatively smokeless sanctuary of the national terminal.

Having now smelt the smoke and experienced it (albeit on a very small scale), even this did not prepare me for the view from the plane as we travelled south to Canberra. As I looked out the window, I could see lines of fire moving through the bush for kilometres upon end.

Interleave Figure 1.1: Driving towards the fires in Canberra, January 2020

Source: participant photograph

Thick clouds of smoke hung over areas where the fire was thickest and I remember thinking this is truly an environmental tragedy. What amazed me though was that while I was transfixed by the fires, unable to pull my gaze from the window, no one else in the crowded plane was paying them any attention. I wanted to stand up and shout 'My god, the ground is burning! Stop reading your paper – we need to do something!', but for everyone else, these fires had become part of daily life.

Reproducing in Climate Crisis

In the Southern Hemisphere summer of 2019–2020, three of us were living in Canberra, Australia's inland capital city, and the other in Auckland, Aotearoa-New Zealand. Like many parts of Australia, Canberra was in the grip of a long drought: the grass was brown, kangaroos had moved down from the mountains into the suburbs to search for food, and the heat was increasingly intense. Canberra's famous street and park trees were dying and the air crackled with dryness. The garden tanks were empty and the forest ponds had dried up. Dedicated citizens set up water stations for wildlife throughout local bushland, recording their activities on digital platforms so that others could join in. Across the Tasman, Aotearoa-New Zealand was experiencing its fourth warmest year on record, with hills usually covered in lush green grass left brown and the earth bearing large crevices and cracks. This especially hot summer season was also extremely dry, leaving the entire North Island in one of the most severe meteorological droughts ever recorded.

The Australian 'fire season' started early. Well before Christmas, bushfire reports became part of daily life. We Australians downloaded the 'Fires Near Me' app, and before travelling anywhere checked our route and destination. The nightly news was filled with images of smoke, flame and heroic, ash-covered firefighters. The scale of the fires was hard to comprehend. Altogether approximately one third of Australia's forests were burnt – more than 8 million hectares of vegetation across the south-east of the continent, an event unprecedented in the last 200 years (Godfree et al, 2021). The fires burned across South Australia, Victoria, Canberra and New South Wales (NSW). Over the summer, the Australian fires became global news. The *Berliner Morgenpost*, for example, developed an interactive map to allow viewers to compare the extent of the burned area to any region in the world.[1] Video images of devastation and survival flooded the internet. In one memorable snippet, a koala staggered from a 42°C forest, coming across a group of cyclists. Reaching for a man's water bottle, it desperately drank, standing up on its hind legs to lean on the bike. Such behaviour from an iconically shy animal was both touching and appalling.[2]

Humans and animals tried to escape the smoke and flames, but diverse habitats were devastated. Humans worked to save their farms and houses as well as the forests. Many were unable to: over 3,000 homes were lost, mostly in NSW. Vast quantities of rural fencing and buildings were also destroyed. Thousands of local and international firefighters volunteered to help save towns, farms and forests. Thirty-three people, including nine firefighters, died as a direct result of the fires (Hitch, 2020). Another 445 deaths were later confirmed to be indirectly related to the fires and smoke. Authorities issued instructions to thousands of holidaymakers travelling in the coastal areas who then spent long hours in the ensuing traffic jams or following significant detours to avoid the fires and return to the relative safety of cities, often with their pets. People living on the fringes of bushland rescued animals and tried to provide them with food and shelter. A group of surviving koalas from Canberra's Namadgi National Park were moved into a special research facility at the Australian National University (ANU). In total, approximately 3 billion nonhuman animals died: 143 million mammals, 2.46 billion reptiles, 180 million birds and 51 million frogs (Australian Institute of Health and Welfare, 2020; Richards et al, 2020; World Wide Fund for Nature Australia, 2020). It was a frightening and intense time, full of anxiety, grief and dread. Almost nowhere felt safe. We were not safe.

Seventeen years earlier, in 2003, Canberra had experienced an intense urban blaze, ignited by out-of-control fires in surrounding national parks and pine plantations in close proximity to Canberra suburbs. Four hundred and seventy homes were lost and four people died. This part of the city is now rebuilt and replanted – the National Arboretum covers part of this landscape. Since this time, Canberrans have been particularly wary of fires: we understand that fires do not only happen 'out there', in the bush, but can enter cities, especially our 'Bush Capital' surrounded by dry hills, farmland and national parks. In January 2020, Namadgi National Park to the southwest of the city was ignited during a military helicopter landing (part of a reconnaissance exercise for the firefighting effort) (see Figure 1.1). This enormous blaze ultimately consumed 80 per cent of the Park. Citizens in that part of the city – including Rebecca and her family – readied themselves to leave, but ultimately the fire did not enter the urban areas. Fires were also close to the northeast of the city. Flying in from Melbourne or Aotearoa-New Zealand, three of us witnessed the long curling line of flames and smoke burning through the forests and farmland that divide Canberra from the sea. In late January, a fire started near Canberra Airport (10 kilometres to the east of the city centre), but was contained after several days.

Figure 1.1: Looking towards Parliament House, Canberra and showing Namadgi National Park on fire

Source: participant photograph

By mid-December 2019, the city was enveloped in smoke from surrounding fires. On some days, Canberra – known as a city of clear skies and clean air – had the worst air quality in the world. Particulate levels were 23 times the hazardous rating (ABC, 2020). Visibility was shockingly low – people's photographs, often shared online, demonstrated the ghostly absence of iconic views (see Figure 1.2).

The sun disappeared into a shimmering yellow and grey that sometimes turned into a deep browny-red. Wind drove smoke in at strange times – the wonderful desert-like cool night air that makes the hot Canberra summers bearable instead brought intense smoke. Doors and windows had to be closed and sealed, and parents were advised to keep children inside. Childcare centres and holiday camps closed. Just as the world started to hear about a strange new virus appearing in Wuhan, China, most Canberrans went into voluntary lockdown. Some started wearing masks.

But lockdown did not mean safety. The smoke kept coming in, and the fires continue to pose a threat. All of us kept our most precious belongings packed and we were repeatedly asked to be 'fire ready'. We had to keep on top of the news, watch the 'Fires Near Me' app and have a clear plan about when we would leave our homes and where we would go. The only places to go were local sports grounds or schools; it was not possible to escape

Figure 1.2: 'Where is our Parliament?' Participant photograph highlighting the severe lack of visibility and making a political statement about the absence of governmental action during the fires and in relation to climate change more broadly, taken a short distance from Parliament House, Canberra

Source: participant photograph

Canberra to places that were usually easy to drive to – the coast (the fires were terrible there) or Sydney (the roads were lined with fires and sometimes closed). If you did not have the resources to fly and relocate, the only option was to stay put and wait it out. The 'Fires Near Me' screenshot given in Figure 1.3 shows the extent of fires near Canberra in January. The app uses coloured diamonds to indicate the level of danger of each fire in a time-sensitive fashion. Rebecca sent this image to her family in Aotearoa-New Zealand to convey the seriousness, scale and number of fires in the region.

Situating the 2019–2020 Australian megafires

How is it possible to make sense of this devastation? Many commentators have remarked that these fires constituted a 'season like no other' (Rowland, 2021: 12). During the fires (and since), two partially contradictory explanatory discourses circulated in popular accounts and everyday conversation. The first, which we call the 'nothing to see here' discourse, figures the fires as typical Australia. This explanation points to the undeniable fact that Australia has long experienced bushfires. Proponents of this account argue that,

Figure 1.3: Screenshot of fires surrounding Canberra on the 'Fires Near Me' app

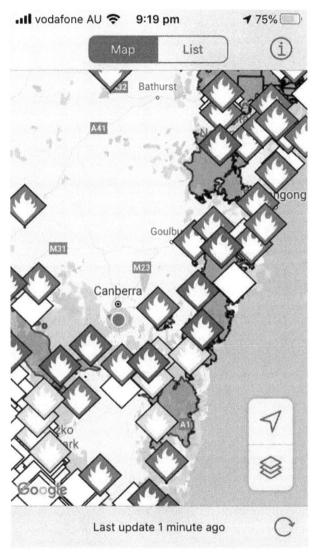

Source: taken by Rebecca; permission to reproduce this image was granted by the Royal Firefighting Service of NSW

although severe, fires are to be expected in Australia and consequently that this conflagration, while spectacular in its breadth and destruction, should not be seen as atypical in Australian climate history. The second discourse, while concurring that Australia is a bushfire country, instead argues that the 2019–2020 fires were extraordinary and clear evidence of global climate change, or what First Nations fire expert Victor Steffenson (2020: 183) calls 'environmental mess'. We call this the 'climate change' discourse. In this account, the intensity of the fires was attributed to the long preceding drought, itself attributable to increased temperatures, caused by human activities such as the burning of fossil fuels. Both discourses articulate political allegiances. The first position was held by the conservative Morrison government (then-Prime Minister Scott Morrison was notoriously absent, holidaying with his family in Hawaii during the initial weeks of the fires; he also made several serious political blunders, famously forcing a distressed pregnant resident from a severely fire-affected town to shake his hand on camera). The second position aligns with the liberal, environmentalist left.[3]

It seems to us that neither discourse persuasively accounts for the 2019–2020 fires. While both acknowledge the historical significance of fire to Australia, neither adequately articulates the significance of that history to our current predicament. In our view, the history of fire in Australia and the current state of our country are biosocial phenomena that must engage with Aboriginal practices of fire management which pre-date colonization and continue to the present day. This book is an attempt to describe particular aspects of this biosociality – those relating to reproduction, care and kinship – as it unfolded in Australia in 2019–2020. This story has implications for many other places recently affected by out-of-control fires – including California, Spain, Brazil, India and Greece – and, in less direct ways, places affected by other disasters such as flooding and hurricanes. How might feminist social scientists contribute to making sense of these calamities and their impacts on human and nonhuman individuals, families and communities as entwined events?

The Pyrocene

In this book, we begin our exploration of the biosociality of bushfires by engaging with environmental historian Stephen Pyne's notion of the 'Pyrocene'. Across a range of publications, Pyne uses this term to highlight the significance of humans' relation to fire in the planet's current ecological predicament. The term is in many ways very similar to terms more commonly used in social theory and sociology, such as the Anthropocene (popularized by scientist Paul Crutzen and widely used in the geo and social sciences and humanities) and the Capitalocene (popularized by political geographer Jason Moore [2017] and feminist technoscience studies scholar Donna Haraway [2017], among others).[4] In each case, these terms describe our current epoch as one in which geological strata, and thus our entire global environment, have been shaped by human activities. The terms are used to make claims that the previous geological epoch, the Holocene (dating from 10,000 years ago and characterized by the retreat of glaciers, the migration of many species and the rising dominance of humans) is now over.

Such claims are scientifically contested. Among those who agree that the Holocene has ended, there is also serious debate about timing. Some date the Anthropocene or Capitalocene from the Industrial Revolution, some focus on the rise of human agriculture 12,000 years ago, while others focus on the development and deployment of the atomic bomb. Other theorists write of the Plantationocene, highlighting the historical significance of colonization and slavery to our current biopolitical situation (see, for example, Haraway et al, 2015).

In contrast to many Anthropocene geologists, social scientists and humanities scholars, Pyne argues that the Pyrocene does not come after the Holocene, but rather is a better term for the entire period since the Pleistocene (Ice Age). Our era, he argues, is shaped by fire rather than ice: 'the Holocene is the Anthropocene. Since the last glacial epoch, warming has been continuous, with minor blips, and throughout those millennia humanity's firepower has made it more and more dominant. Today, there is no aspect of the Earth that we have not altered' (Pyne, 2019a: 187).

The vastness of scale Pyne evokes here arguably runs the risk of ignoring the 'great acceleration' in human geological impacts described by many other scholars and scientists. Although he does signal the current situation as a crisis, Pyne also highlights the long, slow burn of the Pyrocene. In contrast to some accounts of the Anthropocene, his articulation refuses to naturalize the labours of humans in the preceding age (that many call the Holocene). Pyne's contribution is his extensive engagement with and explication of the long histories of human effects on, or coevolution with, ecosystems. It is this work that allows us to connect Australia's long history of fire with our contemporary experience of environmental mess. The Pyrocene describes both the positive, world-shaping practices of First Nation peoples across the world (including Europeans), the decimation of these in acts of colonization, and the negative effects of such decimation and of the burgeoning of nonsustainable fire-related practices (such as burning fossil fuels) during industrialization. Pyne's account of the Pyrocene helps us here to think about the 2019–2020 fires as an historically and geographically situated, relational biosocial event.

Pyne makes large claims for the significance of fire in human history, arguing that Homo sapiens are both products of the Pyrocene and its key actors: 'The firestick became the fulcrum by which to leverage opposing thumbs, bipedal locomotion, big brains, language, and the rest into reconstructing physical environments, which then changed the changer … It's hard to imagine the sapiens thriving, much less dominating, without it' (Pyne, 2019a: 201).

Humans, Pyne asserts, are the only species to deliberately set fires (although three Australian birds – the black kite, the whistling kite and the brown falcon – are also known to use burning sticks to set fire to grass during hunting). Historically, humans used fire to cook food and to manage crops using firestick farming; they also used fire to provide heat for their own and other animals' bodies, including dogs (Haraway, 2003; Rose, 2011). Human's intra- and inter-species sociality has been shaped by fire. According to Pyne, our bodies have also been formed through our use of fire: cooking food meant we developed small guts and big brains. The smoke and heat of fire also allowed food to be preserved, facilitating human movement (Pyne, 2019a: 129, 201). Ecologies and environments have also been sculpted by these activities. Australia is one of the clearest cases in point. As the oldest, driest and hottest inhabited continent on Earth, historian Tom Griffiths suggests that Australia has long been 'the fire continent' (Quince and Phillip, 2020).

Prior to European colonization in the late 18th century, Australia was cultivated and cared for through complex sets of practices developed over millennia (Pyne, 1998; Morrison, 2020; Steffensen, 2020; Gammage and Pascoe, 2021). These practices included deliberate fire-setting and the management of naturally occurring fires, and were specifically tailored to the particular habitats or ecosystems that were the spiritual and material responsibility of the people living on, and with, that part of 'Country'.[5] Australian plants have coevolved with these practices and many require fire to germinate and to flourish. Fire was used to control the growth of other plants and to maintain open spaces for farming, and for human and animal habitation and movement. Australian animals have for tens of thousands of years lived with and benefited from our First Nations peoples' firestick farming (Jones, 1969) – moving into previously burned land to eat the fresh growth, for example. Both histories of these practices and accounts of their contemporary iterations emphasize the quality of these fires, which were carefully planned, well controlled and most often 'cool'. These fires had specific, constructive purposes and hugely positive spiritual and cultural significance, as Steffenson's book *Fire Country* explains:

> There is a large diversity of ecosystems in the landscape – each have their own special characteristics and treasure. Learning all the trees and medicines is a must for understanding how to apply the right fire for the right country. The old people managed the country that needed fire in a certain way, to keep the diversity of ecosystems. As a result, the people and the animals had access to all the places that could supply particular resources they needed to survive. (Steffenson, 2020: 60)

For Pyne, Australia provides an iconic example of the catastrophic outcomes of the destruction of traditional fire practices through colonization: 'it is Australia's contact with Europe that tracks, with eerie fidelity, the acceleration in humanity's firepower that has made the Pyrocene not simply a check on a succession of glacial breakouts but a runaway phenomenon in its own right' (Pyne, 2019a: xii).

European colonizers had little or no understanding of the significance of fire in the Australian context and failed to see the landscape as shaped by First Nations peoples' care and labour. Bringing European concepts of land management, fertility and nature to an entirely different place involved extensive and often catastrophic acts of violence to people, animals and plants. As First Nations peoples were pushed off their land and/or killed, colonizers cleared forests, introduced non-native animals and sometimes used fire in immensely destructive ways, allowing fires to burn too strongly and for too long in the wrong season (Mariana et al, 2022). Long-established and carefully cultivated landscapes, often consisting of large trees and open grasslands (which English colonizers likened to gentleman's parks) (Gammage, 2011) were used to farm destructive hoofed animals and grow non-native crops, or became crowded with shrubs, weeds and trees (Mariana et al, 2022). In Indigenous terms, Country became dirty or sick (Gammage and Pascoe, 2021).

In places designated 'National Parks' (a process that began in the early 20th century), native flora and fauna were sometimes left alone to 'flourish' without fire, which over many decades led to an over-accumulation of flammable material and serious imbalances in plant and animal ecologies. Our cities were built in and around bushland – reflecting settler Australians' own love of the country's unique flora and fauna. Gradually, over the second half of the 20th century, non-Indigenous scientists and officials started to pay attention to First Nations peoples' knowledge about fire and began to deliberately burn forests to prevent out-of-control fires (Weir et al, 2020: 307). Importantly, these regimes were in no way comparable to the sophistication of Indigenous burning practices and often caused grave damage, according to First Nations' experts (Chenery and Cheshire, 2020; Steffensen, 2020; Gammage and Pascoe, 2021). Referring to studies of Aboriginal burning practices in three very different parts of Australia, including Canberra, Weir, et al (2020: 307) show that although governmental regimes of burning were in part inspired by historical and contemporary Indigenous practices, they were often undertaken without 'empowering Aboriginal people to do so themselves, or even engaging with contemporary Aboriginal land managers'. (Interestingly, Canberra's very small programme of Aboriginal fire management comes in for praise in this text see also King [2019].)

Into the 1990s and 2000s, governmental controlled-burning programmes were underfunded, and landscapes became loaded with pyrogenic material; in most parts of Australia, First Nations people were also not permitted to burn as much as they needed to in order to maintain Country in the right condition. With long droughts and increasing temperatures, Australia became a pyre (Gammage and Pascoe, 2021: 147; Mariana et al, 2022).

Up to the present day, political disputes among the major parties and the Australian Greens have also continued to rage about the frequency, intensity and location of controlled burns. The capacity to use fire as a mitigation measure has also been questioned when confronted with weather conditions as intense as those experienced in 2019–2020. Some experts have argued that no amount of burning or logging could have saved the environment when the land was so dry and the heat so intense (Bowman et al, 2021). Organizing sufficient fires is expensive and time-consuming, and deliberately setting fires and allowing lightning strike fires to burn are risky and complex strategies: things can get out of control without the lifelong, millennia-long knowledge that First Nations people bring to this task. Public debate during and after the 2019–2020 fires raised questions about how to include Indigenous expertise in 'cool burns' alongside other technological practices such as using fire retardants, aeroplanes and water trucks (Ross and Quince, 2020), and such discussions are ongoing. Weir, Sutton and Catt argue that 'public debates about prescribed burning rarely grasp the agenda Aboriginal people bring' (Weir et al, 2020: 308; see also King, 2019). The books of Victor Steffenson, Bill Gammage and Bruce Pascoe play a significant role in educating wider Australian publics about First Nations' understandings of the role of fire in caring for Country, exhorting our leaders to recognize the literally life-saving potential of this knowledge.

Like Indigenous fire experts, Pyne strongly argues against traditional European suppressive approaches to fire in the Australian context: 'Fire suppression, outfitted with industrial means such as air tankers, helicopters, engines and vehicles to ferry crews can dampen a landscape's fire load; but if that land needs fire or has the natural means to kindle it, then the consequences of suppression will end in counterproductive conflagrations' (Pyne, 2019a: 193).

Pyne names this 'the fire paradox': 'The more we try to control burning', he writes, 'the worse the burning that results' (Pyne, 2019a: 193). Instead, a mix of strategies is needed. As First Nations fire expert Joe Morrison states: 'People need to see and understand that an unburnt country is not 'wilderness' and how country should be – but country desperately calling for fire to rejuvenate it and restore the balance of risks. Not uncontrolled damaging fires, but fires that are understood, planned, patchy and regular' (Morrison, 2020).

Bushfires (controlled or not) are only one element of the Pyrocene. Over millennia, European cultures developed their own expertise in fire, focusing on the extensive harvesting and burning of ancient plant reserves in peat, coal and oil. As Pyne argues, these skills underpin the colonization and urbanization of many parts of the world, and the intensity of contemporary mobilities of people, goods and capital. They are also the key cause of the current environmental mess: both climate change and toxic pollution result from extracting and burning fossil fuels. Making connections to other forms of global crisis, particularly zoonotic viruses and pandemics, is more difficult and may indicate limits to using 'Pyrocene' rather than 'Anthropocene' or 'Capitalocene' to describe our Age. As environmental historian Tom Griffiths (2020: np) argues: 'COVID-19 spilled over from wild animals to humans and became a pandemic because of ecosystem destruction, biodiversity loss, climate change, pollution, the illegal wildlife trade and increased human mobility.' Humans' capacity to use fossil fuels to power cars, trucks, ships and planes means that both human and nonhuman animals move around in unprecedented ways, facilitating the spread of viruses and bacteria. Pandemics are, as many scientists have argued, increasingly likely in these circumstances (Knowles, 2021). Human consumption of nonhuman animals and human mobilities are also both at stake in zoonotic pandemics. Shaped by cooking, our capacity to eat animal flesh without becoming sick depends on using high temperatures to destroy viruses and bacteria. Cooking meat also requires the capture or farming and storage of animals and carcasses before cooking, which introduces multiple risks of infection. While extensive management regimes typically reduce these risks, practices at the margins – of forests and of regulation – introduce new dangers. The possible source and trajectory of the COVID-19 pandemic from bats through exotic meats to humans typify these risks. Ultimately, the Pyrocene is about much more than fire.

Troubling the Pyrocene concept

As many critics have argued in relation to the Anthropocene (Braidotti, 2013; Colebrook and Weinstein, 2015; Haraway et al, 2015; Haraway, 2016), we must be careful to distinguish groups of humans when theorizing the Pyrocene. Not all humans have contributed equally, although many have in some ways benefited in the short term. Although a global phenomenon, the Pyrocene is unevenly distributed in terms of both culpability and effect. Wealth matters here: because they have profited from them, those who did the most to create Pyrocenic industries are more likely to be able to shield themselves from their effects. Rich people can afford air-conditioned homes and air purifiers, can pay for medical treatments of associated health effects and move to less-affected parts of the world. But as the COVID-19 pandemic has shown, wealth is not an absolute protector and even luxurious mobility can be associated with danger. As we learnt in Canberra in the summer of 2019–2020, only a privileged few can escape the smoke. As the photograph in Interleave 1 shows, the Pyrocene articulates a profound paradox in that the vehicles we use to escape fires are also implicated in the ongoing climate crisis that renders fires more likely.

Racial and ethnic differences are also significant here. Aboriginal Australians living in remote areas (First Nations people are far more likely to live in remote regions than any other ethnic group in Australia) are significantly more exposed to bushfire smoke and other forms of air pollution, including smoke from outdoor cooking fires (Clifford et al, 2015). A report on the 2019–2020 fires by Bhiame Williamson et al (2020) shows that they disproportionately affected Aboriginal people, particularly children aged five and under, as they occurred in areas with higher than average numbers of younger Indigenous families. More than one tenth of the children directly affected by the fires were Aboriginal, even though Indigenous people comprise only 2.3 per cent of the population of NSW and Victoria (the two states where the fires were most fierce). Williamson et al (2020) also articulate the specific harms to Indigenous people created by witnessing the damage to Country involved in out-of-control fires. Loss of trees, plants and animals is akin to losing family for Aboriginal people. Out-of-control fires are also a deeply painful reminder of the enduring systemic failure of Australian governments and citizens to recognize First Nations' expertise in caring for Country. Williamson et al (2020) call on those documenting the experience of the fires and developing policy responses to acknowledge and pay serious attention to these additional, additive traumas. Linguistic racism also runs through written accounts: the 2019–2020 fires were dubbed the 'Black Summer', without any consideration paid to the positive meaning of 'Black' to Aboriginal and Torres Strait Islander peoples. Like Williamson et al (2020), we have chosen not to use that epithet in this book.

Pyne's account of the Pyrocene pays no attention to sex/gender or reproduction, although Australian scholarship on Indigenous firestick farming notes the different responsibilities of men and women in relation to caring for Country with fire, arguing that these were significantly disrupted by colonization and are currently being reshaped through engagement with settler notions of firefighting and sex/gender (Gammage, 2011: 160; Eriksen, 2013a, 2013b; Eriksen and Hankins, 2015). Historically, as feminist archaeologists, anthropologists and historians have argued in studies of many different times and places, humans' use of fire to cook and farm, to build and make was associated with a gendered division of spaces and forms of work, and thus the enacting of 'kinds' of bodies (Avakian and Haber, 2005; Allen and Sachs, 2012). Contemporary figurations and experiences of sex/gender remain shaped by these differentiating histories of human engagements with both wild and domesticated fire. Geographers Nigel Clark and Kathryn Yusoff (2018) argue, for example, that (European) fears of out-of-control fire is connected to fear of unmanageable sexual desire (culturally associated with female and queer sexualities). Australian representations of bushfire control, as we saw in the 2019–2020 media reports, are highly gendered, portraying fire 'fighting' as embodying masculine power (Tyler and Fairbrother, 2018). Australian geographers Joshua Whittaker, Christine Eriksen and Katharine Haynes (2016) argue that such representations and cultural narratives impact decision making in bushfire situations, where men are more likely to stay to 'defend' their homes (thus risking their lives), while women are more likely to leave (see also Eriksen et al, 2010; Tyler and Fairbrother, 2018). Such representations also ignore both Indigenous Australians' long histories of positive engagements with fire and the specific formations of sex/gender in First Nations communities. In engaging with the Pyrocene in this book, we want to critically explore the ways in which sex/gender and reproduction are done in the current epoch. How is climate entangled with sex/gender and reproduction in Australia?

These entanglements are evident in living situations, interpersonal relationships and expressions of distress. A report on the health impacts of the 2019–2020 bushfires argues that homelessness, drug and alcohol use, and domestic violence typically increase during extreme fires (Australian Institute of Health and Welfare, 2020). Qualitative research undertaken by Debra Parkinson (2019) after the 2009 fires in Victoria also points to an increase in domestic violence, as well as the challenges of raising these issues when public discourses emphasise the need for recovery. Academic claims about increased risk of domestic violence, reported in national newspapers, became controversial during the 2019–2020 fires, raising questions about the proper time and place for feminist commentary on sex/gender and critique of the heroic discourses prominent in bushfire-related media. Other media representations, including a popular 2021 ABC TV drama entitled *Fires*, included a small minority of women as firefighting heroes. Similarly, an Indigenous women's firefighting crew, based in Eastern Victoria, made headlines during the 2019–2020 fires (Smethurst, 2020).[6] These representations signal the much-understudied entanglements of sex/gender, 'race' and the Pyrocene, highlighting important questions we will address in this book.

Making Pyrocene babies

Throughout the fires, the ANU encouraged its staff to contribute their expertise to national debate and action. Such contributions achieve the university's 'mission' as 'The National University'. Mary Lou and Celia had been thinking together about reproduction and climate change for some time and felt that the bushfires had highlighted many key concerns about the naturalization of heterosexual biogenetic storying of reproduction, the privileging of some forms of parenting or caring above others, and the poorly acknowledged entanglements of humans with other species and environments.

Keen to explore interdisciplinary research collaborations, Mary Lou and Celia met with Professor Sotiris Vardoulakis, an international expert on air quality, in early 2020. Sotiris was busy writing guidance for the Australian government and public, including pregnant women, about how to manage smoke pollution. They also talked to Professor Paul Dugdale, a public health clinician and academic, who was managing public health advice for Canberra during the worst of the fires and smoke. Sotiris and Paul introduced us to Professor Christopher Nolan, an endocrinologist putting together an interdisciplinary team of clinicians, nurses, psychologists, anthropologists and epidemiologists for a project entitled 'Mother and Child 2020' (MC2020), to study the short-term and long-term health effects of the fires and smoke on women and children in Canberra and the NSW South Coast. We were delighted to be invited to join this team (and are still involved in this project), but also framed a different, sociological investigation to gather qualitative data from women and their partners about their experiences of pregnancy, birth and newborn parenting. Sotiris and Paul agreed to be involved and the project was funded through the Research School of Social Science's Cross-College Grant scheme, through which we were able to employ Rebecca. Extending the team to include Louisa, who visited Canberra in December 2019 in the midst of the fires, was a natural development of her long-term collaboration with Mary Lou on issues relating to pedagogy, sex/gender and reproduction.

As a biomedical investigation, MC2020 focuses on mothers and babies. In this book we look beyond the parent/child dyad to consider the complex entanglements of bodies and worlds that constitute reproduction in all its forms. Thinking sociologically, we ask what it was like to conceive, gestate and/or give birth to a child in the southeast of Australia in 2020. How did the parents of what we might call 'Pyrocene babies' make sense of pregnancy, birth and newborn parenting during the intense fires and the start of the COVID-19 pandemic in Australia? More broadly, what can these experiences tell us about the meaning of reproduction in the current era, often referred to as one of climate change, crisis or even emergency? Although our empirical work focuses on people with babies, hence our subtitle, in this book we take an expansive view of reproduction, including humans, nonhumans and environments in our analysis. Rather than thinking only of mothers and children, we understand reproduction as diverse, interconnected, intergenerational modes of living. For us, reproduction is biopsychosocial, geographically and temporally located in every respect. As we will show, this expansive understanding of reproduction allows us to make meaningful connections between 'making (bushfire) babies', climate, kin, care and COVID-19.

Existing studies of bushfire babies

We quickly learnt from our medical and scientific colleagues that very little is known about the health impacts, whether short-term or long-term, of bushfire smoke on pregnant women, foetuses or infants (Holstius et al, 2012; Black et al, 2017; Abdo et al, 2019). The vast majority of research on air quality and reproduction has focused on the effects of chronic air pollution on foetuses rather than bushfire smoke or mothers, exploring the impact of air pollution on birthweight, preterm birth, infant mortality, respiratory disease, and many other conditions in childhood and adult life (Poursafa and Kelishadi, 2011; O'Donnell, 2017; Klepac et al, 2018).

One of our MC2020 colleagues, Associate Professor Alison Behie, is a biological anthropologist specializing in the physical effects of exposure to bushfires. With her colleague Megan O'Donnell, Behie undertook research on the 2003 Canberra fires and the notorious 2009 fires in Victoria. In two papers, O'Donnell and Behie (2013; 2015) discuss the need to study environmental disasters and their impact on birth outcomes, particularly in the context of climate change. Theirs was the first study to look at the impact of an environmental disaster on the reproductive outcomes in an Australian population. O'Donnell and Behie (2013: 345) specifically examine 'changes to gestational age, birth-weight and secondary sex-ratio of babies born in the nine months following the ignition of the 2009 Black Saturday fires'. Their 2015 study found that contrary to previous research, in a cohort of male babies exposed to the 2003 Canberra bushfires, birthweights were above average. They attribute this to maternal stress and increased glucose levels in the mothers, which acted to accelerate growth. More generally, they suggest that this could indicate an adaptive response to environmental disaster ('heightened environment responsivity'). Their 2013 study of the 'Black Saturday' fires found evidence that maternal exposure to bushfires in the second and third trimesters increased the chances of pre-term birth and lower birthweights in babies, a finding echoed in Abdo et al's (2019) research on the impact of wildfire smoke on pregnancy outcomes in Colorado.

This focus on the foetus is not surprising: feminist research has long argued that pregnant women are typically figured as environments for foetuses in biomedical, scientific and environmentalist literature, as well as in popular culture (Duden, 1993; Roberts, 2007; Salmon, 2011; Sänger, 2015). The existing biomedical literature on the effects of toxins, including air pollution, is no exception. In much of this research, mothers become 'environments of exposure' (Landecker, 2011; Lamoreaux, 2016; Mansfield, 2017), positioned as responsible for at least trying to control exposures to toxins (Possamai-Inesedy, 2006; Crighton et al, 2013; Mackendrick, 2014). In contrast, recent scientific research on epigenetics acknowledges the uncontrollability of environmental pollutants and potential intergenerational exposures, although here again, feminist scholars argue, the focus on the vulnerability of the foetus and maternal responsibility tends to be reiterated, even as mothers are reimagined through the lens of environmental factors over which they have limited control (Mackendrick, 2014; Mansfield, 2017).

Epigenetic and other contemporary medical research also extends the period of maternal responsibility to include a concept of pre-pregnancy maternal health, which tends to frame all women of childbearing age as 'potential mothers' (Waggoner, 2013; 2015; see also Roberts and Waldby, 2021).

Figured as environments or transmitters of generational health, mothers are more likely to be the target of public health and media warnings about the risks of environmental and chemical contaminants, whether linked to transmission while in the womb or via 'toxic' breast milk (Possamai-Inesedy, 2006: 408; Mello, 2015). Mothers navigate this burden in a number of ways, using a range of strategies including following public health information (Crighton et al, 2013) and 'precautionary consumption', that is, choosing the 'right' food and consumer products to limit children's exposure to chemicals (Mackendrick, 2014). Mackendrick (2014: 705) argues that through such labour, women are held 'accountable for children's futures'. This burden of care is mediated by social class and the distribution of risks of environmental hazards for mothers across social groups (Downey, 2005; Mackendrick, 2014; Murphy 2015).

Debates about foetal exposure to bushfire smoke seem to have had little impact on Australian public health discourses to date. The Australian government's report on the health impacts of the 2019–2020 fires, for example, includes only two references to pregnancy, which are both contentless – pointing only to pregnant women as 'vulnerable' without explaining how and stating that more research is needed (Australian Institute of Health and Welfare, 2020). The report presents no data on the health impacts on pregnant people, foetuses or newborns (Oderberg, 2021), nor does it pay specific attention to Aboriginal and Torres Strait Islander children and families (Williamson et al, 2020). Through detailed questionnaires and the collection of biomedical data, MC2020 is designed to gather groundbreaking data about the impact of fires and smoke on mothers and babies. The team also planned to undertake physical examination of babies during their first years of life – initial hopes of collecting placentas and undertaking detailed measurements of newborns were thwarted by the COVID-19 pandemic, which rightly curtailed all non-essential access to birthing suites and biological samples. In conversation with this biomedical research, this book explores how ideas about the vulnerabilities of foetuses and pregnant women were articulated during the 2019–2020 fires and the start of the COVID-19 pandemic, and how parents responded to these articulations.

Pyro-reproduction: key themes and approach

Canadian feminist technoscience studies scholar Michelle Murphy (2016: np) observes that: 'We are living in a historic moment when life on earth unevenly shares a condition of already having been altered by human-made chemicals, a condition that might be called alterlife. Alterlife names a historically new form of life that is altered by the chemical violence of capitalism and colonialism.' While Murphy's focus is on chemical exposure, we find her notion of 'alterlife' generative for our study of reproduction in the Pyrocene, which we will call Pyro-reproduction. Engaging with Murphy's writing via the concept of Pyro-reproduction helps us apprehend how historically new forms of life (and death), kinship, care and embodiment are associated with megafires. At the same time, it enables us to pay attention to the *longue durée* of humans' relationship with fire and the slow burn of climate change – highlighting significantly different temporalities to those associated with human-made chemicals. Thinking of Pryo-reproduction as a form of alterlife also helps us grasp the uneven ways in which capitalism and colonialism distribute healthcare in the pandemic both in Australia and around the world.

In her short essay Murphy (2016) makes four propositions in relation to researching alterlife. First, she advocates for 'non damage-based accounts' of the infrastructures of capitalism and settler-colonialism. We understand this as a call to not look away from damage, but also as a refusal to let counting the carnage be the end goal of research or politics. Relatedly, her second concern is 'finding critical and creative ways of using environmental data to create ways of holding governments … responsible for environmental violence' (Murphy, 2016: np). While the scale of our research does not allow for the collaborations Murphy envisages, the ways in which we tell stories about the effects of fires in this text are intended to trouble conventional ideas about responsibility when it comes to reproduction and climate change. Such an approach forces us, and hopefully our readers, to understand that responses to the bushfires and the pandemic can and must recognize how such events are entangled. Third, Murphy calls for expanding understanding of the 'intergenerational and looping temporalities of industrial chemicals' (Murphy, 2016: np). Similarly, we ask questions about what it means to live with bushfire smoke for extended periods. In trying to apprehend how such events make an impact beyond the visible environmental havoc, we ask: what are the intergenerational temporalities associated with the biopsychosocial consequences of the megafires? How does bushfire smoke loop – that is, how does it activate previous events or harms (for example, decades of governmental inaction on climate change and massive investment in carbon economies) and how might it act unpredictably in the future? How are the increased frequency and intensities of such events changing the reproductive futures of people, plants and animals?

As we discuss in Chapter 2, none of our parent participants identify as Aboriginal or Torres Strait Islander. It is important, nonetheless, to pay heed to Williamson et al (2020)'s argument that extreme bushfires have additional and specific impacts on First Nations families both because of their positive connections to Country and their experiences of the intergenerational trauma of colonization, which involved the loss of rights to care for Country, including through burning. Murphy's fourth provocation is to ask how 'the condition of alterlife invites us to attend to the possibility of alternative life forms, of life otherwise, and of future survival' (Murphy, 2016: np). Here, we consider how reproductive life is changing in relation to the COVID-19 pandemic and the 2019–2020 fires, and speculate on what this means for multispecies survival in landscapes that burn more frequently and with greater intensity. Our investigations lead us into several key arenas: air, breathing and smoke; technologies, digital platforms, data and biosensing; and care, kinship and sex/gender.

Air, breathing and smoke

In recent years, air and breathing have increasingly been integrated into social scientific thinking, from feminist, philosophical and anthropological perspectives, and notably in the work of medical humanities and interdisciplinary others studying breathing and breathlessness in the context of respiratory illness (Richards et al, 2016; Wainwright, 2017; Malpass et al, 2019). There is a small but growing body of literature that attends to the phenomenological and embodied dimensions of breathing, air, smoke and pollution. A key claim of this literature is that 'scholars have tended to ignore the air and the presences it accommodates' (Dennis and Musharbash, 2018: 110). Indeed, air is often framed as 'anti-presence' or a kind of absence: several scholars cite Luce Irigaray's critique of Heidegger, where she accuses him of 'forgetting the air' in his privileging of solidity. In mainstream European philosophy and social theory, Irigaray argues, air is background, the 'loss of grounding', and has remained peripheral (Choy, 2012; Dennis, 2015: 199; Graham, 2015; Oxley and Russell, 2020).

Feminist scholar Magdalena Górska's book *Breathing Matters* offers a posthumanist analysis of breath, emphasizing the relationalities enacted through breathing, where breathing is 'an event of bringing the outside in and the inside out' (Górska, 2016: 28). Górska interrogates how breath helps us reconfigure the boundaries of embodiment, and highlights the transformative potential of breath for thinking about relationalities with atmosphere and the environment. In a year marked by megafires and COVID-19, such transformations and relationalities took many turns that were unanticipated; because of the time and context in which it was gathered, our data provide unique insights into the ever-shifting boundaries between breathing, technologies and environments.

In related work, Louisa has drawn on Todd (2017) to discuss breath as a tool to think with (Allen, 2020). She highlights breath as presence; a 'here and now experience' and an act that is never repeated. It is both singular and relational to the extent that we share the air that we breathe with others (Dennis, 2015; Allen, 2020). Our mutual reliance on air suggests that ensuring its presence 'is a non-voluntary collective life-sustaining responsibility' (Allen, 2020: 8). During the bushfires and COVID-19 pandemic, this sense of breath as a collective life-sustaining responsibility garnered new meaning. Like the First Nations scholars cited earlier, Oxley and Russell (2020: 18) note the way in which 'histories of breath' for marginalized populations must be considered, for example, in relation to exposure to industrial pollutants or the intertwinement of smoking with socioeconomic factors. In our study, the socioeconomics of air and breath were apparent in the ways in which different participants and their networks responded to the threats of smoke and fire.

Technologies, digital platforms, data and biosensing

Technologies and digital platforms play an important part in Pyro-reproduction. Phones, apps, smoke detectors, radios, windows, air filtration systems, virus tests, masks and vaccines all contribute to the making of sex/gender and reproduction in these times of climate crisis. Learning from the Science and Technology Studies and sociological literature on self-tracking and environmental sensing (Nafus, 2016; Pritchard et al, 2019; Roberts et al, 2019), we focus on people's engagement with technologies and digital platforms in both understanding and managing physical risks, but also in (re)making connections of care – for human and nonhuman animals and for their environments. Air-purifying and filtering technologies – from windows through to masks and filtering machines – became essential elements of 'making babies' during the 2019–2020 summer. Since then, of course, masks have become essential to every aspect of human life.

In our study, we were struck by people's take up of these technologies and platforms and wanted to better understand how air quality, measuring air pollution related to bushfires and breath came together during the time of the fires. Like Garnett (2020), we are interested in the different technologies used to measure air pollution and the ways in which these are mediated by diverse dynamics. We talked to public health experts, clinicians and architects, as well as to women who were pregnant and parenting in order to find out the different ways in which people imagined bodies and their biologies in the pandemic. For Garnett, such research involves a rethinking of the relationship between bodies and environments that 'blurs the interior and exteriors of bodies' and troubles ideas about bodily integrity: 'human occupants were revealed as shaping the composition of particles and these particles then behaved in response to the respiratory dynamics of buildings and bodies' (Garnett, 2020: 69).

The consequentiality of air and the governance of/responsibility for air is raised by several scholars: from the way air delineates who constitutes 'the public' in relation to secondhand smoke and smoke-free legislation (Dennis, 2015), to the paradoxical lack of attention paid to the political ecology of urban air in an age of climate change, global interconnectivity and pollution (Graham, 2015), or the histories of deadly air as a weapon in war highlighted by Sloterdijk (2009), who makes this explicit by framing air as a 'life support system'. Engaging with these technologies and with the discourses of risk circulated by public health officials and others produces new understandings and experiences of our bodies, and particularly of breath and breathing. Learning from this research, we are interested in the governance of air and air quality data in the home, local neighbourhoods and cities.

Care, kinship and sex/gender

Reproduction, Kin and Climate Crisis also contributes to and builds scholarship in studies of queer kinship. Key interventions in queer kinship studies have focused on how new technologies of reproduction queer family making and ideas of the human (Mamo, 2007; Dahl and Gunnarsson Payne, 2014; Lewis, 2019; Riggs et al, 2020), documenting how queer kinship is always already racialized (Puar, 2007; Eng, 2010). Our queer approach analyses relations between reproduction, technology, embodiment and climate crisis. We focus on queer relations between the human and more-than-human: like Dana Luciano and Mel Chen, we don't 'reserve queer theory for LGBTQI-identified people or topics' (Luciano and Chen, 2015: 193).

In Australia, the start of the COVID-19 pandemic coincided with the 2019–2020 bushfire season. The first Australian cases appeared in late January 2020. In Canberra, there were only a few weeks between the city starting to feel 'normal' again in terms of air quality and fire risk, and the onset of real concern about this strange new virus. Within only a few weeks of coming out of our houses to breathe the air and mourn the huge losses, we were in lockdown (the final fire in NSW was extinguished in early March; Australia went into its first COVID-19 lockdowns on 25 March). All of the parents in our study were caring for a newborn during the COVID-19 pandemic. As we will show, this situation threw up intense challenges for families: how to welcome and care for a baby without having visitors? How to get enough help with existing children during the exhausting final stages of pregnancy while in lockdown or isolation (due to COVID-19 or smoke and bushfires)? How to socialize a baby, and indeed become a parent, during the critical first year when social contact through mother groups and even informal gatherings at cafes and parks were banned? Once the smoke cleared and people were allowed to go for walks, babies and children were taken outside, but playgrounds were closed and no one was allowed to congregate. We all got used to calling out to neighbours over the fence, but we were not able to get close enough to really admire the new baby or to invite anyone in for a cup of tea. Babies in prams gazed anxiously at strangers' faces or turned away in dismay – they were simply unused to seeing new people. What will the long-term consequences of this be, we wonder? The people we interviewed raised the same question.

In these strange conditions, kinship moved online. Grandparents, siblings and friends tried to connect with new parents, children and babies via Zoom or Facebook. Many of us were also working on these platforms, while some were also trying to educate children. People became exhausted by the mental and physical demands of online communication. So much is lost in these encounters – smell, touch and context. Being with babies is usually a highly physical experience. What does it mean to take these kinning encounters with newborns and their parents online? The biopsychosocial practices of care and kinship were, we argue, queered (set askew) by the non-normative relations associated with the pandemic. In thinking through this issue, we draw inspiration from Haraway's work on response-able and inclusive futures, and related writing on rethinking kin-making possibilities beyond heteronormative nuclear family reproduction in the context of both reproductive justice and ecological crisis (Haraway, 2016; Clarke and Haraway, 2018; Hester, 2018; Clare, 2019).

Writing a book about Pryo-reproduction means thinking about gender and sexuality. We understand these as a set of relations and practices, and focus here on multiplicity and change over time. Like other scholars of queer kinship, we see sex, gender and sexuality as relational and continually in flux. Such an approach continues to be a departure from the majority of the biomedical and sociological literature on bushfire smoke and air pollution, which makes biologistic assumptions about the relations between 'mothers', foetuses and babies based on a binary understanding of sex/gender. In contrast, we do not assume that we know what it means to be a woman, or that a mother must be or identify as a woman, or that any woman is or wants to be a mother. We do our best in the book to be careful with pronouns and to use words like 'women', 'mother' and 'parent' in non-discriminatory and open ways.

STS approaches to care are also key to the questions we ask in this book (see, for example, Mol et al, 2010; Martin et al, 2015; Puig de la Bellacasa, 2017; Lindén and Lydahl, 2021). Framing care as embodied practice, distributed across networks of human and nonhuman actors, these approaches inform our exploration of how caring for the environment and for human and nonhuman others becomes entangled with questions of kinship, embodiment and reproductive justice.

Chapter outlines

In *Fire, A Brief History*, Pyne concludes that:

> Instead of a prevailing paradigm, we may need to scan more broadly. We need to find amid the bewildering scatter of points – of all the fires, data sets, commentaries, policies, news flashes, sciences; of all the lurches, bumps, and glitches that describe the equants and epicycles of climate and biosphere and people – a regression line called a narrative. The Anthropocene provides a possible context for that to happen. (Pyne, 2019a: 199)

In *Making Bushfire Babies* we gather together and analyse a range of data articulating the relations between the 'bewildering scatter of points' Pyne lists, introducing several more of our own. While we agree with Pyne that new narratives are needed for the Pyrocene, we part company when he suggests that fire's 'ancient alliance with humanity allows for a narrative that centres the action on the mind, hand, and heart of the agent most responsible' (Pyne, 2019a: 200). Indeed, what we attempt in this book is to write narratives that do not centre the human, but rather explore what happens when we refuse or trouble this category and try to think differently about relations in the Pyrocene. We learn from participants' experiences that conventional ideas of motherhood, care, kinship and the value of having children are queered in these kinds of situations and thus will be going forward.

Our methods and the various data analysed throughout the book are introduced in Chapter 2. We also include accounts of our own experiences and elaborate the theoretical resources we are drawing on. Chapter 3 weaves together breath, bushfire smoke, the COVID-19 virus and maternal guilt, tracing the ways in which these came together in varying responses to the unpredictable influxes of smoke and viruses. We ask why our participants felt guilty for breathing in smoke despite knowing it was something over which they had little control. The situation presents an impossible predicament, we argue, whereby the only way not to inhale smoke is for the mother to stop breathing. How did the public health production of pregnant women as a 'vulnerable' group shape participants' stories of parental responsibility and care?

Chapter 4 focuses on experts, machines, masks and buildings. During the bushfires, public health authorities issued daily advice about air quality based on data produced by government-owned monitoring stations, weather forecasting and information from firefighting teams. We were fascinated by the various ways our participants responded to this advice. We follow air purifiers through the data, drawing on interviews with experts involved in producing public health advice and providing clinical care to pregnant women and newborn babies, and with citizens involved in air quality monitoring. We analyse online information sites and relevant social media posts, as well as photographs taken by pregnant women and their families of their homes and surroundings during the fires. What do these practices tell us about the intersections and misalignments of public health advice, citizen science projects and everyday life?

Chapter 5 points to how people invent new forms of caring, collectively and individually. During both the bushfires and the COVID-19 pandemic, 'families' were articulated in particular ways by health and other governmental authorities, and by citizens, as key forms of social organization and support. 'Families' were often connected to 'homes', as if they are the same thing. New terms, such as 'care bubbles', had to be invented to acknowledge that this is often not the case and new rules were invented about who was close enough (emotionally and legally) to be allowed to be physically co-present in homes they do not legally share. We asked how pregnant women and parents of newborns sought help in extreme and unprecedented environmental conditions. How did formal and informal pregnancy, birth and postnatal care change in this period? In what ways does climate crisis make more people aware of the challenges of kinship and of the need to think again how we understand kin, including kinship with the more-than-human?

Reproductive futures are our focus in Chapter 6. How are climate, mass ecological destruction, reproduction and population linked for our participants? When and how did discussions of these connections come into their lives? More conceptually, how can we open up questions about the connections between climate, reproduction and multispecies kinship? What feelings are provoked when one is making bushfire babies and imagining their futures?

The concluding chapter turns to the potential impacts of the book's argument. The stories we gather call our attention to the unpredictable and diverse ways in which the conjoined crises of climate and the pandemic give rise to new forms of kin, care and making babies. They also point to the myriad ways we gather and respond to information and advice when we are living in the midst of something which often feels unmanageable and where the limitations of individual agency are palpable. There are many ideas about 'the right thing to do': this is true at every level, from taking a breath, through to going outside and to managing populations. Expert knowledge is always partial, political, situated and fraught, and people invent ways of going on that make sense to them. This book is an attempt to open space for reflection and storytelling that might help us learn to live better now and in the future. Drawing on stories about wombats and orchids in the final chapter, we raise questions about multispecies kinship and what we can learn from nonhuman responses to crises, including new forms of flourishing.

Interleave 2

Coming home to Canberra from Aotearoa-New Zealand, January 2020: Rebecca

We drove home along the Princes Highway and the smoke got increasingly dense as we approached Canberra. I remember researching the type of masks we needed and ordering smoke masks online as we drove down, as we'd heard there was a shortage in Canberra. At a roadside stop near Bundanoon we felt like we'd stepped into a refugee zone: cars of weary families buying up massive amounts of supplies, obviously having just driven from bushfire affected areas of the coast, a feeling of tension palpable. It felt surreal, as we'd been otherwise so disconnected from the 'reality on the ground', having just flown in from Aotearoa-New Zealand. We carried on to Canberra and the smoke was very thick. We have evaporative cooling at our house which we couldn't use with the smoke, as it draws air in from outside to function. It was very hot. The smoke leaked into the house via a grille on the toilet window, so when we arrived home, there was a definite smoke smell throughout the house. I remember thinking that it felt like a very strange decision to leave the Aotearoa-New Zealand summer and clear skies for this smoky, apocalyptic reality. On bad days, particularly just after New Year, we could hardly see the street in front of our house, let alone any of the hills around us.

Interleave Figure 2.1: The view from Rebecca's house, Canberra

Source: Rebecca's photograph

2

Methods in Crisis

How can we study climate, COVID-19, kin and care in particular times and places of crisis? The research for this book was forged in the intense smoke of the 2019–2020 Canberra summer and funded by our university just before the COVID-19 lockdown saw universities batten down their material and financial hatches. With just A\$30,000 in our account and living in lockdown conditions, we set out to explore how we might talk to people about reproduction and climate change. Mary Lou and Louisa had already been writing about young people refusing to have babies as a form of ecological protest. Celia and Mary Lou were members of a feminist reading group about reproduction in which we had been reading, *inter alia*, Michelle Murphy's *The Economization of Life* (2017), Sophie Lewis' *Full Surrogacy Now* (2019), Katherine Dow's *Making a Good Life* (2016) and Catherine Mills' *Biopolitics* (2017). Rebecca was working several casual academic jobs, having recently returned to work after having her first child. Reproduction was on our collective minds, but we were full of uncertainty about how best to research it in the contemporary moment. Suddenly, 'climate crisis' seemed so much more real: not something that will affect coming generations, but a series of catastrophes that forced us choking and frightened into our homes. What analytic resources did feminist and queer theory, new materialism and sociology have to offer in this moment?

After many conversations among ourselves and with colleagues in a range of disciplines, we decided to seek ethical approval to start talking to pregnant women (and their partners if they wished) and to people who had recently had a baby. Our plan was to ask participants to take us for a walk in their local areas while talking us through what happened during the fires. Rebecca is an urban sociologist, and we were inspired by her interest in place and space. We were also very keen to know how people had managed their daily lives and how they might articulate the networks of care and connection in which they were situated. Immersed in queer theory and feminist technoscience studies, we felt strongly that no assumptions should be made about who was caring for who or what during the fires and the pandemic. We wanted to explore what counted as care for our participants, to know what kinds of work were involved in having a child, and how all that had changed during the fires and then the pandemic. We also wanted to understand how experiencing the smoke and then COVID-19 was affecting people's thinking about futures and families.

As indicated in Chapter 1, our research project is part of a large interdisciplinary study of the effects of the 2019–2020 Australian bushfires and smoke: the MC2020 study led by Professor Christopher Nolan at the ANU Medical School (https://medicalschool.anu.edu.au/MC2020study). The MC2020 study is an ongoing collaborative project involving multiple universities, Local Health Districts and Aboriginal Health Services in the Australian Capital Territory (ACT) and SE NSW region. It is a longitudinal cohort study recruiting more than 1,000 mother-child pairs in the ACT and SE NSW to investigate how they have been affected in the short term and longer term by smoke from the 2019–2020 bushfire season and by the COVID-19 pandemic. MC2020 uses a series of four quantitative questionnaires over a 12-month period. The questionnaires, which we helped design, ask participants about their material circumstances and their psychological and social wellbeing at the time of the 2019–2020 bushfires, their experiences of pregnancy and birth, and their experience of the COVID-19 pandemic, and to collect information about the health of the participating mothers and babies 12 months after the fires.

The MC2020 project will provide globally important information about the risks of smoke and fire to mothers and babies. The questionnaires also ask about mental health, social and medical support, living conditions and economic pressures, exploring the connections between exposure to smoke and fire, forms of disadvantage and the physical and mental health of mothers and babies. While we do not draw on these data here, the questionnaires will provide information about mental health, social and medical support, living conditions and economic pressures, and will explore the connections between exposure to smoke and fire, forms of disadvantage, and the physical and mental health of mothers and babies. Other substudies, which are in development at the time of writing, will address issues of prenatal and postnatal care, using qualitative methods such as focus groups and interviews to explore the gaping holes that were exposed during both the fires and the pandemic. One of these subprojects, led by Indigenous public health scholar Stewart Sutherland, focuses on the short-term and longer-term effects of the fires on local First Nations communities, while another project, led by ANU medical professor Christine Phillips, focuses on migrant families' experiences.

Located within feminist and queer sociology, feminist technoscience studies and new materialism, our research was oriented towards more open-ended, conceptual and political questions. We decided to undertake in-depth qualitative interviews with a much smaller group of people (many of whom were also participating in the survey research), and their partners if they desired, but also to 'follow' significant actors like smoke, air purifiers and flows of air quality data. We wanted to explore in detail how the smoke and fires impacted the lives of people who were pregnant or parenting a newborn baby and to think about the materialities of the Pyrocene in Canberra and SE NSW.

As we suggested in Chapter 1, there is little expert knowledge about the risks of bushfires to pregnant women, foetuses or newborn babies. Altogether, there is a lot of uncertainty in this space: uncertainty that was compounded by the onset of COVID-19. In order to better understand these uncertainties, we decided to also interview a range of professionals: an environmental architect, a public health clinician, an air quality researcher, a data scientist, a biological anthropologist, a reproductive endocrinologist and a bushfire management expert. We were interested in how they were working with 'things' such as smoke and air, and how they were working to support or inform pregnant women and parents. No one had 'the answer' to our questions, but they all had many interesting things to say. This book tunes into a rich polyphonic stream of voices, texts, numbers, images and things. Our archive includes transcriptions of audio-recorded interviews, written field notes prepared after the interviews, our own written accounts and photos of our experiences during the fires, texts, images and data from online discussion forums, citizen science websites and Facebook groups, media articles and government and university websites, apps and leaflets, academic papers and books, and participants' photographs, videos and hand-drawn maps.

Our data collection, analysis and writing are shaped by our ontological and political commitments. We are all feminists and have been long immersed in interdisciplinary critical approaches, including new materialisms, queer theory, actor-network theory, feminist technoscience studies, decolonial theory and feminist and critical sociology. We are also environmentalists, although of somewhat varied stripes. Two of us are from Australia and two of us are New Zealanders. Several of us have spent long periods living overseas and have deep attachments to countries and landscapes other than those in which we were born. We are concerned about climate change and about social justice, and are, to put it simply, 'for' some worlds and not others. Like everyone we know, we feel distressed by many of the events of 2020. We are mourning the lost animals and forests, and have concerns about people's and animals' exposure to smoke. We are worried about the parents who experienced intense anxieties and we care deeply about the social isolation and economic troubles many have experienced during the fires and the ensuing pandemic. Of course, the pandemic continued as we wrote this book: although at times the situation in Australia and Aotearoa-New Zealand was relatively 'good', there were many rapid changes, and eventually three of us became infected. Like viruses, bushfires will also come again. We are not disinterested bystanders in this project. We are involved. We are all involved.

Theoretical influences

Donna Haraway's question 'What is decolonial feminist reproductive freedom in a dangerously troubled multispecies world?' (Haraway, 2016: 6) is a key provocation for this book, as is her insistence on bringing debates about human numbers into feminist engagement with ecological crisis. This argument is developed in *Making Kin Not Population* (Clarke and Haraway, 2018), where several authors, including Michelle Murphy, extend an understanding of kinship beyond biogenetic or blood relations. The title of our book is inspired by this text. It signals our contention that making kin and making babies are intrinsically connected and should be thought together rather than oppositionally.

In her contribution to *Making Kin Not Population*, Adele Clarke traces the history of feminist efforts in relation to reproductive justice, arguing for accounts that critically bring together questions of reproduction, population, environment and kin, and contest the 'dehumanised "thingness" of "population" and population control' (Clarke, 2018: 14). Drawing on Haraway's notion of the Chthulucene (her alternative name for our current epoch), Clarke asks 'how the broadest kinds of accountabilities can be brought into play, especially through generating, maintaining and valuing kinships and other mutualities that go far beyond the biogenetic' (Clarke, 2018: 16). In her chapter, Haraway (2018) calls for new ways of counting and assembling populations in the context of ecological crisis. She argues the need to go beyond population numbers and consider both the 'born ones' and the 'disappeared' people and animals that have perished as a result of existing systems of inequity, exploitation and extraction. The stories we tell in this book are accounts of loss and survival, human and more-than-human.

Ontologically, we align ourselves with a performative or 'ontics' approach that argues that the world comes into being through the intra-action of 'words and things', to quote John Law (2008), Karen Barad (2007) and Michel Foucault (2000 [1970]) in one sentence! Borrowing Haraway's (1988) language, we are interested in the 'material-semiotic', understanding our participants' articulations of their experience as stories or accounts that are necessarily formed in both material circumstances (they are 'situated knowledges') and in particular versions of language and discourse: struggling for words to describe the colour of a bushfire-affected sky is not an accident – culturally we don't yet have sufficient language to articulate the Pyrocene. Calling our participants' words 'stories' does not indicate we think they are not true or not important – clearly we value them – but rather is intended to contest conventional research traditions that rely on human testimony to articulate 'facts'. We take the same approach to the words of experts, to our own writing about the fires and, indeed, to published scientific and biomedical literature. All of these are stories that matter, articulated in and through particular assemblages of living and nonliving things and discourses, in particular times and places. Our approach to all these texts could be characterized as 'response-able reading' (Murris and Bozalek, 2019).

We have tried to materialize this approach in the book's design. We wanted to present readers with as many rich stories as possible and to create accessible entry points for those who do not share our intellectual histories. The Interleaves are sections containing verbatim transcription from audio recordings, written field notes or our own personal accounts, or images produced by us or our participants. Chapters contain analytical readings of the themes of these stories and engagements with the relevant academic literature. These sections are also stories – but they are stories shaped by particular traditions of academic thought and modes of analysis. The structure of the book, then, expresses intertwined polyphonies and tries to listen both for the resonance and disharmonies in and among the different accounts, both visual and textual. The analytic sections are written to be read in sequential order, but readers may want to start, as we did, by immersing themselves in the stories and images we gathered. This can be done by reading through the Interleaves first.

Interviews with parents of newborns

During 2020 and 2021, we interviewed 25 mothers (and sometimes their partners) about their experiences of the bushfires. Almost all these interviews were conducted by Rebecca, in participants' homes or in a local cafe or park. Conversations with some participants were conducted over Zoom, where they had moved interstate, were based on the far south coast of NSW or had indicated that they preferred this mode of communication. Interviews lasted between one and two hours and were audio-recorded and transcribed verbatim. Participants were recruited in several ways: some by word of mouth and snowballing, others by indicating their willingness to be contacted on an MC2020 questionnaire. After completing an interview, participants were also invited to share information about the study with friends. We decided to use this dual approach because funding constraints associated with our substudy meant we were required to complete all of our data collection before the end of 2020. This would not have been possible if we had only recruited solely through the MC2020 questionnaire because of various institutional complications associated with obtaining ethics from external organizations. We obtained ethics permission from our university to interview participants in our substudy in August 2020, and finally completed ethics processes associated with MC2020 in late October 2020 (gaining ethical permission to recruit via MC2020 databases from the ACT's Health Research Ethics Committee).

Eighteen participants were living in Canberra at the time of the bushfire smoke. Four were residing on the NSW South Coast: two in the Bega Valley Shire (approximately 230 km southeast of Canberra); and two in the Shoalhaven region (approximately 200 km from Canberra towards the coast). One participant who usually lived overseas was visiting her family's holiday house in a small rural town in the Snowy Mountains at the start of the bushfires and smoke, but was evacuated to Bega and then to Canberra. Two participants had moved away from Canberra as a result of the bushfire smoke and/or the COVID-19 pandemic, to Melbourne and Brisbane respectively. Basic demographic questions were covered at the start of the interview, including age, ethnicity, gender, sexuality, highest level of education, job, number of children at home and their ages, whether they live with other dependants, and whether they own or rent their home.

All participants identified as Anglo-Australian, 24 participants as female and two as male. Twenty-five identified as heterosexual and one as bisexual. Seventeen participants were married and nine were cohabiting or in a de facto relationship with their partners. Ten of the participants were first-time parents; the others had two or more children. Only one participant had an adult dependant living with them who they were caring for in addition to their children. A total of 69 per cent owned their own homes (this is slightly above the Canberra norm of 67 per cent home ownership); the others were renting. Our participants were, for the most part, highly educated: 69 per cent had a bachelor's degree or above, 19 per cent had a diploma or certificate and 12 per cent had completed secondary school. Participants' occupations are set out in Table 2.1. While the majority of participants were on some form of maternity leave, their employment status was relatively evenly divided

Table 2.1: Parental interviewees' occupations

Industry	Number	%
Public sector	8	31
Private sector (IT and finance)	5	19
Health-related fields	4	15
Tertiary education	3	12
Tourism/retail	2	7.5
Primary education	2	7.5
NGO/charity	1	4
Not employed	1	4

between full-time and part-time roles, with two participants employed on a casual basis, one self-employed and one not currently employed.

The high number of public servants and people working in tertiary education reflects the dominance of these sectors in Canberra and our profiles as researchers. The relatively high number of professionals and the educational levels of participants is also reflective of the higher than average socioeconomic demographic composition of Canberra compared to the rest of Australia (according to 2016 Census data, almost 36 per cent of the population of Canberra had a bachelor's Degree or above, compared to 22 per cent in Australia [Australian Bureau of Statistics, 2016]). Canberra is also a predominantly White city: 67 per cent are Anglo; 2 per cent are Aboriginal or Torres Strait Islander. People from Chinese and Indian backgrounds constitute the largest ethnic minorities. Overall, MC2020 has struggled to reach ethnic and sexual minority communities, despite a range of strategies, including doing interviews for community radio, television and magazines, posting information on relevant Facebook sites and approaching local churches. Our own failure to recruit people from minority groups reflects time pressures and lack of resources, as well as COVID-19 restrictions. We tried, perhaps not hard enough, but did not succeed. We are hopeful that the subprojects mentioned earlier, focusing on First Nations people and migrants, will have greater success and are supporting those colleagues in that work.

Our interviews with parents started by asking if they had completed the MC2020 questionnaires and whether it had triggered any thoughts or reactions. We also asked participants to tell us what was happening in their lives at the time of the bushfires: their stage of pregnancy; where they were living; and how they coped with the smoke. For most participants, talking about the bushfires and smoke came easily; it sometimes brought up vivid memories and strong emotions. This meant that in many of the interviews there was no need to prompt with formal questions. Some participants explicitly noted their relief in telling their story. The interviews were typically interspersed with the pauses and interruptions that accompany childcare: babies babbling, banging toys or waking from naps and older children seeking attention. In two interviews a male partner was fully involved in the conversation, while in several others partners of the participants were peripherally involved, interjecting at points, making us a cup of tea or passing through the interview to help tend to the baby.

The experience of conducting interviews in-person and via Zoom were, unsurprisingly, quite different in terms of building a rapport and enabling a flow of conversation that takes into account body language and situational knowledge. While most Zoom interviews worked relatively well, technological lapses occasionally halted the flow of the conversation. But these mediated interactions can also be rich and insightful (Howlett, 2022). The Zoom interviews allowed Rebecca a (somewhat static) view into people's homes: ranging from a blank wall to dynamic scenes of home life, with children or other family members passing through the screen and waving, the chaos of everyday life unfolding in the background. Zoom interviews also allowed a degree of comfort and informality for participants, and saved participants the labour of travelling with young children to an external location for the interview or tidying their homes to welcome an interviewer into them. It may have also enabled time-pressured people to participate: some who opted for Zoom interviews in Canberra explained that it allowed them to speak freely in the limited window of their baby's nap time. Spending time on Zoom had clearly become normalized for a lot of our participants during the pandemic.

In-person interviews in participants' homes also provided a rich experience of physical environments: participants could point to the vent that leaked the most smoke or the view that was otherwise obscured during the smoke. In many cases, we also witnessed participants' interactions with their partners and babies. We could get a better sense of their immediate geographies and imagine their experiences of 'sheltering in place' from the smoke. Other interviews were conducted in cafes. In almost all these interviews, participants were alone. This worked well for the most part: participants were able to talk more freely without attending to their children – some explicitly said it was a welcome break – but cafes are also noisy and this meant the sound quality for transcribing was sometimes poor. The risk that participants feel uncomfortable or conspicuous speaking in public with a recorder in front of them never seemed to be a problem.

One part of each interview focused on people's housing situation at the time of the fires, exploring how their homes were impacted by the smoke. These questions were, in part, motivated by the research teams' own experiences of the smoke and the differing approaches we took to minimize its impact. We were interested in whether participants had been forced to leave their homes or whether, like Rebecca and Celia, they had done so by choice. If so, where did they go? The majority of our participants were living in Canberra and most of them did stay in their homes – in fact, only two left the city. One evacuated to Canberra to escape a more intense fire risk (first inland and then at the coast). Importantly, quite a few opened their homes to relatives and friends escaping from fires, including those on the NSW South Coast. Other participants who live on the coast were forced to leave; indeed, one of the most harrowing stories we heard (discussed in more detail in Chapter 3) involved a terrifying evacuation with a two-month-old baby, whose mother described trying to provide her with cleaner air by breathing through her own face mask and then directly into the baby's nose and mouth. The baby, she reported, was exhaling black smoke.

Canberra housing is notoriously poor when it comes to environmental issues: many houses date from the mid-20th century and have not been adapted to address current ecological conditions (increasing temperatures, increased risk of intense fire and long droughts). Even new homes are often poorly designed to deal with smoke or fire – we discussed this with the director of a local environmental architecture and science firm, as described in Chapter 4 (see also Williamson et al, 2022). Many participants provided us with detailed accounts of the adaptations they made to prevent smoke coming into their leaky homes, the technologies they purchased to try to filter the air, and their experiences of buying and using face masks (something that was to become so familiar only weeks later when the COVID-19 pandemic became evident). Official advice was limited and somewhat confusing: people shared information and ideas, devising various tricks with wet towels, masking tape and air filtering machines.

A third of our participants had already given birth or gave birth during the worst of the bushfires and smoke: three gave birth before the fires started, five during the fires, six straight after the fires but before COVID-19 and ten during the pandemic. We wanted to know how experiences of birth were impacted by the smoke or the pandemic. Women due to give birth during the bushfires were apprehensive about smoke being present in the hospital (as it often was in prenatal visits). One participant commented that she was terrified that the smoke might impact her breathing while giving birth – breathing being the key technique she had learned to get through the experience. Others commented on their lack of awareness of smoke during the labour; for many, the intensity of the experience far outweighed observations about smoke inside hospital rooms. These issues are explored in more detail in Chapter 3.

Sometimes we were interviewing participants many months after the fires and their baby's birth. We asked, then, if they had developed particular parenting practices to manage the effects of smoke on the newborn baby and if they had any concerns about how the smoke or the COVID-19 pandemic has affected their baby, directly or indirectly. Approximately one third of our participants gave birth during the lockdown in Canberra and all recounted how significant this was for their birth experience. For one mother, a slight temperature after a difficult labour on the first days of lockdown saw her, her baby and her partner being used as "test cases" for implementing lockdown procedures in a regional hospital. Another mother spoke of the oddities of the COVID-19 protocols: despite strict procedures, she was asked to walk around the hospital while in labour because there was no room for her. Rather than exposing herself to further COVID-19 risk, she chose to walk in a bushland area nearby. Others recounted anxiety about social distancing constraints in addition to their existing anxieties about the birth, particularly the challenge of only being allowed one support person at the hospital (in addition to the logistics of organizing care for their other children).

We anticipated that the lack of interaction with other parents and babies might have had adverse impacts on our participants. For one woman, this manifested in failing to clearly articulate and address early concerns about her baby's health, which later did turn out to be important. In retrospect, she felt that support over the summer and during the pandemic in terms of access to specialist advice and maternal health support was really lacking, which made her especially concerned that mothers with fewer resources, or first-time mothers, might not be able to access the services they required. This was a commonly shared concern.

Although ten of our participants were having children for the first time, many had at least one other young child. We were interested to know how they took care of these children while pregnant or once they had had the new baby. We wanted to know, for example, how they made decisions about going outside. One participant told us about cutting short a shopping expedition over concerns about smoke data she was googling in real time on her phone. She told us of making calculations about incoming smoke and the distance she had to travel from the shopping centre to reach her parked car. This same participant discouraged peers in a Facebook group for local mothers from doing too much research about the fires: she was concerned that they might become overwhelmed by exposure to information about the negative effects of the smoke. Other mothers reported watching the skies to decide when to let their toddlers out for a quick play in the garden or park, and many were dismayed to find that childcare centres were closed and that shopping centres, indoor play spaces and museums were often no less smoky than their homes. The National Museum of Australia, just down the road from the ANU, did become a refuge for many parents of young children during the extremely hot days (it is a new building with air conditioning with large open interior spaces) though even institutions such as this were posting warnings on their Facebook pages that due to 'the likelihood of poor air quality inside our building', their opening hours might change at short notice. Many similar institutions were shut. Little did participants know that within a few months, being stuck at home with children without access to childcare, school or places of leisure would become a legally mandated global norm.

In order to better understand what motivated the steps participants took to protect themselves during the summer, we also probed for information about the types of health information to which they turned. These included a range of apps, websites, sensory cues (what could they see and smell) and official announcements. In asking these questions we wanted to know what advice people paid most attention to over this period and how they then translated this information into adjusting their own routines. Overall, we got a sense that people found there was a lack of sufficient and specific health information that could help them be confident about making good decisions to protect themselves, their foetuses and babies, and their other children. For instance, participants told us conflicting stories about the significance of the smoke on the health of the foetus, making differing claims regarding when in the pregnancy the foetus is most likely to experience adverse impacts through smoke exposure. One of the experts we interviewed is a local data scientist who decided to establish an online information portal providing hourly updates on smoke in Canberra. Almost every Canberran parent we spoke to had regularly accessed this site. In Chapter 4, we discuss this phenomenon and the complex ways in which participants used their bodies and various machines to 'sense' when the smoke was dangerous to themselves, their foetuses and children, and even their pets.

We also wanted to learn about participants' affective responses to the fires and smoke. One participant in retrospect described the smoke as "acrid", "oppressive" and "apocalyptic". Another described the way the smoke infiltrated the sanctum of her home like a "snake", reporting intense fear about its impact on her foetus. People's feelings were complex and often unclear, especially when recalled in later months of clear skies or refreshing, cold rain. As we will discuss in Chapters 3, 4 and 5, people's level of concern was not a reliable predictor of what actions they took in relation to the smoke. Participants adopted various approaches to researching information and taking action to shield themselves from air pollution.

Moving beyond participants' experiences and feelings associated with the bushfires, we also wondered how living through this experience might influence their thoughts about having children in the future. What, if any, were the implications of the bushfires for the way they think about the relationship between climate and reproduction? Increasingly, we hear reports of women of reproductive age pledging not to have children because of what they perceive as inhospitable futures associated with climate change (Hunt, 2019; McAdam, 2019; Olsen, 2019). Would the experience of being pregnant and parenting a newborn in the midst of a climate catastrophe influence people's future planning relating to reproduction? Would it change the ways that they felt about people having children in general, in the context of climate change? Their answers to these questions are discussed in Chapter 6.

Interviews with professionals

We also interviewed people working in medicine, architecture, air quality monitoring, public health and bushfire management, and asked them to share documents and websites that they produced to educate members of the public about the risk of bushfire smoke to pregnant women and newborns. These interviews covered a range of topics and were initially intended to help us understand what professionals believe the risks to be. It was fascinating to hear how divergent these beliefs were and to have confirmed to us that there is little agreement about the level and type of risk (hence the MC2020 project!). We were also interested to learn about the work these professionals did to manage the risks of fire and/or to help others to understand and manage them. Some were actively engaged in preparing information for the public, others were treating pregnant women and/or babies, and some were involved in monitoring air quality and/or thinking about how homes could be designed to protect inhabitants from smoke. We were also keen to talk to a bushfire management expert to learn how extreme fire events might be more effectively prevented. All of these interviewees lived in Canberra or the NSW South Coast during the fires, and we also often ended discussing their own experiences as well their professional views. Speaking to these interviewees gave us additional insight into both the fires and the pandemic, often from older age groups than our participant parents.

Making maps, sharing photographs and visualizing smoke

This book engages with the multiple materialities of the Pryocene and the emergence of COVID-19, including, *inter alia*, smoke, air purifiers, masks, Facebook groups and wet towels. Such 'things' can be hard to follow in research terms, especially in domestic settings. One way to 'see' them is to collect visual records of their appearance (importantly, such records are themselves framings or enactments). During our research, we gathered images of bushfire smoke and fire, including those in publicly available media, in photographs and videos taken by our participants or by us, and from records of smoke-caused air pollution on Facebook groups and governmental websites and apps. Some of our professional interviewees were closely involved in producing and circulating images and data, and many of our parent participants had spent a lot of time engaging with this information. In these interviews, we asked participants to 'talk us through' relevant graphs and other visualizations.

Contemporary life is powerfully structured by amateur photography: so many social media apps feed on a constant supply. Bushfires are also highly photogenic – they produce shocking visual changes that are often eerily beautiful. Most of our participants had a stock of photos they had taken during the fires and were happy to sort through them to find images that did not feel too personal to share. (We specifically excluded photographs of people out of ethical considerations around consent to be photographed and privacy.) Going through the images either during the interviews or later also triggered memories, prompting discussions of sensory experiences such as vision and smell. Sometimes the photos were mundane: alongside dramatic images of bushfire, we also received images of brown, lifeless gardens

Figure 2.1: Fire-ravaged bush, taken from a moving car, NSW South Coast

Source: participant photograph

or driveways blanketed in haze. Some were taken inside homes: window-framed vistas capturing the day-to-day reality of what participants could see while cloistered in their homes. One participant sent a short video of her terrifying night-time evacuation with a three-week-old baby: without sound, the camera moves quickly through each of the car windows, pitch black except for distant lines of flame (see Figure 2.1 for a still of this video). Cars have played a paradoxical role throughout the study. In this memory, cars are literally life-saving. Yet the significant pollution associated with people's car use is also, undoubtedly, a driver of where we have ended up – getting into our cars in order to escape natural disasters.

In an interesting adjunct, a friend of Rebecca's learned we were looking for images of the Canberra smoke and put out a call on Facebook. People jumped at this opportunity and we ended up with a collection of more than 100 images that we have permission to share and reproduce.

Sunsets sometimes turned a deep browny red in the midst of the fires. The freakish beauty of the sky at night was often remarked upon and photographed (see Figure 2.2). Meteorologists were consulted to explain how the smoke from the fires was having these effects. Ben Noll from Aotearoa-New Zealand's National Institute of Water and Atmospheric Research explained the phenomenon being experienced across Australia's east coast, and across the ditch in Aotearoa-New Zealand as 'scattering', a phenomenon whereby a beam of sunlight hits a smoke particle in the atmosphere. This sends some of the light's wavelengths off in different directions and happens millions of times before that beam reaches your eye. Dust particles can help to create more scattering in the mid and upper atmosphere, which can increase the vibrancy of sunsets and sunrises.[1]

We use images throughout the book not as 'Pyrocene porn', but as examples of figurations of smoke and fire to critically explore. Mostly these are not professional images, designed to shock or captivate, but rather amateur attempts to capture something significant. They are also part of stories; participants told us about how they used images to get their families and friends in other parts of the world to understand how serious things were. 'Before and after' paired images became an important genre at this time: media articles used this device to great effect, as did our participants. This genre was also an important part of early COVID-19 photography, where people published images of empty streets alongside their previously teeming earlier versions. There is often something nostalgic or mournful in these pairs – a yearning for a lost world. In one example from the NSW South Coast, a participant captured a gleaming cruise ship in her local harbour in glorious sunshine and then the same view cloaked in heavy smoke. The first image carries an eerie foreshadowing of the early days of the COVID-19 pandemic in Australia, when passengers on board a cruise liner were allowed to enter the country without adequate quarantining, unwittingly spreading viral infection.

We also gathered visual data in the form of hand-drawn maps made by participants. At the end of each interview, we invited parents to draw on a piece of paper or on their computer, providing two sketches of their social networks and supports. The first map reflected what they anticipated

Figure 2.2: The Namadgi National Park fire on the outskirts of Canberra

Source: participant photograph

in terms of social networks and support they hoped to depend on while pregnant and looking after a newborn baby. Sometimes this first map was superimposed by another sketch of how these social networks/support and places actually played out during the period of the bushfire smoke and the pandemic. Of course, we told participants that there was no correct way to draw the maps, and it was fascinating to see how different participants undertook this task. For us, the sketches were as methodologically significant as the conversations that took place alongside the drawing of the maps. We reproduce several of these 'care maps' in the book and will spend time discussing their form and content, mostly in Chapter 5. The mapping exercise was not completed by all participants, however, and some were seriously logistically challenged – attempting to conduct the interview on a Zoom call because of COVID-19 restrictions meant that some participants valiantly attempted to hold babies in one hand while endeavouring to draw a map with a mouse in the other. Sometimes this meant the map became haiku-like. In the example in Figure 2.3, the participant used the 'heart' icon to show how isolated she felt, alone with her husband and mother, with all the love of her wider social networks at a distance due to COVID-19.

Our hope was that the care maps might provide us and the participants with recollections of people, places or things that were particularly important to them that may not have surfaced during the interviews, and thus help us to achieve our aim to focus on things as well as people. We were interested in the thickness of participant's kinship networks and what they encompassed. We did not anticipate that these maps would be highly detailed, although some participants surprised us with what they

Figure 2.3: Participant's care map of their social network during the bushfires and COVID-19, drawn on a computer, names removed

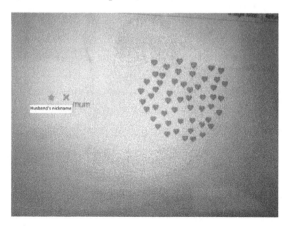

Source: participant drawing

Figure 2.4: Participant's hand-drawn care map, showing the differences between hoped-for and actual support

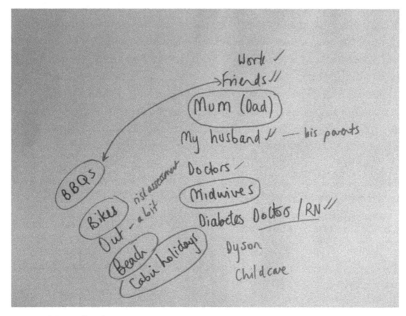

Source: participant drawing

included in their maps and how interesting they seemed to find the exercise. Nonhumans appeared here: on several maps, air purifiers feature as a key part of people's social network, along with families, friends, and maternal and child health services. Some, as in Figure 2.4, even mention the brand of purifier. These machines, which became impossible to purchase in Canberra at the height of the fires, had become highly valued actors in participants' social networks. Others drew particular radio stations or apps as part of the networks that made their lives possible. As we will explore throughout this book, both the bushfires and the COVID-19 pandemic created radical forms of social isolation for pregnant people and parents of newborns. This was often reflected in the maps. Smoke and the risk of infection meant staying at home alone, or with only a partner and sometimes also a toddler for company. It is perhaps not surprising in these extreme conditions that technologies and media forms rise in emotional and practical importance.

Our own accounts

Some way into the project, we decided we needed to produce our own accounts of our lives during the fires and how we have experienced the connections between reproduction, kinship and climate. As a new research group, we recognized that these personal reproductive histories are embedded in our readings of, and responses to, the interview transcripts and other data we collected, and that we needed to try to make this more explicit in our interactions with each other. This process also helps us to queer thinking about kinship, climate and reproduction via representation of the myriad ways of seeing, feeling and responding to the ways people intra-act with these phenomena. We present these stories in the spirit of collaboration with our participants, who we treat as expert informants on their own lives. Of course, we also have to be careful about this: unlike that of our participants, our anonymity is not protected here. Our stories, like theirs, are emotionally fraught and complex. During the fires, some of us were also dealing with very difficult circumstances: the death of a beloved friend; serious illnesses and accidents in family members; and children with mental health challenges. It is worth repeating: 2020 was a difficult year!

Re(imagining) reproduction: data, analysis and writing

It is one thing to conduct interviews (and a difficult and energy-absorbing thing at that) and quite another to work out how to analyse the resulting data. Writing about this analysis is yet another task of great complexity. We spent most of the money we had paying Rebecca to conduct the interviews and to undertake a literature search. We were lucky enough to have some funds for professional transcription, however, and also experimented with automated digital services (which, we worked out, could at least provide a relatively cheap first version for Rebecca to carefully edit). We ended up with over 200,000 words of transcripts, 13 care maps, more than 100 photographs, images and videos as well as our own stories. We had also collected media stories and data from online sources such as the Canberra Air Quality Facebook page. We conceived all these data as a set of stories or accounts, told in different forms and wanted to see what happened when we read them against and with each other.

We tried several ways of doing this. Building on an actor-network theory approach, for example, we decided to 'follow the actor' – 'smoke' in one instance – to see where and how it appeared in participants' accounts, in images and in forms of digital data (scientific recordings of air quality, for example). We also followed air filtration machines, tracking how they acted and how their actions were reported by both parents and experts. In other iterations, we took a more classical sociological approach, focusing on themes or tropes to track where concepts such as kinship or care appeared in the various data. We also experimented with (re)writing narratives, taking participant's accounts and summarizing them into shorter, more condensed versions and looking both for what was unique or singular in any particular person's story, but also what was shared across several.

Writing the analytical sections for the book also became a very mixed process. Typically one person took the lead in starting a shared online document, but ultimately everyone was involved in writing or rewriting every chapter. We have tried to smooth out the book's tone, but not too perfectly. We want readers to remember that it was written by four people and that its purpose is to record and analyse polyphonies. We hope the inclusion of long extracts and images will also help convey this multiplicity. This focus on multiplicity is intellectually and politically important to us. Our aim in conducting this research and writing this book is to ask questions and to tell stories that help us to (re)imagine reproduction in the current era.

Interleave 3

The emotional impacts of living through bushfires: a discussion with Katya (interview transcript)

Rebecca: Did the bushfires and smoke and COVID, did that have sort of any impact on that decision-making process (re having more children)?

Katya: Just going back a bit, too, about the bushfires and COVID and just how much of a mental impact this had on me, I developed severe anxiety and depression throughout this time. To the point where I've actually been getting clinical hypnotherapy done since July, June, July, I started seeing her, just because I could not cope. So it got to the point where I couldn't even open up the blinds, I didn't want to look outside, you know, it was so fearful of what life was going to be like, you know, since all this that I didn't know if I could physically live in this life.

And the bushfires and COVID combined definitely had a huge impact on that. Adding to be a new mum on that and feeling like you're not doing the best job that you possibly can, I needed professional help to actually get me out of bed, and to actually be a mum, be a partner, do the laundry, do dishes, just do something because I physically, emotionally could not do anything. And it got to the point where I would lock [daughter's name] in a room for 15 minutes just so I could have a big cry, just so I could even give her a hug.

Interleave Figure 3.1: View from a South Coast kitchen, taken shortly before evacuation

Note: When fires are close by, the sky becomes red and then black, and the lack of visibility obscures the horizon. This is disorienting spatially, temporally and affectively.

Source: participant photograph

Rebecca:	Oh gosh, that's hard. Have you found that the clinical help has been helping you?
Katya:	Oh, the hypnotherapy has been the best thing I've ever done in my life. It's helped me in more aspects than just the bushfires and COVID, it's helped me with … so, I have been … so she wanted me to see a GP, and the reason why she said I've actually got chronic Post Traumatic Stress Disorder from all of this, because I was having reoccurring dreams and waking up and not being able to breathe, like, thinking I've had smoke and stuff in my lungs and things like that. Worried that I'm going to lose my daughter, so I'd had, like, vivid dreams of her passing away and being burnt to death and things like that. So it really had … yeah, it really had a mental impact on me, and she just said, "We can definitely help you." And she said, "You actually need it." So it was chronic Post Traumatic Stress Disorder that

I was going through, and I had no idea, I thought it was just postnatal depression, which is such a common thing. And then I would talk to my friends about it going, "Oh, yeah, I've got postnatal depression", like, completely know what you're talking about, and then I'm on a different scale again.

3

Breath, Breathing and 'Mum-Guilt'

The material presence of breath and embodied act of breathing offer an 'organizing concept' (Choy, 2020) for our thinking in this chapter. We trace breath and participants' accounts of breathing to see where they lead in making sense of their experiences of bushfires and the pandemic. Drawing on feminist new materialist thought that recognizes breath as intra-active phenomena (Barad, 2007; Górska, 2016), we configure breath as a mode of reflection and attention to the material politics of living through crisis. Here, breath acts as a form of sense making, 'a force that not only materializes, recognizes and manifests social power relations but also forces social and environmental transformation' (Górska, 2016: 253). In the discussion that follows, we suggest breath is a material force that shapes the lived experiences of participants by materializing mother subjectivities responsible for the health and wellbeing of their children in these crises. Such responsibility is bestowed in smoky and virus-filled atmospheres over which humans exercise minimal (if any) control. When mothers realize the impossibility of this task, some experience what one participant characterized as 'mum-guilt'. This is a feeling of personal 'failure' to prevent children's exposure to the effects of smoke and the COVID-19 virus.

This work contributes to a theorization of breath and breathing as feminist politics (Irigaray, 2004; Ahmed, 2010; Górska, 2018). Who gets to breathe, and who doesn't, can provoke questions about social, political and economic privilege and how this is sustained (Górska, 2016). Within such scholarship, breath is recognized as 'a lively and deadly force not only physiologically but also affectively and socially' (Górska, 2018: 253–254). As Sara Ahmed (2010) explains, breathing serves as a powerful metaphor for claiming presence and breathable existence in spaces of marginalization and discrimination like queer and post-colonial politics:

The struggle for a breathable life is the struggle for queers to have space to breathe. Having space to breathe, or being able to breathe freely is

... an aspiration. With breath comes imagination. With breath comes possibility. If queer politics is about freedom, it might simply mean the freedom to breathe. (Ahmed, 2010: 120)

The pursuit of breathable lives has received recent international attention in relation to racial discrimination and anti-Black violence in the US. Black American George Floyd was choked at the knee of a Minneapolis police officer while saying "I can't breathe". His last words were an uncanny repetition of Eric Garner's, who was also killed in a New York City Police Department (NYPD) chokehold in 2014. This phrase and its symbolic meaning became pivotal in the ensuing Black Lives Matter movement's call for an end to racial discrimination and violence. This movement reinvigorated protests in Australia about First Nations Australians' experience of police violence and deaths in custody, particularly the story of Dunghutti man David Dungay Jr, who died while being restrained in prison in 2015 calling out that he could not breathe (Anthony, 2020). In such instances, the universal right to breathe (Mbembe and Shread, 2021) becomes an aspiration for political justice and social transformation.

Tracing breath in participants' stories about bushfires and the pandemic reveals inequalities regarding who bears principal responsibility for protecting children in crises. A respiratory analysis, as Magdalena Górska (2016: 251) writes, 'can ... provide insight into relationalities that accentuate contemporary trends in the development of neoliberalism and its consequences at both local and global levels'. Within the 'risk society' (Beck, 1992; Lupton, 2012b) the intra-relationalities of breath and discourses of neoliberal reproductive citizenship see women caught in their own regulation as 'good mothers' who vigilantly prevent children's exposure to smoke and COVID-19. We argue that when breath full of smoke and the COVID-19 virus is conceptualized as a *lively force,* mothers cannot be conceptualized as primarily bearing this responsibility. Within a new materialist framework, agency and contingent responsibility are a matter of intra-acting, and not something that someone (or something) possesses (Barad, 2007). Breath serves here as a tool to challenge binary logics that constitute contemporary ideas about motherhood, whereby you are either a 'good mother' (without guilt) or a 'bad mother' (with guilt) for exposing your child to smoke and COVID-19. This chapter attempts to generate 'breathing room' (Choy, 2020: 589) for women where they might experience alter-possibilities (Murphy, 2018) and feel less guilt in moments of crises.

Conceptualizing breath and breathing

Before exploring where breath and breathing appear in this study, we explain how we work with these concepts. In mobilizing breath, we contribute to recent scholarship that draws renewed attention to the act of breathing and the related practice of smelling (Malpass et al, 2019; McLean, 2019; Allen, 2020; Oxley and Russell, 2020; Stephen, 2021). Breath is a relatively underexamined phenomenon within the social sciences; however, we are writing in a moment when it has surfaced as a significant issue. As Timothy Choy (2020: 586) notes, it is a 'challenging and important time to breathe together' because there are 'so many multiple, overlapping, resonating, and yet incommensurate callings-out of respiratory distress and systemic breathing disorderings, as well as agitations for somethings-else'. One of these 'callings-out' is the global pandemic which has drawn attention to breath because the virus is transmitted by aerosols expelled as breath (World Health Organization, 2020). The air we breathe has suddenly become 'suspicious' (Harms, 2020), inaugurating a plethora of governmental regulations such as mask wearing, social distancing, isolation measures, border closures and lockdowns that have upended normal life. During the devastating bushfires of 2019–2020, attention to breath was also heightened when smoke became too thick and oppressive for people to breathe, sometimes forcing evacuations. In both moments of crisis, how people breathe and whether they can do so adequately influences daily life and its possible activities.

As long as we live, we breathe. This material reality is another reason we employ breath as a mode of attention in our analysis. Examining an act so fundamental to being must surely reveal something novel about the conditions of our material existence. The importance of breath to life means that conventional depictions of breathing are framed within revered medical knowledge. From this perspective, breathing is understood physiologically as a process of respiration that comprises two phases, inspiration and expiration, as explained by pulmonologist Michael Stephen:

> With a signal from the brain, the diaphragm contracts downward, expanding the lungs in an instant. In this way, the breath of life is drawn into the body, and contained in it are millions of oxygen molecules. The lungs seamlessly pass the oxygen off to the red blood cells, which, with the help of the heart, deliver these molecules of life to the cells of the brain, muscle, kidneys, and other organs. Continuing the circuit, carbon dioxide, produced as oxygen is consumed by our tissues, is whisked through our veins and back to the lungs, and then expelled into the atmosphere as the diaphragm now relaxes. (Stephen, 2021: x–xi)

This physiological depiction of human breathing is fundamental to the formation of Western understandings of embodiment (Górska, 2016). In this biomedical rendering, air and the human body are distinct entities which pre-exist the act of breathing. Air is understood to exist outside the body before it is inhaled and becomes breath, which is then expelled into the external atmosphere. Human bodies and air have boundaries that become blurred once air enters the body, but ultimately remain perceptually discrete. There are of course other cultural and spiritual ways of conceptualizing breathing. For instance, in Hebrew the word for breath is *ruach*, which also means 'spirit of life', recognizing more than a physiological understanding of this act (Stephen, 2021: vii). In Pranayama or yoga breathing, breath is conceived as comprising four parts; inhalation followed by an air-filled pause, and exhalation, also followed by an air-filled pause (Rosen, 2002). Our discussion does not dismiss these ways of conceptualizing breath, but rather seeks to contribute to this existing body of thought. We add to these theorizations by asking: 'What does feminist new materialist thinking bring to understandings of breath and breathing in times of crisis?'

Within a new materialist paradigm, breathing is understood as intra-active phenomena. Intra-action is a neologism coined by Karen Barad (2007) in her work on quantum physics and feminist philosophy to reconfigure conventional notions of causality. In her development of this concept, Barad challenges interactive understandings of causality, where something is seen to cause an effect in something else. For instance, a causal understanding of breathing is that it is enabled by the lungs contracting and expanding, a process made possible because lungs and air precede the act of breathing itself. Applying a Baradian conceptualization, breathing is understood as a process of intra-action where the act of breathing comes into existence at the same time as lungs and air materialize. Breathing subsequently becomes a consequence of mutually constitutive differentiation, as Górska explains: 'breathing materializes and becomes intelligible in an intra-active manner of simultaneous constitutiveness and differencing of multiple material-discursive, naturalcultural, human-nonhuman, organic and inorganic forces; of rhythms, flows and movements that are enacted and enacting situated naturalcultural, sociopolitical worlds and with specific effects' (Górska, 2016: 51).

The elements (or *relata*) present in the moment of intra-action when breathing materializes (for example, smoke, COVID-19 virus, pregnant bodies, air purifiers, masks and whether it is humans or nonhumans that breathe) differentiate this experience in what Barad calls 'differential patterns of mattering' (Barad, 2003). In other words, the phenomena of breathing emerge as specific and local 'sets' of agentially intra-active relata for example, smoke, lungs, COVID-19, pregnant bodies and neoliberal discourses of motherhood. Within this intra-active process of becoming, such relations materialize boundaries and properties which themselves become intelligible as mother subjectivities that manifest experiences of 'vulnerability', 'risk' and 'guilt'. What such a conceptualization of breathing eventuates is an understanding of how this repetitive and seemingly uniform process in humans is experienced and constituted differentially, depending on the relata present.

Understanding breathing in this way has implications for our analysis of participants' experiences of bushfires and the pandemic. This conceptualization recognizes the unboundedness of human-nonhuman phenomena like pregnant bodies, smoke and breath. When no human or nonhuman entity is ontologically prior, and instead comes into being in specific sets of intra-relations, then distinctions between 'inside' and 'outside' the body become blurred. Notions of individual agency and responsibility no longer hold in this model because there are no bounded subjects (or objects) to enact them. Agency and responsibility are instead distributed as a product of the intra-actions of relata in any assemblage. This conceptualization attributes agency to nonhumans that are seen to actively shape or 'give a push to' (Vannini, 2015) human action. Nonhuman elements such as smoke and viral-laden breath are viewed as vibrant entities actively involved in producing human behaviour. The subtlety of this shift in conceptualization is demonstrated in the following example. Instead of recognizing pregnant women's decision to stay indoors to avoid smoke as an individual act of will, we might attribute this 'decision' to smoke's agency to produce physical effects like breathlessness which compel this action. The idea that pregnant women control their exposure to smoke as an act of human exceptionalism is unsettled when smoke is conceptualized as a vibrant and intra-active element of the bushfire assemblage.

Thinking with breath within a feminist new materialist paradigm enables an untethering of guilt around inhaling smoke, or COVID-19 virus, from conventional discourses of pregnant 'mother's responsibility' for their children. An understanding of breath as an intra-active phenomena, as Górska explains,

> problematizes the distinction between concepts such as 'inside' and 'outside' by troubling notions of corpomaterial boundaries in the worldly metabolization of oxygen; it complicates notions of self, other, and environment in challenging individualistic conceptions of humanness and articulating its transcorporeal character that defies bodily and subjective boundaries of the self; it also problematizes human exceptionalism by embedding humans in the intra-actively constitutive atmospheric, material, and social dynamics of living. (Górska, 2018: 250)

What occurs in this conceptualization is a recognition of the distributed nature of agency as a consequence of intra-active relations in any assemblage. Within this framing, it is redundant to suggest that women have control over unborn babies, smoke or COVID-19 virus because, like everything else in the world, women come into being in an intra-active and indivisible social dynamics of living. However, this does not mean that the actions of pregnant women (or any human) are free of accountability; rather, it is that this accountability is conceptualized differently. As Barad (explains, 'the acknowledgement of "non-human agency" does not lessen human accountability; on the contrary, it means that accountability requires that much more attentiveness to existing power relations' (Barad, 2007: 219). Humans are responsible for the world of which we are a part, not because we are its orchestrators, but because in a distributed understanding of agency, 'reality is sedimented out of particular practices that we have a role in shaping and through which we are shaped' (Barad, 2007: 35). In this sense, responsibility to human and nonhuman 'others' is an ontological inescapability, because we are 'of' rather than 'in' the world.

Materializations of breath

When we follow breath in this research, where do we find it? Breath appears in the numerous references participants make to the pervasive smell of smoke during the bushfires. The ability to smell is a function of breathing through the nose and a sensory perception only available while awake (Carskadon and Herz, 2004). Through their talk, participants evoke vivid depictions of the "stink" of smoke which they describe as "oppressive", "disgusting" and "horrible". Lily explains how "I felt sick with the smell, like, the smell was just too nauseating for us in [coastal town]". Several participants remarked on its pervasiveness indicating "it just kind of smelt, you know, you could smell the smoke everywhere". Delineating the quality of smoke, Helen said it had "that smell like after you've been camping – there is just smoke through everything". Another quality of the smoke participants highlighted was its ability to cling to other objects, which meant "you couldn't hang [out] washing ... because it would just ... you'd bring it in and you'd be like, 'Oh, we've been camping, like, our towels smell like smoke'". For Anita, the inability to remove smoke from her baby's pram left outside when the fires came within 700 metres of her house meant she had to discard it because "I was like, I can't put my newborn in this again, like, I just couldn't. I tried to clean it and I couldn't".

In her research exploring the pleasures of smoking cigarettes, anthropologist Simone Dennis (2018) maintains that smoke *renders our breath visible*. Smoke operates in the same way in this study. In describing the smell of smoke, participants draw attention to their breathing and the affective atmosphere its acrid aroma produced. Smoke's vibrancy is illuminated here as a force that provokes responses in participants such as "disgust", "nausea" and "oppression". This is not conceptualized as a causal effect where smoke causes participants to feel ill; rather, smoke, pregnant women and feeling sick simultaneously come into being in the moment of their intra-relation. Smoke in this instance produces pregnant women as "nauseated" subjects at an ontological rather than simply a psychological level. In paying attention to breath, it is possible to apprehend how the materiality of the world, in this instance in relation to 'smoke', eventuated particular forms of affective embodiment.

Breath also surfaces in participants' references to employing their sense of smell to gauge the severity of the smoke each day. Knowing how intense the smoke would get was important for ascertaining if certain activities would be possible. As will be discussed in Chapter 4, most participants consulted official national news sites for fire and smoke updates, or regional versions, where the local mayor might provide information specific to a geographical area. Many checked air quality apps, but became frustrated when these and other official media sources were not regularly updated or precise to participants' location:

Connie: I remember, like, at first, you would only get a very …
            like, an average over a couple of days or something, and
            it wasn't super helpful because within a day, things would
            change so much … I didn't think the information was
            that useful, because it was very broad.
Rebecca: Yeah, because they had sensors in three different parts of
            the city.
Connie: Yeah, that's right, yeah, and I don't think anything was
            particularly near us, or they weren't particularly accurate
            for where we were. So we often found what we were
            experiencing was different.

Due to the inaccuracy and sometimes discrepancy in air quality data, participants began to rely on their own sensory perceptions. Gina was four months pregnant with her first child when the bushfires began. An administrator working at a university who we interviewed on Zoom, Gina appeared very composed when we spoke to her; but shortly into the interview she revealed that her participation in the MC2020 questionnaires had evoked a lot of emotion about how "crap" the period of the bushfires smoke was for her. She noted that she never felt entirely safe during that period; anxiety about the impact of the smoke on her baby was a constant companion. She explained how she engaged in a process of checking multiple sources and then settling on her own sense of smell to determine the day's activities:

Gina: So yeah, I would say, just a combination of what I could
            see and smell, like, instantly inside the house, like, when

you wake up, you know, you can smell it. And some days were particularly stronger than others, and you kind of just knew that it was going to be a bad day. And so, like, when I woke up and I saw that it was bad, I could smell it really bad, I would check the app to see … kind of just to reiterate what I was seeing and smelling and how bad it really was, sort of thing.

In this case, the act of inhalation to detect smoke has consequences for how the day is structured – for instance, whether "Today might be an okay day to get a walk in" or "to go out to the shops or whatever, what would be a good time to do that". Breathing acts here as a 'doing-in-thinking' (Unmüßig, 2021) whereby participants rely on smell and other sensory data such as sight to make decisions about what activities are feasible. Here 'thinking' is not conceptualized as occurring before the 'doing', but 'doing-in-thinking' intra-actively comes into being in the same moment. Tracing breath's circulation in this way subsequently offers a more sensual and embodied understanding of living in this moment of bushfire crisis.

Fear over not being able to breathe due to the presence and density of smoke was another way breath materialized in women's accounts. For some participants, this fear manifested in concern about how they would give birth in smoky conditions. Matilda worked at a university and was in her early forties. Rebecca interviewed Matilda in her home, which had views out to the mountain range to the west of Canberra, while her six-month-old daughter slept and her four-year-old was at daycare. Matilda shared several traumatic experiences over that period: illness, an evacuation and an almost daily struggle to breathe. While she ended up giving birth about a week after the smoke abated, Matilda was anxious about how she would be able to breathe during labour, given that smoke had been visible in the birthing rooms on her prenatal visits to the hospital. This worry was intensified by her experience of already finding it harder to breathe because her baby was pushing against her lungs:

Matilda: Look, I was scared, because you know what labour is like, you need every ounce of breath to deal with the pain, to deal with the task of pushing out a baby. You need everything to be optimised, your health, your mind, your support structures, the air. And I was thinking, how am I going to do this? Because I would sit here exactly where you're interviewing me now [speaking to Rebecca], I was sitting here, dizzy from the smoke, because I had a huge belly. You can't expand your lungs, and then the air you're breathing is smoke-filled.

Matilda was not the only participant to highlight how she was already experiencing difficulty breathing and that smoke compounded this sensation. Rae described herself as having a sensitive respiratory system as a consequence of being asthmatic as a child. We interviewed Rae via Zoom, as she sat on the floor of her family's holiday home playing with her baby son. Her husband sat close by interjecting at points. Having flown into Australia from their home in South America, she was based in a small country town in the mountains south of Canberra, from which she, her husband and parents had had to evacuate only weeks before she was due to give birth:

Rae: I remember when we arrived in Sydney, there was a lot of smoke at the, like in the middle of November ... And I just remember waking up and not being able to breathe very well at night. I guess that kind of every time it was really smoky I'd have that feeling of not being able to breathe ... I remember I would wake up and I hadn't seen the smoke, but I was just like, I feel like I can't breathe properly. I'd look out the window, and go "Oh right, this is why, so much smoke".

Fear of not being able to breathe was so overwhelming for Katya that it triggered recurring dreams where she would wake believing her lungs were full of smoke. When she consulted her GP, she was diagnosed with Post Traumatic Stress Disorder, which she attributed to experiencing the two crises – the bushfires and the global pandemic – in quick succession, on top of a medical emergency one week before the bushfires when her infant daughter stopped breathing and had to be rushed to hospital:

Katya: I've actually got chronic Post Traumatic Stress Disorder from all of this, because I was having recurring dreams and waking up and not being able to breathe, like, thinking I've had smoke and stuff in my lungs and things like that. Worried that I'm going to lose my daughter, so I'd had, like, vivid dreams of her passing away and being burnt to death and things like that.

Katya was a resident of a town in the South Coast region of NSW, where the threat of bushfires was severe. This danger meant that she and her husband had to evacuate with their two-month-old baby, resulting in a harrowing car ride where they both took turns blowing air into the baby's mouth. At one point prior to the evacuation, Katya explained that the baby had been "breathing out black smoke".

While fear of not being able to breathe was experienced by many during the bushfires, it was particularly pronounced for these pregnant women. By way of explanation and in accordance with a feminist politics of breathing and the struggle for a breathable life (Ahmed, 2010), we draw attention to another feature of the bushfire assemblage. This element is neoliberal discourses of 'risk' which renders pregnant women 'doubly vulnerable' during this time. The notion that pregnancy makes women more 'vulnerable' to an array of environmental risks, including smoke, has a long and well-documented history in feminist literature on pregnant embodiment (Duden, 1993; Searle, 1996; Ruhl, 1999; Salmon, 2011; Lupton, 2012b). As Lupton (1999: 63) argues, 'most medical and many lay discourses tend to represent the pregnant body itself as inevitably deviating from the norm, as vulnerable and susceptible to a range of ills and risks'. These can include detrimental effects for the foetus if pregnant women are exposed to alcohol, drugs, smoke, prescribed medications/herbal remedies, toxic chemicals and fumes, vaccinations, overexertion, underexertion, poor diet, peanuts (prompting peanut allergies in children) and listeria-carrying foods and diseases. The invisibility of many risks in the form of unspecified 'germs' and uncertainty about the effects of the newly emergent virus COVID-19 on unborn children intensify this sense of vulnerability. As predominantly middle-class educated women, the participants in our study were well versed in information about their increased 'risk' (see also Lupton, 2011). We do not, however, conceptualize this heightened knowledge as producing a fear of not being able to breathe in any conventional sense. Instead, pregnant women intra-actively become fearful subjects within a bushfire assemblage that includes breath, smoke, neoliberal discourses of risk and pregnant embodiment (to name only a few relata). Such a theorization has implications for our thinking about 'mum-guilt' and responsibility, as we will demonstrate in the following discussion.

Breathing and risk

Most participants voiced anxiety about the effects of inhaling smoke on their unborn baby. This concern surfaced in comments like:

Gina: I would say that I was fairly stressed, I guess, about the smoke inhalation, what it would do to my baby, you know what stage the baby was growing at, you know, would it affect the development of his lungs or anything like that. So I guess that was just the most stressful time.

Such anxiety was fuelled by media reports that depicted citizens' exposure to smoke as the equivalent of smoking a pack of cigarettes a day (Nowroozi and Alvaro, 2020). As Delilah said, "There was, you know, lots of kind of ... anecdotal stuff flying around about, like, Canberrans and being exposed to, you know, the equivalent of X cigarettes every time they're outside when it's higher than this level." Similarly first-time mother Alison laughed and commented: "Yeah, it was just a bit gross when you're like, am I basically smoking in pregnancy now?" The effectiveness of anti-smoking campaigns has resulted in moral judgement and stigma for women who continue to smoke during pregnancy (Wigginton and Lee, 2013). These campaigns have raised public awareness of the potential detrimental effects of smoke exposure to unborn babies, such as low birthweight, pre-term birth and infant mortality, and increased respiratory disease in childhood and later life (Lupton, 2012b). Cigarette smoking (along with alcohol and drug consumption) attracts particular contempt in discourses of maternal responsibility. As Salmon (2011) notes, this is evidenced in the employment of words like 'kill' and 'abuse' in popular commentary to describe their effects on babies (Lupton, 2012b).

Participants' anxiety was partly attributable to an absence of existing research providing reliable information about the effect of bushfire smoke on the unborn child (O'Donnell, 2017). This lacuna led some to seek information by using Google, special interest Facebook pages, or asking their obstetrician or GP:

Connie: [J]ust being a bit concerned about the pregnancy, and I remember doing some research and, you know, seeing that there was really not much out there ... I just felt like no one really knew anything, like, the support that I wanted was for someone to explain to me how it all happened and what was happening and what the effects potentially would be. And I felt like, like I said, with my GP, my midwife and the people that I spoke to about it didn't seem to have any more information than what I had.

For Connie, a public servant in her late thirties who was 30 weeks pregnant during the worst of the smoke, this paucity of information was a motivating factor in participating in the MC2020 study, which she hoped would gather evidence about the long-term effects of bushfire smoke on women and children. In the absence of data, participants revealed concern and uncertainty about how the stage of pregnancy might be significant for whether a baby would be impacted, or the severity of any effects. There was a discrepancy in perspectives here, with some participants believing smoke inhalation was *more* dangerous in the last trimester because major organs like the brain were undergoing rapid growth. Other participants believed the last trimester was *less* dangerous because vital organs were predominantly formed and therefore less susceptible to malformation. Renee, a senior public servant with three children, conveys some of these logics when she says: "I was also worried, like, brain development, because at that point, as you get into the end of the pregnancy, like, all the brain development and things. And again, I kept having conversations with myself going, 'I'm not my first 12 weeks, surely that's riskier. I'm in this safer zone?'"

Participants were worried about the effects of smoke inhalation not only for their unborn child but also their other children. This anxiety was evident in describing the challenges of looking after toddlers who were confined indoors during the bushfires. Public health advice was to stay out of the smoke as much as possible (Australian Medical Association, 2020), which meant spending entire days inside. Participants subsequently engaged children in a range of indoor activities such as "bird spotting" from the window, puzzles, colouring, drawing or storybook reading to keep them entertained. For some children like Matilda's four-year-old son, remaining inside was untenable because he was "an active child who needs to be outside to be in his happy space". To manage his needs, Matilda described monitoring the smoke's intensity and letting him out when it subsided:

Matilda: So on the really severe days, he only went out for a little bit of time, but then on the severe but not as severe days, we would allow him to go to a playground. A couple of times he was allowed to ride his bike on the local school's basketball court, he was learning to ride. So he was allowed a brief, you know, period outside on the not very bad days, not the severe. But yeah, we explained to him and he understood.

Fear of the effects of letting children go outside was also apparent in lockdowns during the pandemic, only this time it was inhalation of the COVID-19 virus, rather than smoke, which worried mothers. For Lisa, a graphic designer and mother of two, this concern raised a dilemma about whether to send her children to their daycare:

Lisa: Like when it was bad in lockdown, I wished for more help with [child's name] definitely. That was the hardest thing when I was super pregnant and he was just going crazy at home, we couldn't even go to the park or anything. That was hard. I mean, technically, I could send him to daycare, but I felt really anxious about that, and I talked to people about it a lot, like, am I making the right decision here about keeping him home? And the general consensus was, yes, this is unprecedented, just do what you need to do. But selfishly, I was, like, I just want to send him so that I have a break. [Laughs] So that was probably the hardest thing.

Lisa's story – told to Rebecca in a cafe while Lisa nursed her six-month-old daughter – was interlaced with anxiety and emotion that often bubbled to the surface. Her uncertainty about keeping her toddler son home may well have been exacerbated by her general concern for his health, stemming from his need for heart surgery when he was eight weeks old (and after a traumatic birth experience). Lisa also described worrying about miscarriage during the bushfire smoke, lack of information about the effects of smoke, memories of the 2003 bushfires and, later, concerns about her daughter's low birthweight.

Official information about children's susceptibility to COVID-19 and its effects for pregnant women were similarly scarce in the early stages of the pandemic, when there was considerable conjecture about how the virus was spread (She et al, 2020; World Health Organization, 2020). However, the general sense that pregnant women are more vulnerable held, and uncertainty about COVID-19's effects heightened participants' concern about their baby's health. Several described their anxiety about attending regular maternity checks in health facilities and hospitals where ill people were concentrated. The sudden onset of the pandemic and the implementation of unprecedented governmental restrictions for citizens to 'go into lockdown' left health professionals in a state of panic and disarray regarding these new rules, as Renee describes:

Renee: I went in to see the midwife and the receptionist said, "You're not supposed to be here", like, in a really panicked way. I went, "Oh!". And I know now that I had actually been quite anxious getting to that appointment, I'm thinking I've made this huge effort and, you know, potentially … it seems weird now, potentially, like, risked my baby to come to this appointment.

Other participants worried about how their carefully prepared birthing plans, designed to make them feel safe, would be thwarted by new movement restrictions and person limits in hospitals (Wilson et al, 2022). Government announcements about the cancellation of surgeries (Tomevska, 2021) left Lisa concerned that the elective caesarean she had booked would be cancelled. After "hearing stories about Italy that the strain on the health system caused by the virus would mean hospitals would have to turn people away … and if that happened here", Shelley worried where would she give birth and whether it would be safe. Suddenly, going into labour, which already constituted as a risky endeavour within contemporary discourses of maternal health, had become even riskier.

Once participants had given birth and brought their baby home, fears around breathing-in-the-virus remained. Several described how the usual celebrations and visits from family and friends bearing gifts and home-cooked meals failed to happen. While family time alone getting to know their newborn was valued by some participants, others lamented an absence of much-needed emotional support and childcare from significant others. The idea that babies are particularly vulnerable to serious illness in the first 12 months (Lupton, 2012a) was a concern for several participants, especially as COVID-19 was an unknown entity and this exacerbated their feelings of risk. Gina describes how in her attempts to protect her newborn from exposure to the virus, she restricted visitors, made them use hand sanitizer and ensured they kept their distance:

Gina: It's pretty awful, to be honest, like, you're worried about, like, when we first had him, you know, everyone was so excited and they wanted to come see him. And we wanted to have people over, I wanted to have family and friends and whatever else over, but we just didn't know who they had seen and who they, like, you know, just the, like, the community contact, we just didn't know who's been seeing who and what exposure they have had to COVID.

          So we tried to limit our visitors as much as we could during those first couple of weeks. I mean, you do that anyway, you know, before kids have vaccines, but we really tried to minimize how many people would come and visit. If we did have people come and visit, we made them, like, hand sanitize and whatever else.

Managing anxiety is a technique learned by citizens of the risk society (Beck, 1992). Lupton (2012b: 331) argues that 'the concept of "risk society" is relevant in positioning of foetal and maternal bodies in contemporary discourses and practices'. The notion of the 'risk society' refers to a new era for individuals (in Western societies) characterized by an increased awareness of daily risk and preoccupation with controlling it (Beck, 1996). This new sensitivity to risk is attributed to an overdependence on medicine and other forms of science to simultaneously inform us of risk and safeguard against it (Ruhl, 1999). In relation to pregnancy, this has occurred with the advancement of biomedical technologies such as ultrasound, which is now routinely offered to all pregnant women. Such technologies enable the imaging and surveillance of foetal bodies for genetic disorders and developmental 'abnormalities' (Sänger, 2015). These advancements in prenatal screening bring the experience of pregnancy into public view and have the potential to identify a plethora of 'risks' for the unborn child and mother. As Possamai-Inesedy (2006) observes, the accessibility of knowledge about the risks women face in their pregnancy not only offers them new forms of agency, but also produces additional types of risk for them. Such knowledge is accompanied by the assumption that 'women should take care to avoid risk as much as possible [and] has the effect of rendering pregnancy as a perilous journey, requiring eternal vigilance on the part of the woman travelling through it' (Lupton, 1999: 66).

For citizens of the risk society, there is a recognized shift towards individualization where agency to shape destiny is bestowed through personal decision making. This is opposed to a notion of a future that is determined by a monarch or government that instigates rules and metes out punishment to control citizens. In a form of neoliberal governmentality, the ideal citizen is one who is autonomous, self-regulated and expected to take responsibility for their own actions and welfare. For pregnant women, this translates as being charged with the primary responsibility for caring and maximizing the potential of their child, even before it is conceived (Waggoner, 2015). Social institutions associated with health and medicine and their expert practitioners, along with media organizations, reproduce the imperatives of self-regulation among citizens. During the bushfires, this was evidenced when public health authorities declared pregnant women should wear masks to reduce their unborn baby's exposure to smoke (Minister's Department of Health, 2020). Via these tactics, pregnant mothers learn to feel responsible for the health of their unborn baby and other children, as well as at fault when it fails (Lupton, 2009). The management of the health of one's pregnant body is a feature of 'reproductive citizenship' (Salmon, 2011), whereby pregnant women are required to take personal responsibility for their actions and its implications for their children. Pregnancy has subsequently become 'remoralised' as 'an ethical practice' (Weir, 1996) producing mothers as 'good' or 'bad' depending on whether they make 'the right' or 'wrong' choices to protect their children from smoke and the COVID-19 virus.

'Mum-guilt'

Feelings of 'mum-guilt' associated with breath and breathing were apparent throughout participants' narratives. Sarah had gestational diabetes and used swimming to help manage this condition. Each morning she would check the air quality app and if the readings were good, she would head out to the pool. However, this decision caused her significant angst because the physical exertion of swimming meant breathing more heavily and inhaling additional smoke particles that were potentially harmful for her baby. The responsibility of managing this risk produced a constant and agonizing dilemma for her:

Sarah: It [pregnancy advice] always says swimming is great for pregnancy and it always says swim, do yoga and all these things … But when I'm exerting myself … am I getting more of the particles in, because that did seem to be what the studies kept saying over and over is that if you exert, you're going to bring in more, but I just thought I have to balance up the risk of the gestational diabetes and not exercising ... and then minimise my exposure [to smoke] for the rest of the day ... So that was kind of how ... I thought through the balance, the constant balance. And the days where I got it wrong, like Sydney, I got really upset with myself, really devastated and then just had to move on.

Sarah expresses 'mum-guilt' here in several ways. Her decision to go swimming makes her feel guilty because it (implicitly) places her own diabetic health needs over those of her child. Having to breathe more deeply while swimming also produces guilt for exposing her baby to additional smoke particles. Sarah also refers to a day when she went to work in her Sydney office and, while sitting at her desk, felt black ash fall on her shoulders from the ceiling. She had forgotten to bring her mask and explained that when she got home she had a "foul headache" and experienced her worst worry about the effect of smoke on the baby. In her own words: "I just thought, what have I done permanently to him?" This guilt led her to be vigilant about always remembering her mask because it "Doesn't matter how uncomfortable it is and whatever. I'd wear it in the car ... I think people think, 'weird!', but I don't care what you think! ... I've got a baby!"

Another example of feeling guilty about breathing smoke was offered by Matilda who, to escape poor air quality in Canberra, travelled to the South Coast "to have a rest" in a "smoke-free seaside" town. When fire threatened this area, residents were evacuated to the beach:

Matilda: ... being in the thick of it literally, with singed leaves falling down and hot ash burning our eyes as we sit on the beach, and I'm sitting there thinking, "Sorry baby, sorry [baby's name]", sorry everyone, you know, and then trying to waddle back as fast as I can to evacuate in the car. And your respiratory effort is higher because you're walking up a hill from a beach. And I'm like, "sorry baby again", like "I'm inhaling this bloomin stuff".

Elsewhere in her interview, Matilda, who was struggling with debilitating illness, in conjunction with the bushfires, indicates how this made her feel unusually "vulnerable" and "disempowered". These circumstances meant she was "unable to do much. So, I really had to let it go". Despite recognizing that debilitating illness, bushfires and inhaling smoke were beyond her control. Her sense of guilt emerged when she apologized four times for having to breathe. This is a heart-rending moment in understanding pregnant women's experiences of the bushfires which starkly illuminates an impossible bind for them. It reveals how within a notion of reproductive citizenship where women are responsible for children's safety (Salmon, 2004), they are left only with the (illogical) option of not breathing. We see this denial of breath as part of a feminist politics of breathable lives (Ahmed, 2010) that highlights an unbearable burden on women and leaves them guilty about their own right to breathe.

Participants' feelings of guilt about breathing smoke extended beyond their own breath to that of their children. Anita's family was evacuated during the week between Christmas and New Year when the fires were severe. She describes how there were 48 hours when it wasn't possible to venture outside because the smoke was so dense that it made daytime pitch black and it was impossible to breathe. The fires continued to burn for several days afterwards, although the smoke began to ease, so Anita remembers letting her children, who had been cooped up for a week, play outside. Recounting this decision, she says:

Anita: [O]bviously the fire was burning so close for so long, we
            sort of just adjusted to it and relaxed a bit. And now I look
            back at photos of that time, and it's, like, the girls are
            outside, and I can see the smoke and I'm like, "What was
            I thinking?" [Laughs] But obviously I was just partly, like
            my ... one-year-old at the time, she just had to go outside,
            like, she lives outside usually. And I think also I just got
            used to it, so I didn't realize how bad it was.

Matilda similarly berates herself for allowing her son, who was desperate to play outside, to go out without a mask:

Matilda: [A]lso knowing for [child's name's] sake as a small child, on
            some days, he has to go outside because of the consequences
            for his mental, emotional wellbeing, you know, he has to
            go outside, even if it's for 20 minutes. Admittedly, we didn't
            put a mask on him, I never remember him wearing a mask,
            which is bad, bad form.

Against a backdrop of public health advice to 'keep out of the smoke', both participants constitute their actions as those of 'bad mothers' for relenting to their children's need to play outside. Previous studies on motherhood have established the ideal 'good mother' is perpetually occupied with caring for her children, unfailingly meeting their needs and acting upon expert advice about their welfare (Lupton, 2012a). These actions are entangled with moral meanings and judgements about women's mothering practices (Lupton, 2012a). Subsequently, the decision to let children play outside, against public health expert advice, makes participants feel like 'bad mothers' who are 'morally wrong' and 'guilty' of not conforming to 'good' mothering practices.

'Mum-guilt' for breathing was also evidenced in participants' narratives about the pandemic. Describing the difficulty of enduring lockdown restrictions with a newborn, Gina relates how activities like visiting a cafe to relieve the monotony of childcare ceased. Summoning the phrase 'mum-guilt' employed throughout this chapter, she explains: "I think as well, like, even now, like, if you go out, you feel guilty about it, like, you shouldn't be out because there is a slight chance that you may get something and then, you know, the mum-guilt kicks in and whatever else." The guilt Gina refers to here eventuates from a worry about her newborn breathing in COVID-19 at a cafe where the air is perceived more "suspicious" (Harms, 2020). This concern implies that mothers are responsible for the air their children breathe, something which Sarah raised directly when she said: "I think it, maybe it was just being pregnant is like more you're completely responsible for their air." Feeling responsible for an unborn child's air is tied to contemporary conceptualizations of the pregnant body as containing the Other within the Self, in an ambiguous blurring of boundaries (Lupton, 2012b). The unborn child is perceived as 'precious', 'fragile' and particularly 'vulnerable' to external harms, to which the mother's womb offers a 'warm nurturing, safe, protective' buffer (Lupton, 2012a: 1). We suggest that the idea that mothers might control the air their unborn/born child breathes is a fantasy of human control over the material world. Within discourses of maternal responsibility, however, women are expected to protect children from harm, and an inability or unwillingness to do so can result in 'mum-guilt'.

In their attempts to control the air their children breathe, participants describe implementing regulations around contact during the pandemic. These range from restricting who was able to visit their home to banning all visitors during the baby's first few months. While such controls were designed to keep their newborn safe, some participants recognized they also had negative consequences. For example, these rules increased feelings of isolation, severed important forms of emotional and practical support, and prevented participants from extending help to others. Denying significant others the ability to see the new baby also resulted in guilt for a number of participants:

Katya: I feel guilty, I've got friends who have never met [baby's name]. I couldn't be the support that I wanted to be for my family in Melbourne and vice versa. You know, even her great grandmother is ... in a nursing home, and we can't see her. So yeah, I definitely feel a lot of guilt. Her grandmother hasn't seen her since she was born … So yeah, there's a lot of connection there that she just hasn't had, and as a mum, yeah, you feel guilty for it. You know, it's out of your hands but, you know, you … yeah.

Katya's guilt over restricting visitors extends to the adverse effects she perceives this having on her baby's ability to form social connections. Later on in her interview, she explains she wanted her daughter to be around her cousins "so she can see what older children are doing and how they walk and how they play and how they speak for her development". For Katya, this absence of contact, intensified by the closure of mother's groups, meant "it 100 per cent had an impact on her development, yeah, for sure". Similar feelings were expressed by other participants who worried that without contact with people outside the family, their child's development would be impaired. As Helen reveals, "there was a period there that I was worried about her [the baby's] social development. 'Cause she just didn't see any other babies for such a long period of time". While contact restrictions were mandated at government level during lockdowns, some participants extended them beyond these periods. This strategy to keep their baby safe from COVID-19 provoked simultaneous feelings of guilt for denying contact with others and potentially impeding their infant's social development. In such instances, participants were caught in a paradox where being a 'good mother' meant simultaneously being a 'bad mother', resulting in feelings of 'guilt'.

Smoke's nonhuman agency

According to Harms (2020: 277), 'breath and air elude control'. This statement is of relevance for the current study with the modification that it is 'breath and *smoky* air' that elude participants' control. Our theorization of breath and smoke as vibrant nonhuman intra-active agencies is significant in reconceptualizing maternal responsibility during a period of crisis. As explained earlier, this is because when agency and responsibility are understood as a distributed product of the intra-active bushfire assemblage, women cannot be held individually responsible for the health of their children. This offers a transformation in thinking about 'mum-guilt' not as something individually born by women, but as eventuating from a specific coagulation of human-nonhuman relata, including discourses of reproductive and neoliberal citizenship and maternal responsibility. Such an understanding is only possible when the agency of nonhuman things to produce human action and feelings is acknowledged. In this section, then, we demonstrate this nonhuman vibrancy with reference to the way 'smoke' from the bushfires shapes human behaviour.

The research team have encountered smoke's vibrancy via their own engagements with bushfires as recorded in their personal accounts of this time. However, reminders of the agency of smoke have continued since the bushfires have ended. While working from home in Aotearoa-New Zealand during the peak of Omicron infections, Louisa smells smoke and wonders if the activity of analysing the interview transcripts (in which she is currently absorbed) has finally gotten to her. She notes the smell's metallic tinge and looks out the window to see an enormous cloud of dense grey engulfing the skyline. As the intensity of this aroma is unbearable, she races outside to rescue the washing and hurriedly shuts all the windows, even though the summer heat is stifling. The whole incident only lasts 20 minutes, a minuscule timeframe compared to the 40 days of smoke endured by Canberrans. It is, however, a potent reminder of just how powerful and traumatic the fires were. During ten years of living at her current address, she has never encountered a fire and wonders what the material world is trying to tell her with the appearance of this one.

Smoke's agency is evidenced in its ability to shape participants' daily activities and in some cases cancel events. As previously described, participants routinely checked air quality apps, monitored wind direction and triangulated information from multiple sources to seize moments to go outside. Gina explains what her approach involved: "I kind of kept an eye on the air quality ... on the government websites ... So I would regularly check ... how bad is it today? Alright, it's really bad. Now I'm going to knuckle down and just try not to go outside and ... you know, really ... limit my exposure to it." Smoke's presence limits Gina's activities to indoors and conversely when it recedes, it enables her to go for a walk or head to the shops for groceries. Gina's actions are not conceived here as acts of individual will premised upon her assessment of the presence/absence of smoke. Instead, smoke is understood as a nonhuman agency that intra-acts with Gina's breath, eventuating her action of either remaining in or leaving the house. Another example of smoke's vibrancy is provided by Libby, who had planned a weekend away with her husband at the beach. Setting off in the car, they began to encounter roadblocks due to fire risk and Libby realized the drive would be too difficult. After persevering for three hours, the trip had to be abandoned as the roads were inaccessible and smoke made driving visibility treacherous. In this example the intra-active agency of smoke and other relata (cars, fires, air, humans and roadblocks) thwart Libby's holiday plans and force a car journey in which she and her husband unwillingly "did one giant round trip!".

The way in which smoky air eludes human control is also witnessed in participants' stories about its inescapability, despite their attempts to contain it. Peppered throughout the interviews are descriptions of innovative strategies participants actively employed to wrestle control over the smoke. These comprised sealing windows and doors in their homes with tape or wet towels and using essential oils or vinegar in water under fans to diffuse the smoke. Other strategies included the use of air purifiers that became highly prized commodities during this period as they were believed to make the air better to breathe. While some participants were sceptical about their efficiency, the act of having one was in itself reassuring, as Naomi explains: "It kind of felt like I was being more proactive and trying to clear the smoke out. So I don't even know if it actually helps [laughs]. But it kind of felt like a placebo sort of thing." Reducing time spent outside and vigilantly wearing masks outdoors or even while in the car made some participants feel safer. Others tried to escape the smoke by travelling to other parts of Australia or delayed their return to smoke-filled regions. Drawing up fire plans and pre-planning routes to the hospital should they go into labour were also approaches that were taken. While some participants engaged in research about the effects of smoke exposure in pregnancy to feel more in control, others actively avoided seeking information and silenced fire alerts on their phones so as not to feel overwhelmed with information. In all instances, participants were resigned to smoke's presence and their inability to eradicate it. Capturing the sentiment that doing something they knew to be ineffectual was better than doing nothing, Sarah says: "We just had to do whatever we could do, to do that."

Conclusion: an exhalation (and air-filled pause)

So where has following breath and breathing in this chapter led us? Thinking with breath as an organizing concept invites nonlinearity in understanding and conceptualizing women's experiences of bushfires and the pandemic. Via this approach, we have attempted to contribute to recent emerging materializations of breath (Oxley and Russell, 2020) as well as a feminist politics of breathing (Górska, 2018). By following breath, it is possible to see how through the act of breathing participants *become* particular kinds of subjects – in other words, subjects who experienced 'guilt', 'fear' and/or 'vulnerability' and perceived themselves as 'bad mothers'. While breathing can undoubtedly eventuate positive dispositions such as those of 'calmness', 'happiness' and 'contentment', it is important to remember, as Choy (2020: 568) notes, that we find ourselves in a historical moment of 'respiratory distress and systemic breathing disorderings'. Crises like bushfires and a global pandemic make breathing especially challenging on various physiological, geographical and political levels. Given this historical context, it is unsurprising that breathing eventuates primarily negative experiences for participants.

From a new materialist perspective, *breathing makes these experiences at an ontological level* rather than simply causing participants to feel or do certain things. For example, the presence of COVID-19 does not cause pregnant mothers to feel fear for their unborn babies in any conventional sense. This fear materializes in and through breath, in the moment in which breath, virus, pregnant bodies and government lockdowns intra-act. This conceptualization recognizes the agency of nonhuman things like smoke and viruses to shape human subjectivity and action, and simultaneously elude human control. Breath subsequently configures who we are and shapes our relationships with human-nonhuman others *at the level of being*. In any intra-active event of breathing, we materialize as certain subjects contingent upon the relata present in that temporal moment. As a nonhuman agentic force (along with smoke, fires, air quality apps, air purifiers, masks and the COVID-19 virus as examples), our breath opens and closes possibilities for acting and thinking about ourselves. In a sense, we are held hostage to breath and what it enables us to become. We have to breathe to live, but breathing is no simple task, especially when you are pregnant during a crisis.

What breath has been able to *do* in this analysis is challenge 'the binary logics that constitute contemporary notions of human subjectivity' (Górska, 2018: 250). Breath challenges the dualist logics within discourses of maternal responsibility, reproductive citizenship and risk society that posit women as either a 'good mother' (without guilt) or a 'bad mother' (with guilt) for exposing children (born and unborn) to smoke and the COVID-19 virus. A new materialist orientation to breath helps disrupt notions of 'inside' and 'outside', and complicates notions of self, other and environment. This theoretical framework challenges individualist conceptions of humanness, recognizing that pregnant women are not discrete bounded entities that have sole (or even primary) control over the health and wellbeing of their (un)born children. Within this theorization, pregnant women are recast as part of a complex web of material relations that they do not fully control rather than the agentic centre of the world. What this reconfiguration does is to release participants (at least at a theoretical level) from 'mum-guilt' by recasting the experience of keeping their babies safe during crises, like the bushfires and COVID-19, as unachievable through 'individual' action.

Via a new materialist conceptualization of breath and breathing, it is possible to acknowledge that human exceptionalism is a fantasy. Breathing is not within our control, a fact long recognized by free divers, who are the most adept humans at resisting the need to take the next breath (Fong, 2018). New materialist thought recognizes that pregnant women and how they are viewed within discourses of reproductive citizenship are intra-actively constituted through the material and social dynamics of living. When the nonhuman agency of the world is taken into account, responsibility is configured as relationally distributed and not something that women hold or enact individually. Via our exploration of how the involuntary act of breathing is guilt-filled for women, we suggest that bushfires and the pandemic as environmental and viral crises elude human control. This does not mean that humans cannot be held accountable for these crises. Nonresponsibility is an untenable position within a new materialist ontology and its notions of response-ability (see Allen et al, in process). However, within a feminist politics of breathing, we maintain that the 'guilt' pregnant women experience through each breath they take is inequitably apportioned to them and negates the accountability of the rest of the world for environmental and viral crises.

Interleave 4

"We both really love data": Shalev NessAiver's story (interview transcript)

So it was probably around November, I think, when it started to get bad, and I'd been doing a lot of research into just baby health and development [during] the whole pregnancy. You know, we both really love data information and, you know, we're science-oriented. So when this started happening, I did all the research. I looked around and I read a bunch of papers, and put together a picture. And I was pretty worried because there's quite a lot that could happen.

So I began to see there was a pattern, right? It became fairly clear that if you figured out where the fires were and where the winds were blowing, you could tell when it was going to be really bad. So … in the morning I started doing that and I would just message her or tell her in the morning: "Okay, today, like, you've got to be really careful, don't go outside in the middle of the day. Here are the times when it's probably going to be better." You'd start to see repeating wind patterns where over one period of time when the temperature dipped, it would blow in and then another one would come from a different direction and clear it out. So I was able to kind of give her a little sense of, like, you know, "in these couple of hours, that's when you should go outside. Everything else is probably going to be bad, but we should go shopping right now".

And then I realized, well, look, there's a lot of people here, and I'm sure other people could benefit from this. So I just – I tried to do the simplest possible thing I could do, which was to provide information … I do a lot of web development, so I just made, like, a little mini webpage, and then took pictures of that. Since I was already doing it for her, I just put it on a Twitter account and started publishing that.

Interleave Figure 4.1: Neighbours gather to observe the fire

Note: Coming together to observe the smoke and flames was common during this period – the spectacle of the fires was at once captivating and disturbing.

Source: participant photograph

As the months rolled on, the wind patterns changed and more fires sprung up. So it was less useful to say, like, "Here's what's going to happen", because all I could really say is "It's probably going to be smoky all the time". But I was able to pull data from some automated sources, and display that in a way that I felt was a little bit easier for people to read and access. And then I put up a little FAQ. I felt that people were under-appreciating the severity of what was going on. They're like, "Oh, it's business as usual. It's just smoky". And, you know, in my mind, I'm very health conscious about all these, you know, there are lots of things in our environment nowadays which are not fine, I think, but which we're exposed to regularly.

We already had an air purifier, which was helpful. So I put up a bunch of stuff – I did the research, on how to figure out which air purifier to get, ... because air purifiers will give you a number as to clean air delivery rate, and, you know, when you're actually trying to figure out if this works for your house or not, people were confused. I had friends asking me, like, "So what should I do? What should I get?" So I tried to make that clear and just put up ... basically questions that I kept getting repeatedly I put on the website, so I didn't have to answer them over and over again.

And then also data acquisition was a bit tough because at the beginning, the ACT government air monitoring didn't really update very frequently. It was, like, this rolling average of the past 24 hours, and I spent a lot of time trying to figure out if I could extract the current number from the rolling average. And the answer is you can't because you lose information when you take an average, and you cannot reconstruct that information. But there are a couple of other places that they had, like, an agreement with the Air Rater app people to send their data in pseudo-real-time. I think an hour delay was the max. And there was a way of accessing the same EPIs, the same sources that the AirRater app was using that I could pull directly and just put it into the website.

Smoke, Machines and Public Health

Although bushfires are a standard part of the Australian summer, and despite the fact that there have been catastrophic fires in the recent and more distant past, including in Canberra, until 2020 there were no public health campaigns about the dangers of smoke inhalation that occurs over days or weeks, and no information for specific groups of people (Vardoulakis et al, 2020). Information about what to do in fire seasons has focused on emergency escape plans (which every citizen is exhorted to make) and house and garden preparations to suppress fires near dwellings. Those of us living in Canberra were 'fire ready' that summer – bags packed with key essentials and plans made as to where we would retreat if necessary (the showground, the local oval), but none of us had plans for how to live with smoke.

This infographic (Figure 4.1) was co-designed in January 2020 by ANU colleagues to try to fill this void, and was translated into 11 languages. It was created as a visual summary of a dedicated website where more extensive information was made available along with links to relevant resources. Against a silhouette of Australian bush and a huge smoke plume, the infographic gives advice to citizens about how to take care of each other during bushfire smoke events. Near the end of instructions, at the bottom right of the page, a simple graphic depicts an older woman with a walking stick, a pregnant woman, a crawling baby and a small cat. 'Help others', readers are told, implying that these are the figures of vulnerability who may require care.[1]

As discussed in Chapter 3, the pregnant women in our study recognized themselves in these images and were willing to think about themselves as in some ways more vulnerable than nonpregnant others. We could argue that they were model citizens in this regard: obliging, responsive, concerned and caring. Most of them followed all the other instructions on the infographic – they stayed indoors, reduced their physical activities, and tried to protect their mental and physical health. Some of them wore masks and many made

Figure 4.1: ANU bushfires infographic

National Centre for Epidemiology & Population Health
Research School of Population Health
College of Health & Medicine

Australian
National
University

Source: infographic reproduced with permission from the PHXchange, ANU

plans to evacuate in the case of fire. To greater and lesser extents, they all obeyed the exhortation to follow governmental advice on bushfires. What was less clear, however (unless they went to the more detailed website), was how they should 'follow air quality information', another instruction on the infographic. Where was this information to be found? And what does 'following information' mean? (It is rather different, we suggest, from 'following advice'.) What were the actions one should take once air quality information was found? And what were the risks of not doing so? In these challenging circumstances, what should a pregnant person or parent of a young baby do?

Seeking expert advice

Unsurprisingly, and again acting as good citizens and mothers, many of the women in our study asked the health professionals involved in their maternity care for advice about these issues:

Renee: I spoke to my midwife about it, just mentioned, like, "What should I do?", and their advice was "Just take it easy and try and stay out of the smoke." They were very upfront, like the only advice they could give was to stay out of it. But they also said, like, "Babies are really resilient and if anything, the mother will be affected before the baby will." So, they tried to be very reassuring, but they also, you know [trails off]. You could sense they needed to be careful because there's no medical rules and not a lot of medical research. I don't know if there is any but certainly they weren't speaking from a basis of, like, "This has happened before, and this was proven." It was more just "Try and stay out of it and the baby, you know, you've got to look after you, the baby will look after itself hopefully."

This consistent finding – that clinicians were unable to provide specific advice to women or to explain the risks of smoke inhalation to foetuses or mothers – was in some ways a surprise to us. Trying to work out what was going on, we interviewed various medical and scientific professionals about what they understood the risks to be and how they were communicating these to patients or citizens. In the first instance, Celia spoke to Professor Paul Dugdale, the acting Chief Medical Officer of the ACT, who was responsible for providing health advice to citizens and the government in Canberra at the height of the smoke events in early January 2020. Paul described the intensity and pressure of daily morning meetings in the emergency services command centre, where he would listen to the firefighters discussing the current state of fires, wind and smoke, and analyse the Bureau of Meteorology's data and predictions for that day's air quality. His job was to translate this information into public health guidance:

Celia: Do you remember giving advice specifically for pregnant women and if so, what that was and why?

Paul Dugdale: I can't remember if I gave advice on it, but I remember thinking it through to, you know, a small extent. I mean, I think, the womb is protective and the baby in the womb, I wasn't too concerned about. Once the baby's born, it's a different matter. They're opening up their lungs and using them. One of our operating theatres at Canberra hospital was the smokiest place I saw in the whole thing. It actually made my eyes water and we were still operating in there.

Paul is a public health clinician, not an expert in pregnancy or foetal or infant health. His sense that babies would be protected in utero echoes what many of our interviewees were told by midwives. We continued to wonder, then, why pregnant women might be seen as vulnerable, so we interviewed one of Canberra's leading endocrinologists, Professor Christopher Nolan, who specializes in maternal diabetes and has a particular interest in the impacts of bushfire smoke. Chris reported that during the fires, the majority of his patients were worried about smoke and a small minority were very concerned. He described the corridors of Canberra Hospital as "billowing" with smoke – people were unable to see from one end of the corridor to the next. We asked Chris what he remembered saying to patients who expressed concern:

Celia: So, if … a patient said to you, "I'm worried about my baby", what would your answer have been?

Christopher Nolan: Yeah, so at the time I was actually looking at literature about effects of bushfires, wildfires, really, most of the information was from the US, and it's pretty scanty information. There's a little bit from fires, the coal-mine fire in the Latrobe Valley. There were studies done on that. And from those studies, it seems that there potentially is a risk of slightly early birth, but it's not a big effect. And … from the coal mine fires, there appeared to be increased incidents of gestational diabetes, and hypertensive disorders in pregnancy, but not consistent across the studies. And the data is not strong.

So, what I was saying to women is that … "We really don't know the extent of the risk to your baby." That advice would be to sort of "Try and avoid smoke as best you can, such as ... staying inside when the smoke is bad outside." But a lot of the houses in Canberra would collect smoke through the day, and then it was actually better outside at different times. So being aware of smoke levels was important, and to try and keep smoke out as best you can, trying to mitigate the risks of exposure is one thing. But from the studies that we could see, the risk doesn't seem to be super high, but ... that there potentially is some physiological effect of the bushfire smoke.

It seems clear that clinicians were operating in a research vacuum – indeed, this is the underlying impetus for the MC2020 research project, of which Chris is the lead researcher.

As mentioned in Chapter 1, another ANU colleague, biological anthropologist Associate Professor Alison Behie, has supervised PhD research into the effects of bushfire smoke on foetuses by Megan O'Donnell. O'Donnell's work focused on pregnancies that took place during the 2003 Canberra and 2009 Victorian 'Black Saturday' fires (O'Donnell and Behie, 2013; 2015). Her research found that babies born during these events, particularly males, tended to be larger than expected:

Alison Behie: So, she looked at the Canberra fires and then the Black Saturday fires to try ... [to investigate] what's going on from an evolutionary perspective ... And some interesting things came out. So, in Canberra, for example, babies were bigger. The baby boys were a lot bigger after, and that was really unexpected. And whether that was a missed gestational diabetes thing, because medical testing was harder to do and women sort of fell through the cracks, we don't really know, but we couldn't come up with a real biological, like, an evolutionary ... reason, unless it was bigger boys are maybe stronger?

Celia: How solid a finding is that?

Alison Behie: I mean, it was a smaller sample size, it was just Canberra, but ... it held true across all the ratios and competence intervals and it was a fairly robust finding, but odd. I mean, most of the other stuff we've found has been preterm births and low birthweight, which sort of tracks with other studies and is what other people see [in their research].

As Alison states, this finding remains counter-intuitive from an evolutionary, bioanthropological perspective and is at odds with other findings about babies born during disasters that tend to show the opposite. All of this uncertainty was unsettling for pregnant women in our study.[2] Alongside the smell and taste of smoke in hospitals, the inability of clinicians to allay participants' concerns was something they found hard to manage:

Sarah: One of my appointments I went in and the smell of smoke was like so thick, [like] someone had lit a barbecue inside those rooms from one of my diabetes appointments! And they were all upset too, the poor staff – they are in it day after day. They said "This hospital air conditioning can't cope, it's just not good." And I remember mentioning to one obstetrician in particular. I said, "Look, I'm a little bit worried about the smoke and what it means in this last trimester." And he said, "Yeah, it's terrible, isn't it? Now about your iron levels, they are showing you are a little bit low." And I'm like, "That's it? You are a doctor. I'm not a doctor. Aren't you supposed to tell me that it's going to be okay? Or some idea about the impact?" I was just so worried about my baby ... Other staff, I think, were a little bit more worried, but that was probably at the start to be fair. He probably became more worried as it went on ... But this year has been really unprecedented, so I try not to judge anyone. We looked after ourselves.

Libby, herself a paediatrician, gave an interesting account of how clinicians and friends reassured women in the face of "not knowing":

Libby: We found that, you know, the helplines ... yeah, my midwife was fantastic, but she didn't know anything about it because there isn't, you know, and the helpline's the same, there's nothing in their training or their ... so they don't have any information for you that you can't access more and better elsewhere, I guess. So, we asked, but ... everyone was kind of going, "Well, we don't know. We actually don't know." And I find particularly when you're pregnant, or in fact have a small baby, everyone is very keen to reassure you. So, everyone's very reassuring about how it's fine, and actually that's not what the research says at all, and I find it a bit condescending in that, "Oh, it's all, okay. It's all fine." I'm like, "Well, actually it's not, it's not, and I'd really love it if you stopped telling me that it was." And instead said, you know, "I really acknowledge that this is frightening and that we don't have enough information, and that really sucks, you know, from what we can see, the good news is blah, blah, blah."

As we will show, in the absence of professional advice and/or the presence of relatively empty reassurance, pregnant women and parents of newborns developed their own methods of 'following air quality information' and taking care of themselves and others. The sociological literature on ecological disasters shows that this is a common and often meaningful approach in the face of potentially life-threatening uncertainty: people act to protect their bodies, their families, their property and their sanity (Erikson, 1994; Convery et al, 2008; Whittle et al, 2012; Mort et al, 2020). While scientific and governmental uncertainty can be unnerving, it can also be invigorating. Sometimes, citizens take the initiative, forming collective banks of knowledge and enacting community-led forms of care (Tironi and Rodriguez-Girault, 2017; Calvillo, 2018; Liboiron et al, 2018; Tironi, 2018). In 2022, for example, Australian citizens at risk from rising floodwaters across NSW and Queensland rescued one another in private dinghies and other vessels in the absence of assistance from emergency services. This chapter explores what the parents in our study did to try to understand and act in relation to bushfire smoke, articulating the intricacies and challenges of contemporary Pyrocene parenting.

Before we go on, it is important to note the divergent experiences of our interviewees according to their physical location during the summer. Some were in Canberra the whole time, and were strongly affected by smoke and the threat of fire, but did not have to evacuate or deal with fires in their immediate environments. Others were on holiday or lived on the NSW South Coast and were exposed to the immediate danger of fire and intense smoke. Many were forced to evacuate from temporary or permanent homes and some ended up moving from place to place on the coast, seeking relative safety. Others left the coast or Canberra for places of greater safety, such as Melbourne or Sydney or other regional places less affected by fires or smoke (sometimes inadvertently finding themselves in greater proximity to fire). Pregnancies and babies played important roles in decision making about moving. Some of our participants were too sick to move, others had babies or children with health issues and many had partners who had to keep going to work. Even though flights were "crazy expensive", as one woman put it, money was rarely a hindrance, although other materialities often got in the way. At points in the crisis, it became impossible to safely leave Canberra by car, for example: the highway to Sydney and the main routes to and from the coast were closed due to fires.

"Weird experts"

The lack of clear public health advice and the apparent ignorance of clinicians presented our participants with a range of problems and questions: when was it safe to go outside to exercise? Was it reasonable to let young children play in the back garden? Could a window be opened at night? Should they wear a mask or buy an air purifier? In response, many developed a set of practices to both manage resulting anxieties and to make daily life decisions. These typically combined bodily practices (seeing, smelling, tasting) with some kind of analysis of 'data' and/or tuning into scientific advice. One Canberra woman described this brilliantly (note: this interview took place many months after the fires and during the COVID-19 pandemic – like many other participants, Sarah can no longer remember technical language acquired during the crisis):

Sarah: [There were] some days where it was just disgusting, and then, yeah, like I was saying, a couple of days we were like, "I can actually see blue sky!" And, you know, monitoring the numbers of the – can't remember what the measurement was now, but it was measuring the smoke particles in the air – and we all became weird experts on what was, like, an appropriate amount of air pollution. And if it was under a certain amount, then I'd be like, "That's it, that means I can go to the pool today" or "I can sit in the backyard."

For almost all our Canberra participants, these decisions were a balancing act. It was important to keep exercising – to keep one's gestational diabetes under control or to feel confident that one was fit enough to manage labour – and to keep young children from going stir-crazy, but going outside often felt dangerous and could make you sick, either immediately or in the long term. The effects on foetuses and children were hazy but possibly profound. For women or children with asthma, the concerns were even higher. How could such decisions be made?

Assessing smoke levels with your body

In their book on health biosensing, Roberts et al (2019) argue that bodies are always-already sensing their internal and external environments, and that technological or device-led biosensing practices (using Fitbits, ovulation biosensors, genetic tests or falls detectors, for example) are typically interwoven with these embodied processes:

Living bodies are full of sensings. What might be called biosensing practices go hand in hand with life in general. Hormones, such as cortisol … are themselves biosensors that detect and signal change in bodily state. To have (or be) a body, to experience in the widest sense of that term, is perhaps a matter of sensing practice, of plural 'heterogeneities doing things' (Bennett, 2009 122). If bodies sense, then biosensing devices are a provisionally stabilised version of what variously takes place in bodies all the time. (Roberts et al, 2019: 13)

Assessing air quality is a clear example of such interweaving. Our participants used a range of bodily senses to assess smoke. In the quote given earlier, for example, Sarah talks about seeing blue sky. For all of our participants, looking out at the world was an important way of judging smoke levels. Many reported having a visual "indicator" or "geographical things" in the view from their home – if they couldn't see that thing (a mountain, an iconic building), they knew the situation was bad:

Matilda: As you can see, you can see Mount Ainslie from here, you can see Mount Majura from here, and you can see Black Mountain from here. So, we would say on less smoky days, "Look, we can see the mountain! We can see Mount Majura, we can see Mount Ainslie, we can see Black Mountain! Wow, what a miracle!" So, we would have our own little geographic things that we would look at from our front balcony to indicate what sort of day it was. We could watch it [the smoke] coming and going as well. It was creepy. It would creep in, and you could see it coming.

The photographs participants supplied were often of grey skies and invisible views. "Normally", they would tell us, "you could see the mountains from here" (Canberra is a city ringed by a set of small mountains), or for those in coastal areas, the beach would be filled with people – boring photographs for sure, but important indicators of the smoke's intense, "creepy" and insinuating qualities. As mentioned in Chapter 2, sometimes people could supply us with 'before and after' pairs to highlight more precisely what was missing. Unfortunately, these pairs make little sense in black and white, so we have not reproduced them here.

Participants also used their noses and mouths to assess smoke levels: other scholars might call this 'atmospheric attunement' (Choy, 2018) or 'attuned sensing' (Calvillo, 2018). As we noted in Chapter 3, many negative words were used to describe the smell and taste of smoke: gross, disgusting, oppressive, awful or horrendous. People became experts in sniffing out smoke – where it was entering their houses through vents or gaps – and described it as somehow alive or intentional; it was "creeping" or "like a snake". Some experienced the smoke as deeply distressing and did all they could to escape it. At its very worst, the smoke raised existential questions about the impossibility of living when the air is unbreathable; a horrifying spectre of dystopian futures.

Being attuned to the smell, taste and look of smoke felt very important to our participants. Interestingly, however, our expert interviewees mentioned that the smaller particulate matter in bushfire smoke is imperceptible to humans (either visually or through the nose and throat). These smaller particles – known as PM 2.5 (particulate matter less than 2.5 micrometres in diameter) – are understood to be dangerous because of their ability to travel through our bodies into the lungs and then the bloodstream (they are not blocked by nasal hairs, for example). From a scientific perspective, lay people's belief that they can make good judgements about air quality via their senses is not accurate.[3]

Blocking smoke's passage and wearing masks

Public health advice such as the ANU website advises people to block smoke's pathways into their homes. Many of our participants undertook to do so: taping up windows and doors, putting up plastic 'contact' (adhesive plastic) over vents, and laying wet blankets and towels along door and window frames. Some reported becoming "obsessive" about this – one Canberra woman was embarrassed to admit to climbing ladders in the late stages of her pregnancy to do this work, but was pleased to have finally been able to convince her husband that the vents in their home were not necessary:

Sarah: I've been saying to my husband for years, "Can we seal up these vent things because I don't think they do anything?" And he said, "No, no, no. They have to be there for some, for some ventilation." This is in the walls. And then there was this great article in the *Canberra Times*. I said, "No, they're just there as regulations from the fifties when people had gas heating so that they didn't accidentally asphyxiate or whatever." So, we sealed those up. I think it was Christmas, sorry, New Year's Day, which was actually one of the worst days, that orange-grey day. And yes, I, I try not to tell people this, but I was up ladders with the contacts, putting the contact around the vents because we've got evaporative cooling and heating. So that's, I don't know how many vents in the house, while my husband was getting spack filler and cleaning, you know, doing the things, I sealed up the whole bathroom … Look, how much difference it made? [rhetorical question]. We got T-Rex tape and put it around the French doors of the girls' room. We had gaffer tape above the dishwasher where there's this gap, but you can feel it when the air blows when you're standing there at night, I think. "Oh, okay. There's another one." But it did make a difference. If air purifiers are to be believed when I got a Dyson that actually told me. We would come in, put it on and it would drop down. So obviously we were able to clean the air inside a little bit. But again, how much of an effect it made... [trails off].

The ANU infographic and website also advise people to wear masks to manage smoke. It takes some effort now to remember the connotations of masks before the pandemic. When the smoke levels got very bad in Canberra, pregnant women were advised to wear P4 masks, which have particulate filters. These were hard to acquire, so the government allocated two to each pregnant woman, which could be collected at local pharmacies. Some of our participants decided to wear them; many didn't. The optics of mask wearing at that point in time were complex – some participants were asked, while at the hospital, why they were wearing one. One decided it was too frightening for her two-year-old son. Another described strangers in the street telling her that as a pregnant woman, she should put one on. Renee remembered being dissuaded by midwives from wearing a mask:

Renee: They ran out of masks. I got prioritized for a mask because I was pregnant, but we ended up being able to purchase them later on anyway, but I couldn't use them. Like, I spoke to midwives and they said, "If you're struggling to breathe, using a mask is actually going to be worse anyway."

Women had complex views about the function of masks. Sometimes they described them as making it easier for them to breathe; at other times, the masks were described as filters for the baby. Matilda, shared a photo of herself: "Sat on the couch, a huge whale of a woman, like, massive stomach with this mask, I look like something from ... [trails off]. Yeah. Just sat there breathing in smoke." Here Matilda describes the effects of the filtered air on her brain:

Matilda: But what I came to realize once we started using that mask from his [husband's] workshop, the spray-painting mask or whatever, the filter, as I said, you think inside [the house] is good, and you put that mask on and you can actually breathe properly, and your whole brain feels different when you put it on. It's like having clean air, and my brain sort of cleared, and then I took it off and it was, like, "Oh! And this is inside! Not good!" [Laughs]

As the fire season ended in March 2020, Australia went into its first COVID-19 pandemic lockdown and masks took on an entirely new significance. As discussed in Chapter 3, the risks of breathing were reconfigured: rather than reducing particulate matter, masks were meant to filter out the virus. Gradually over that year, we learnt to breathe through masks and to accept them as part of daily embodiment. Over the course of the pandemic, citizens and experts have become increasingly aware of the potential dangers of air and the significance of quality ventilation in enclosed spaces. The public health focus on fresh air and ventilation – and, indeed, the privileging of being outdoors – seems to be in direct contradiction to the previous exhortation to seal up homes: one set of directions focused on the movement of air; while during the fires the emphasis was on rendering spaces impermeable to smoke.

Following air quality data

As discussed in Chapter 2, our Canberra participants were almost all middle class and highly educated. It is unsurprising, then, that they often turned to 'data' to find answers in the face of confusing advice from clinicians (see Rapp, 2004). The ACT government provided air quality information on its website, updated daily, and it was also possible to obtain information from AirRater, an app designed by Australian scientists (and recommended by the ANU website). Daily briefings on television, radio and online, featuring the Chief Medical Officer, the Head of the Fire and Rescue Service and the Chief Minister, provided advice about air quality and risk of the fires encroaching on the city. Listening to these briefings and/or following air quality reports became a regular activity for many of our participants.

Air quality is typically described in terms of concentration of particulate material (PM). Outside of fire season, Canberra is a city of clean air – air pollution is not typically a matter of concern or debate. Particulate concentrations were not something Canberrans were necessarily au fait with (participants' failure to remember the term some months later is not surprising for this reason). From late November to early February 2020, Canberra experienced approximately 40 days when the air quality was above hazardous levels (above 200 PM 2.5) (Brown, 2020). At times during the summer, Canberra's particulate levels rivalled the most polluted cities of the world: on New Year's Day, air quality levels reached a 24-hour PM 2.5 level of 855.6mg mμ3 (Lal et al, 2021). Like many journalists, our interviewees reported these facts with horror:

Lisa: And especially because it was in the media by that stage as well, like, oh, you know, 'Canberra has the worst air quality' and everyone was kind of, like, "What??? Not us. We're the Bush Capital! … It's always clear."

Invidious comparisons were sometimes made with poorer countries where low air quality might be expected and where ecological privilege cannot be assumed. Here the astonishment of loss of ecological privilege – a feeling that profoundly shaped 2020 in relation to both the fires and the pandemic – is clear: *Canberra is not supposed to be like this*:

Alison: We actually lived in India for a while, for about a year a few years ago. Not in Delhi, thankfully, we lived way up in the mountains in Tamil Nadu. So, the air quality was actually great there, it was the same sort of elevation as Kosciusko, it was, like, tea plantation territory. But I was just, like, "This is so fucking ironic: 'Who could raise a child in Delhi? How do they live?'" And then I come back to Canberra I'm, like, "What has happened?" [Laughs] Because you look at all the relative indexes, you're, like –
Rebecca: We're worse than Delhi! [Laughs]
Alison: Yes! [Laughs] And Delhi in winter is the worst over there, like, around December is the worst time, January, I was just, like, "Ergh! Serves me right."

Following air quality data isn't something that people in Canberra had been trained to do. In Delhi, air quality, infant mortality and morbidity are clearly catastrophically linked, with 15,000 premature deaths of children under five being recorded in Delhi in 2017, for example (Mariel et al, 2022: 436). Mariel et al's research found that concern about this matter, and willingness to pay for amelioration, was linked to social class. Capacity to care about air quality and plans to reduce pollution are, not surprisingly, income-related. In India air pollution is worst in low-income areas – the proximity of industry and high traffic roads are important causes. Bushfire smoke is less differentiating, although air quality research in Canberra did show higher levels of smoke in lower socioeconomic status areas of the city, due to geographical features such as mountains.

In Canberra, the official air quality advice was based on three monitoring stations located in different parts of the city and provided what our interviewees, in their newly developed language of "weird expertise", described as a "24-hour rolling average". Such information, as one participant argued, might be useful for documenting car- or industry-related pollution in cities, but does not help much in hourly decision making in a crisis. It was not specific enough either spatially or temporally. Indeed, there were times, as Sarah says, where it "had been so wrong". Some of our participants were moved to develop capacities to interpret and cross-correlate with other data – for example, about wind direction:

Sarah: So I was trying to balance up between what I could see
            and … what the data was saying, because quite a few
            times that had been so wrong where it said it was okay,
            and then I'd refreshed and gone, "Oh, no, it's just…" You
            know, remember how it would sort of just waft in and
            then it was coming from that direction, that direction,
            that direction? … And that's the other thing I think we
            did – we just became experts at what's the wind direction?
            Like some sort of salty sailor, like what direction is the
            wind going to be tonight? … If it was coming in from the
            coast it would often bring this beautiful clean air. And that
            was it. Those were the times we'd open up the windows
            and then it would be that nine o'clock, the wind would
            change and then we would run around shutting them all,
            yelling "We need to get the contact back up!"
Rebecca: So did you check with the Bureau of Meteorology for the
            wind direction?
Sarah: Yeah, exactly. Yup. Yup. And it usually was about nine
            o'clock. I remember quite a few times just saying, "I smell
            it! Quick!" And yeah, my husband took a couple of weeks
            actually to understand.

Across our Canberra interviews, a key solution to this problem of untimely
and nonspecific data repeatedly arose. This story is also told in Interleave 4:

Rebecca: And how did you make those judgements? What kind
            of measures were you using? Were you looking at the air
            quality apps?
Delilah: Yes. And there was a guy, some guy on … Do you want
            to know who it was?
Rebecca: Yeah, that'd be great.
Delilah: I'll see if I still follow him [checks her phone]. CanberraAir,
            who was just some local dude who gathered up the data
            and put it out in this nice, helpful way. Sometimes you'd
            be, like, "Well, that was, you know, ten hours ago data, like,
            that's not what I need." I'm trying to remember how he
            presented the data though. I can't remember, the pictures
            aren't showing up for some reason. But yeah, I would
            usually check that. My dad was checking something else
            and so we would often just sort of be, like, "No, no, no,
            mine says this or that." But yeah, that was the main way to
            decide whether it was okay to go outside that day or not.

Shalev NessAiver is a data analyst, educator and computer programmer, who in an interview with a Canberra journalist describes himself as 'an avid biohacker' (Smith, 2020). His CanberraAir website, Facebook page and Twitter account relied on a network of air quality sensors that quickly mushroomed across the city that summer. Citizens interested in air quality purchased 'Purple Air' monitors and started gathering data through the PurpleAir Citizen Science project's website (www2.purpleair.com). In an attempt to support his pregnant wife and to materialize his concerns about air quality, Shalev started to collate and analyse this data. Deciding that the information might also be of interest to others, he built a simple website that depicted real time PM 2.5 concentrations and wind direction, making temporally and geographically specific assessments and forecasts of air quality. In simple language, he told people what the data meant. In an interview with Rebecca, he explained:

Shalev: So, I was able to get updates on the current air quality much faster than the main Canberra website was … I remember I was seeing on Twitter, people were, like, tagging the government saying, like, "Why can't you put this up there?" … Eventually they put it up there, but even so, I found there was still some value in what I was doing in presenting it a bit more concisely, and just very easy to see. "So, what does this mean? Okay, so the numbers are up and down, what should I do with that?"

And there were a couple of different places I could actually pull data from at that point, and people would ask me for, like, historical data sets sometimes, and people were trying to do various … mini-research projects or trying to figure things out. So, I fielded a whole bunch of questions. People would email me about, like, "My child's going to a sport, you know, their usual sports thing, but I don't know if we should do that", and all sorts of different questions about lifestyle and what should be happening right now.

So, yeah, I mean, I think it was a lot, you know. I used the Twitter feed a lot at first, and then eventually I think the website became the more central place and people would just reach out. And also Facebook, I just copied the tweets from Twitter to Facebook. So that worked for a different subset of people who use that more.

News of Shalev's work spread on social and mainstream media, and many of our Canberra participants mentioned this site. Shalev reports that the site was getting about 18,000 unique hits per day (Smith, 2020). The level of time- and place-specificity helped women to make quick decisions about when and where to venture outside.

Although welcome, detailed information sometimes created doubts about using one's body to make decisions. Sometimes there were tensions between what was felt or seen and what websites like Shalev's were suggesting:

Rebecca: And so were you using that just in the mornings to help with your decision making around work or were you using it throughout the whole day?

Libby: We were checking ... yeah, pretty much ... probably not hourly, but something like that, you know, because [as a doctor] we are making clinical decisions for other people's health as well, and certainly I'd always check it before I went outside, you know, before I decided I'd go, "Okay, I need to change locations now." So, you know, you'd check it, you see, okay, and you'd look, alright, prediction-wise, what way's the wind coming? Are we likely to get better or worse in the next hour? You know, if it's poor right now, am I better off waiting an hour and then leaving, or am I better off actually leaving now because it's going to get worse? So, lots of guesswork.

Importantly, the very existence of the website (at least for those who knew about it *and* who were able to act on the advice) felt comforting. In contrast to the relatively spartan announcements of public health officials (which were intended to reduce alarm), the details that CanberraAir provided felt like care. Describing Shalev, Sarah said:

Sarah: He took it on himself to do that. And I thought, "Well, it [the smoke] makes someone else feel like we do! There's one other family!" He was tweeting them [air quality data]. Yeah. It just actually really helped my mental state because I felt like somebody else cared and was doing something about it, you know? 'Cause that's often the way these things work, isn't it, someone has to be motivated to do something about it, do it themselves.

Shalev's project is a classic citizen science project insofar as it made visible forms of data that might typically remain in an expert realm so that citizens in the know could inform themselves and act accordingly (Aoki et al, 2008; Braschler, 2009; Calvillo, 2018; Gabrys et al, 2019). In addition to its significant effect on many women's decision making and mental wellbeing during the fires, Shalev's work has a lasting legacy in terms of establishing both a system and an expectation among Canberrans for citizen-led, granular information about air quality. We have been lucky insofar as the summers of 2020–2023 have not been 'bad seasons' – the drought broke in the winter of 2020 and temperatures have remained relatively low. We are constantly warned, however, that we should expect more extreme fire events. When these happen, we have little doubt that concerned citizens will follow Shalev's lead in collating and sharing data. Like many other forms of health-related biosensing projects, such interventions will no doubt become an increasingly important part of our digital landscape and daily life in the Pyrocene. Indeed, as we drafted this chapter in late 2021, reports were emerging of Australian citizens using portable CO_2 monitors to test air quality inside buildings in order to facilitate decision making about COVID-19 infection risk (Salleh, 2021) and buying personal oximeters to measure blood oxygen levels to help make decisions about when to go to hospital if they tested positive for COVID-19.

Biosensing smoke, like biosensing exercise, ovulation or stress, is a subjectifying practice. Earlier, Sarah described her and her husband becoming like salty sailors in their attention to wind direction, for example. Biosensing also produces forms of collectivity or community around data and bodies – what Roberts et al (2019) call 'living data'. The online sharing of citizen-produced data (in this case from Purple Air monitors) is a key part of constituting such communities. Shalev's central role in gathering and analysing data from citizen science projects and governmental sources is somewhat unusual. None of the women in our study were gathering outside air quality data themselves (although many were observing indoor data on their air purifiers), but this speaks to the unusually urgent times of the fires. Other sociological studies of air quality monitoring describe much slower, long-term citizen engagements around air pollution (for example, Ottinger and Sarantschin, 2017; Calvillo 2018). Reproductive life, going forward, will likely increasingly involve both individual environmental and body monitoring, and collective community pooling of relevant data about air quality (see also Liu, 2017; Calvillo and Garnett, 2019).

Cooling and purifying air

Although our Canberra participants used CanberraAir and governmental information to make decisions about when to venture outside, most of the time they stayed at home. Many Canberra houses were built in the 1950s and 1960s, and many of these are 'leaky' (they have gaps and holes where air can enter and escape uncontrollably). To understand that better, we spoke to Jenny Edwards, the Director of Light House Architecture and Science, a local company that specializes in environmental newbuilds and home renovations. After the fires and during the pandemic, she told us, many people realized the significance of air quality to their health and wellbeing, and came to notice the gaps and leaks in their homes. Such leaks – long-documented in the environmentalist literature on buildings as problematic in terms of temperature change and energy loss (heating or cooling) – took on a new significance:

Celia: So, I guess that's often about heat rather than air, isn't it? … Has it become more about air?
Jenny Edwards: It's become more about air, absolutely. So, yeah, until this year, conversations about indoor air quality were pretty rare, and that's what last summer did, particularly in Canberra where we're so used to having these beautiful, cool, fresh nights. And so suddenly people were switched on to that.

The bushfires also changed people's attitudes towards the technologies already installed in their homes. The bushfire season was a time of extreme temperatures for Canberra. We regularly experienced daytime temperatures of over 38°C, and nighttime temperatures atypically remained high (as an inland city, Canberra's temperature usually drops significantly at night, as Jenny mentions). Over the last few decades, government incentives were offered to install ducted gas central heating (using hot air rather than water), so many people installed evaporative cooling systems (which rely on leaving doors open to circulate air that is then cooled through water) rather than air conditioning. During bushfires, evaporative cooling systems draw smoke into buildings and cannot be used. Many people, then, were left without the capacity to cool their homes. Fans could help to move air around, but temperatures were often very high. Both Jenny and our parent interviewees commented on this problem:

Renee: We haven't been in Australia very long and my husband's, like, "What *is* this country?" Like, the first summer we were renting in a house that had no air conditioning and it was sweltering, not this summer, the last summer [2018–2019]. Pretty much our house was like a clay oven. And then this one [2019–2020, the summer of the fires], well, we've got evaporative cooling upstairs, so we couldn't use the evaporative cooling. So, we had all the win[dows closed] … yeah, everything was shut off … We had the purifiers and pedestal fans in the kids' room to try and cool them down.

People concerned with air quality, particularly pregnant women but also those with asthma or other breathing difficulties, were encouraged to buy air purifiers. These standalone devices of varying sizes can be purchased at big box stores or online and typically cost A$800. During the summer of 2019–2020, they became rare and much-prized items. Air purifiers even made their way onto some of our participants' drawings of their support networks during the fires. People described both their own and others' quests to buy a purifier: sending their husbands out like hunters; asking family members to buy them in other, less-smoke-affected cities to buy and ship; or telling stories of driving hundreds of kilometres to find one. Many of our interviewees described being able to "just throw money at the problem" to buy one, while others received them as gifts:

Matilda: So that little smoke purifier did mean something. It was a gift from a friend, which was very sweet, and at a time when I needed that sort of sweetness. And so that was nice. But also it was just respite, I guess, it provided respite having a room with slightly better air. It didn't solve the air problem at all but it did make a little bit of difference. It was a very small one, it was reassuring, it was sweet. It had a sweetness attached to it.

Treated almost like icons, purifiers were moved around houses to provide their reassuring stream of clean air. In the early stages of the fires, some women described taking a purifier to work; others talked about collective fundraising campaigns to purchase them for childcare settings; while paediatrician Libby said that she offered her patients the opportunity to reschedule their appointments even though she had an air purifier in her rooms. Families' sleeping arrangements were altered to focus on the purifier – children moved into their parents' bedroom; whole families slept in the living areas; or difficult decisions were made about who had the highest need (an asthmatic child or a pregnant mother?). Some women described trying to stay as close as possible to the purifier at all times:

Sarah: When I came back from Sydney, we had people over and my [husband] said, "Oh you have to go outside and talk to them." I said, "I'm sorry, I can feel it in the back of my throat, I need to go inside." And I was basically just a little bit rude and I said, "Sorry, I'm going inside. I'm going to sit next to my Dyson." And that was in early December.

As well as filtering air, these devices provide digital readouts of particulate levels: sometimes this is a number, other times a coloured warning (green for good through to purple for danger) (see Figure 4.2). Unsurprisingly, this function created ambivalent responses. Some participants described being

Figure 4.2: 'Ludicrously bad' PM 2.5 concentrations recorded by a domestic air quality monitor

Note: The value attached to devices monitoring air quality is captured by this image of one participant's air quality monitor in their kitchen. Have such devices maintained their place in the heart of the family home post the fires or was this a fleeting attachment? Where are these devices now?

Source: participant photograph

reassured by the display of numbers – somehow this meant that the machine was working – while others remembered with some horror how often the display indicated that the air quality was very poor. Some also reported that it was hard to see smoke inside their homes, so having the machine helped to make judgements. Machines provided "peace of mind" and helped to "take the edge off mentally", as Gina explains:

Rebecca: And how did you find it in terms of using it? Did you feel it did help quite a lot?
Gina: Yeah, yeah, I think it did ... [I]t was good because, like, it kind of shows you ... like, it had different LED lights and

stuff on so when the air quality was really bad, it would go red and you could really hear it, like, revving up, sort of thing. So, it did, it was just more a peace of mind, sort of thing. Like, I could hear it, I could see it, I knew it was doing something. Something at that point was better than nothing.

Rebecca: So I think you said that it felt reassuring seeing the numbers go down?

Sarah: Absolutely. I probably put a lot of confidence in the Dyson brand because they are expensive and I felt like it was actually working with the smell. I don't know whether it's just because I was preggers, but you get such a strong sense of smell anyway, but I sort of felt like it smelled better. The air was fresher. But when we got the second Dyson that had the little reading, you could see it fall. And I thought "Yeah, pretty good." Like there's mixed messages about how effective they are, but I felt pretty good. And my god it took the edge off mentally! I don't know what I would've done if we hadn't sourced one from somewhere because we were still trapped.

As in other fields of biosensing (Roberts et al, 2019), engaging with the air purifiers' measurements of particulate matter recalibrated users' understandings of acceptable and unacceptable health risk:

Rebecca: Do you feel like it was a little bit of a mix of kind of looking at that data, but also just using your own judgement to look outside and be like, it looks not too bad?

Renee: Yeah, I mean, it was pretty bad every day. We kind of used the data as the line though. Okay, look, it's not super bad, you could still smell it and you could still see it. Yeah, so we did rely on that to kind of help us make the decision when we could go outside. But we certainly didn't wait 'til it was good, because it was just never good. You had to just get it to moderate. And even though we were all, except for my husband, we were all classified as sensitive groups and you weren't supposed to go out in 'moderate', you're like, "Well, I've got to get these kids outside!"

The digital readouts also contributed to some participants' feelings of 'weird expertise'. Even when it was not entirely clear what the readout referred to (what are particulates anyway?) or what they signified in terms of danger (what levels are dangerous, and how long do you have to be exposed to them to be affected?) they came to mean something. Like most biosensing data, these readouts delivered the most meaning when connected or triangulated with other data derived from other sensing practices (the look, smell and taste of smoke most importantly perhaps, but also wind direction and speed):

Gina: So, I did look at the app and to see what the air quality was. But I mean, as soon as you wake up, you look outside and if you can't see much, then you know it's going to be a pretty bad day anyway. So yeah, I would say, just a combination of what I could see and smell, like, instantly inside the house, like, when you wake up, you know, you can smell it. And some days were particularly stronger than others, and you kind of just knew that it was going to be a bad day.

In many fields of health biosensing, clinicians and other experts express ambivalence about patients or citizens' use of data (Roberts et al, 2019: 153). Studies show that doctors typically consider such data inaccurate, excessive and unhelpful (West et al, 2017). Although we have some sympathy with this view – clinicians are bound by decision-making protocols and need specific kinds of data that help them follow these – in the environmental arena, citizen- (or patient-)derived data can be hugely important to challenging and thus developing existing medical knowledge and practice (Ottinger, 2010; Rabeharisoa, Moreira and Akrich, 2014; Ottinger, 2016; Ottinger and Sarantschin, 2017). As Michelle Murphy notes:

Many different disciplines and communities of experts make knowledge about chemical infrastructures, but in piecemeal ways – some experts study chemicals in fish, other experts engineer smoke stacks, while others diagnose illnesses. Yet others feel chemical infrastructures by working and living in sites saturated by industrial chemicals. Quotidian acts of breathing, drinking, and smelling can become knowledge-making moments in chemical infrastructures. (Murphy, 2013: np)

It would make sense that citizen-derived knowledge becomes significant in areas where medical and scientific knowledge is underdeveloped, such as the effects of toxic chemicals and/or bushfire smoke on foetal and maternal health. Participants in our study were proactive in their attempts to make informed decisions and did so in the medical and scientific vacuum that the MC2020 study is trying to address. Our hope is that scientific and biomedical studies and advice could learn to take seriously the activities and experience of citizens that materialize the injunction to 'follow information' *and* to recognize that 'following information' might suit some people better than others. We return to this argument at the conclusion of this chapter.

Fires near us

It is important to note that participants living in areas more directly affected by fires on the south coast of NSW were much less concerned about smoke than those in Canberra, where only two fires came close enough to threaten homes. Our South Coast participants did not have a lot to say about smoke and were typically unaware of information sources about particulate levels. This is because they were focused on something much more dangerous: out-of-control fire. Several were evacuated from their homes or from coastal holiday accommodation due to a serious risk of fire (none lost their homes, but some came very close to doing so, and several personally knew people in that situation):

Rebecca: Did you have any information available to you about air quality in [coastal town]? Was that something that you looked up or was there anything –?

Lily: Oh, like, I didn't worry about it as much as "What fire level are we on? What can we do?" kind of. That would have worried me more than what the air quality was, yeah.

When fires are nearby, information becomes essential, most importantly in terms of making decisions about when to leave the area and where to go. The Federal government encouraged all citizens not only to follow the news on radio, TV and/or online, but also to download and monitor the 'Fires Near Me' app (a live, map-based app, described in Chapter 1). All participants were using this app, which was both a trusted source of information and intensely anxiety-provoking. One participant, who evacuated several times during the summer, described her ambivalent experience:

Rebecca: What about the RFS [Royal Fire Service] apps, did you have …?

Bridget: The Fires Near Me app. Yeah, we had that, which was fairly useful, except [that you need electricity and phone coverage – she gives an example when she didn't] … because obviously you need a phone to use the app. And the radio! … You'd get in your car, turn it on and [it'd] be, like, "Go onto the Fires Near Me app!" and it's, like, "Yeah, you're really thinking this one through, aren't you?" [Laughs] So we were using that here, but it gets to a point where it's really overwhelming because you get the app, and it's just, like, there's this fire everywhere. I had to switch off a few times because I'd keep being, like, "Oh, [husband's name], oh no, there's another fire at [place name], or

they're saying there's a fire at [another place name] now!"
Because even the house fires and stuff come up on that. So
any form of fire, and so we were just getting notifications
nonstop. And I was finding, like, I'm like, "Bridget, your
stress level, you need to just keep it under control." So I only
started looking at it if I felt like there was a need, because
you need it, this isn't going away. Like, [neighbours] down
the road had said we're not getting rain until at least mid-
February or March. So I sort of had to put in some, like,
self-preservation strategies to not freak out completely.

People also relied on word of mouth from neighbours and social media. The
dizzying speed of the fires and the chaos involved in wind direction changes
meant that information was often changing and confusing. Sometimes it
was better not to get too much:

Anita: I found Facebook really hard because, like I said, everyone
            I know was affected, everyone was sharing everything, and
            it wasn't always useful, because there's a lot of crap people
            were sharing. And I think in a way that caused more stress
            because you didn't really know what to trust, and if you
            should, you know, be following this advice to – I don't
            know – do something that seemed stupid. [Laughs]
Rebecca: There was quite a bit of social media going on. Did you
            have any relationship to that at the time?
Hannah: I tried to sort of keep my distance from it, because I didn't
            want to … be kind of drawn into feeling like I need to sort
            of take drastic measures, if that makes sense. So I wanted
            to prevent feeling overwhelmed by it all. Because I think
            social media, there's a lot of sharing of expert opinions. But
            then there's also a lot of people just posting their opinions
            and I think sometimes you wonder, okay, how verified is
            that claim?

In these times of intense and realistic anxiety, many women had to devise
strategies to try to stay as calm as possible, working out who to trust. There
are clearly tensions relating to 'weird experts' and the management of stress
in times of crisis. Knowing who to listen to, how much to listen and when to
listen are just some of the questions that were playing on participants' minds.

Again, issues of geographical specificity were important. In the face of
fast-moving fire fronts, information provided by the Australian Broadcasting
Commission (ABC) did not feel precise enough. Looking back, Anita was
very impressed with her local government representatives:

Rebecca: So you did find that Facebook was probably one of the most up to date sources in conjunction with those other –

Anita: It was up to date ... but it wasn't always trustworthy. We ended up following the council, like, the leadership, the mayor and this other guy, I think he's, like, the media guy, I don't actually know what his job is. But their leadership was outstanding. And they were putting stuff up really, really regularly and so the [names of her local area] ... [T[hings like ABC we trust, was really good, too, but because it was the local council, it was a lot more specific, so things like exact roads. And the area we live in is very small, isolated, you know, like, there's only max a hundred people that live here. So ABC, like, it wasn't going to report on our exact area.

In contrast to this kind of praise, one of the biggest political news stories of that summer was when the former Prime Minister Scott Morrison, who had already been criticized for being on holiday in Hawaii for too long, travelled to the South Coast of NSW to view the devastation of Cobargo, a tiny town that had been seriously affected by fire. Keen to convey his compassion, he was filmed grabbing the hand of a distressed, pregnant resident despite her resistance and being angrily told to leave the area. This frequently replayed scene encapsulated the feelings of many coastal residents that large city dwellers had no idea how terrible their situation was. One year later, when Celia travelled through Cobargo, she saw many notices and posters that spoke to this feeling and a resilient community response (see Figures 4.3 and 4.4).

These kinds of local, community action and care during and after the fires are a long way from the anonymity of national apps and the aloofness of federal politicians, who, after all, are often considered blameworthy for environmental disasters. From the relative safety of Canberra, Delilah's conversation with Rebecca also articulated some of this politicized affect:

Rebecca: Were you using the Fires Near Me app or any of those ones?

Delilah: Yes. The New South Wales RFS one was the one we were probably ... using the most often. I would say the thing that was more worrying wasn't the kind of immediacy of the fire risk, it was just that general feeling over that summer period of the climate's fucked, like, we have – there's no going back, we've stepped over the line, you know, the government's fucked it up for all of us and we're going to face this every summer from now on and ... yeah, what a grim place to live in. [Laughs]

Figures 4.3 and 4.4: Notices in shop windows, Cobargo, one year after the fires

Source: Celia's photographs

Conclusion: "even with everything we've put in place"

Living in a grim place where you feel that the climate's fucked can create despair, especially when it comes to physical effects you can't control. Paediatrician Libby reported a conversation with her husband that articulates feelings of helplessness in relation to her future baby's health:

Libby: As I said to my husband now, crying one day, "It's like, even with all of the things that we've put in place, you know…" I looked at him and said, "We're going to have a smoker's baby, darling." Because even with everything we've put in place, we've at least had that level of exposure. And that's for people who, you know, made a huge amount of changes and conscious decisions about how to bring this baby into the world. That's really distressing.

Later on in the interview, Libby confirmed that her fears were realized, although she did also describe her and her partner as "lucky", in that their baby had avoided worse health issues:

Libby: We didn't have any placenta calcification, but we did have a smoker's placenta.

The idea that being exposed to the bushfire smoke was equivalent to smoking cigarettes while pregnant surfaced across our interviews and in media stories both at the time of the fires and later in 2020. The similarity was said to be visible in placentas. There is some evidence to suggest that exposure to bushfire smoke is associated with inflammation and impaired placental function (see Basilo et al, 2022).

In Australia today, smoking while pregnant is an extremely maligned practice, both medically and socially, that carries connotations of out-of-control maternity that are classed and racialized. For the middle-class, educated women in our study, such behaviour was out of the question, so giving birth to a "smoker's baby" or even a "smoker's placenta" was a highly troubling experience. Our interviewees considered themselves thoughtful, caring parents who would do all they could to ensure their babies' health. The uncontrollability of exposure to bushfire smoke threatened their capacity to attain this goal and left many of them experiencing anxiety, 'mum-guilt' and distress. Almost all of the interviews were undertaken after the babies were born, and most of them had been healthy since birth. The few who were not had developed conditions that may or may not have any connection to smoke exposure – only time and further research (including the MC2020 study) will be able to clarify this. What we can see here, however, is the powerful belief of middle-class, white Australian parents that they can and should control external threats to their babies, both before and after birth.

Such beliefs express privileges – economic, political and physical – that are part and parcel of contemporary gendered and racialized subject formations in the Global North. Such privileges are also both challenged by the enormity of climate crisis and the COVID-19 pandemic, and, as we show in this book, are reshaped and reformed through them. With enough money, people can purchase technologies to filter out smoke or have space for personal privacy in pandemic lockdowns. Although it is often unclear how effective these measures were, as our interviewees have noted, they did provide some 'peace of mind' or at least a sense of 'having done all you could'; ultimately, taking these measures was, for many, an experience of agency, however restricted.

Analysing these kinds of privileges, feminist, queer and anti-racist theorists and activists analyse the uneven distribution of reproductive rights and practices, building arguments for reproductive justice. In her work on environmental toxins such as endocrine-disrupting chemicals, Murphy (2013: np), for example, argues that 'unchosen rearrangements to the embodiment of nonhumans and humans' (bushfires and COVID-19 are clearly both examples of these) 'can be acts of structural violence that destroy the possibility of future life and produce life unborn'. Defining reproduction as 'the sustaining of capacities to live intergenerationally', Murphy suggests that the politics of 'distributed reproduction' should focus on the effects of such acts of violence on these capacities:

> [W]hat is crucial to the politics of distributed reproduction is not the maintenance of proper heteronormative human and nonhuman bodies, but instead is the sustaining of capacities to live intergenerationally ... how [can] unchosen rearrangements to the embodiment of nonhumans and humans ... be acts of structural violence that destroy the possibility of future life and produce life unborn. At stake is a simultaneous recognition of intergenerational injury and a valuing of queer, altered, and othered life. The figure of life unborn, then, expands from a concern of the conventional politics of abortion (and a figure of the Christian right) to a concern of the politics of sustaining multigenerational life and already altered life within uneven conditions of past, present, and recurring violence patterned in the material work of capitalism. (Murphy, 2013: np)

What is important to us here is Murphy's insistence that the politics of reproduction should focus on 'already altered life', what she elsewhere refers to as 'alterlife' (Murphy, 2017). Across her work, Murphy refuses a vision of a pure or unaffected life, insisting that no living being – no matter how privileged – can escape 'unchosen rearrangements of embodiments'. In alterlife, we are all affected and, as we have seen in this chapter, experts might not be able to provide us with advice about how best to live. Uncertainty abounds and control starts to feel impossible. For educated, middle-class, white Australians, this can be uncomfortable, even distressing territory.

Public health clinician Paul Dugdale, who we met at the start of this chapter, focused on how people were thinking things through, making their own judgements about how to manage their own or other's health in the context of extreme fires:

Paul Dugdale: The public health advice is to ask people to think it through and to be sensible and to think you can work this out. You may not know what to do and how do you work it out? Well first of all, you assess your circumstances. You talk with your friends and the other people who help you work things out and you work out your circumstances and you work out what you're going to do. And you know, you, you are good enough for that. And it was similar advice to health professionals working in the hospital, they said, "What should I do?" Well, we didn't know so, "You're a professional, you know, think it through!" Like, we're thinking it through at one level and then all other health professionals have to think, "Well, what will we do?" Like in all their different branches of medicine. And the public had to think it through and they had to be sensible, creative, collaborative, seek help, give help. And the circumstances were so incredibly varied … Like if you're heavily pregnant, you're not going to be one of the people that's going to stay and fight [a fire]. Don't even think about it. There are other people that can [do that].

Paul was really pleased about Shalev's website and impressed by the way people were engaging with citizen science data:

Paul Dugdale: So, you know, people sitting in their homes waiting for an official warning from the authorities is not the way to have your community respond to a disaster. They've got to be thinking it through. So … doing some, you know, amateur air quality testing, good on him! And also I loved it that people were going on to the internet and looking at the air quality advice.

This attitude has strong resonance with existing STS research on biosensing, which shows that the sharing of data and collaborative talk can lead to less stressful decision making and more nuanced practices in a range of health-related arenas. As Roberts et al note:

> Only exceptionally does the data from a biosensor afford immediate unambiguous observation, understanding or actions in relation to bodies and self. Usually, data has to be collected, accumulated, transformed, rendered in graphical form, subjected to analytical processes of modelling, assimilated to other data sources or interpreted in the light of scientific and clinical knowledges that introduce a welter of assumption, presuppositions, representations and norms with them. Biosensor data hardly ever aligns directly with experience in any of its modalities. It has to be worked on, and this work is porous, distributed and expansive. (Roberts et al, 2019: 21)

As we have shown in this chapter, this is especially true in the area of smoke and air quality, and its effects on pregnant women and their babies. There is so much uncertainty in this field. Indeed, working out how to live with climate crises (either specific disasters or the long, slow burn of incremental change) is currently a matter of experimentation at the individual, household and community levels, as well as nationally and regionally. As citizens, we are all learning to tinker with our bodies, our machines and our homes in order to survive. In their study of extreme heat events in Western Sydney (which are increasingly frequent), for example, Lopes et al (2018) found that disadvantaged families living in homes without air conditioning had developed a range of strategies, including draping wet sheets over tables and playing with babies underneath, evacuating the upper levels of their homes, and trying to stay physically very still.

In their analysis of health biosensing, Roberts et al (2019: 8) argue that 'Added to the indeterminacy of health measurement, the lines between body and environment are blurred. Bodies are so plurally entangled in the world that it sometimes hardly makes sense to speak of them as separate from an environment', a point echoed by Murphy earlier. Again, this entanglement is particularly highlighted in our case study. Breathing, as we argued in Chapter 3, is fundamentally both about the environment and the body: air comes in and out of our bodies, and we make this connection in our unconscious and conscious acts of breathing. The world is made as we breathe. It thus makes little sense to talk about bodies as separate from environments in bushfire events, or indeed more generally. We are imbricated in our worlds, particularly through breath.

Bodies and technologies also blur in our data. People often talked about their bodies, or parts of their bodies, as filters and sensors. The boundaries and relations between our bodies, environments and technologies are constituted in actions/practices. As many feminist theorists have argued, being pregnant is already a form of blurring or deindividualization. Being pregnant during the fires intensifies this experience.

In this chapter we have focused on smoke and the fires, but it is important to remember, as discussed in Chapter 3, that the COVID-19 pandemic started right at the end of the fire season, producing significant new concerns about health and specifically breathing. The breath of others quickly became dangerous in a variety of ways. New apps and biosensing devices are currently in development to assist citizens in making judgements about air quality and health risk. Extensive platforming has been an inextricable part of the pandemic ('Check-In' apps in particular) and assisted breathing technologies constitute a significant part of treating serious COVID-19 infection. As we will discuss in Chapter 5, the pandemic has also had a huge impact on the ways in which collectives can be formed and lived.

The forms of collective DIY action Paul Dugdale calls for in the face of biomedical uncertainty about bushfire smoke resonates well with the ANU's exhortation to 'help others' on the bushfire smoke advice sheet. It speaks also to forms of politics promoted by Murphy and other feminist, queer and First Nations scholars focusing on (re)distributive justice. What is at stake here are forms of care. We will turn to these concerns in the next chapter.

Interleave 5

Evacuating while pregnant: Matilda's story (interview transcript)

[F]or December, we decided to take a small car trip, a holiday. So it was just as the smoke was getting bad. I had my RFS app and we took off to Western New South Wales where we managed to escape some of the smoke, and it was wonderful. And then we drove back into [village] for two nights to stay … it was terrible. The smoke was thick, the place was filled with smoke, and my partner has asthma. We had a small child, and I was pregnant. And so collectively, we were an at-risk family, each of us individually and then as a group, we were all at risk due to our bodies, various, you know, things going on.

What we noticed was that there were basically roadblocks, and we decided to leave the accommodation early, and all that was coming towards us down the road were bulldozers and fire engines, and utes with firefighting equipment strapped on the back. As we drove out, the visibility was really poor, and that was quite scary. Not to mention the health effects of that level of smoke, and they were closing the facility and they had to get everyone out within two days.

[W]e had friends down the South Coast … who said to us "What a horrible holiday. Just as you're pregnant, just as you're able to get out of bed and not be so sick. Why don't you come down, stay with us for a few nights, we'll put you up in our ground-floor apartment?" … So we had two nights there, which were really nice, and then on New Year's Eve, my son woke up … I thought it was like 2 am, because it was pitch black, and it wasn't, it was … I was putting him back to bed, I said, "Go back to bed, it's the middle of the night", and he ended up wetting the bed because he was getting up, because his body clock was saying it was morning, and he wanted to go to the toilet, and I said, "No, no, just go back to bed."

Interleave Figure 5.1: A coastal evacuation

Note: The large number of cars shows that this town was experiencing peak season crowds. Australians typically drive to their holiday destinations.

Source: participant photograph

Anyway, all these sirens and cars were driving past the house, which was unusual and then I heard the people upstairs running around and I thought, something's going on. Went outside and the clock said eight, my watch said eight, my mobile phone said eight, but it was pitch black with black leaves falling out of the sky, and that was the massive bushfires, and all the people from surrounding towns were coming into [coastal town] for evacuation.

Then we evacuated back to Canberra through really thick smoke again with poor visibility, and it was terrifying. The drive was terrifying.

Summer holiday, January 2020: Celia's story

Later in January, we managed to get down to Bermagui for one of our two previously booked weeks. The people down there were keen for visitors to come and we were keen to get away from Canberra. We drove down and managed to have quite a good holiday. Bermagui was almost empty of visitors – although there was a big contingent of Northern Territory firefighters staying there who we saw most days – filthy and exhausted after a day's firefighting, or getting ready to go in the morning. It was moving to see all the community action – food being cooked, clothing stalls, support in the library, etc. The drives down and back were really upsetting. That part of the South Coast has great emotional significance for me, as I used to go there every holiday as a teenager. On the way home we stopped in Cobargo for a coffee. So incredibly sad to see it ripped through. The fires started again in this area as we left Bermagui. As we drove into Cooma and out again, we were in a huge and frightening dust storm – one of the worst drives of my life. The car was shuddering and visibility was extremely low. We had to continue but it did not feel safe. As we drove into Canberra, there was a fire near the airport. That was also the day that an American firefighting plane crashed near Cooma, killing three crew.

5

Kin, Care and Crises

Care, kinship and climate, and their ambivalent terrains (Puig de la Bellacasa, 2017: 5) are our focus in this chapter. Feminist technoscience studies scholar Maria Puig de la Bellacasa attends to the maintenance of care in interdependent worlds. This maintenance, she argues, has 'ethical and affective implications'. She urges 'staying with the tensions between these dimensions' (2017: 5). It is these tensions that animate our analysis. While our initial focus in developing this study was the bushfires, COVID-19 is now woven into all of our lives. The pandemic and bushfire smoke are intertwined in our participants' accounts. Across 2020, taken-for-granted rituals and relations became impossible, or only possible in very small windows, or with particular people/professionals: COVID restrictions resulted in maternal health nurses parked in cars outside houses interviewing mothers to be about their babies' health before quickly slipping inside homes to take measurements that weren't possible from a distance. Exploring COVID-19, the smoke and fires together, we see how plans for care and kinship associated with birth and new parenting were, sometimes very hastily, renegotiated – often in ways that participants felt were unsatisfactory, although not always. A few participants pointed to silver linings in the ways in which normative expectations in relations to kinship were necessarily disrupted.

In this chapter we have separated stories about fire from stories about smoke and about COVID-19. While we are thinking about how these crises are interwoven, examining each distinctly helps us see how care is queered by, and resonates through, each event. In 2020, our participants became interdependent in ways that they could not have foreseen, and sometimes this was a source of added tension (for example, when families found themselves negotiating evacuation orders in the midst of fires). During the pandemic, participants sometimes felt robbed of dreams of interdependence that they had carefully cultivated with a pre-pandemic mindset. In interviews, we asked how and when our participants looked for help and who was able to answer that call. Here, we also attend to how they accessed institutional care in times of crisis, and the absences they felt in terms of medical care. Care maps our participants created (some of which are reproduced in Chapter 2) trace the ambivalent terrains of care that surfaced in these intra-actions and entanglements.

While we resist drawing neat lines between privilege, care and climate, Michelle Murphy, in an article entitled 'Unsettling care', draws on the work of Shelley Colen (2009) to reinforce the point that care is not merely political or economic, nor is it merely reparative: care is always geopolitical; it is always stratified (Murphy, 2015: 725). Puig de la Bellacasa (2017: 91), in conversation with Donna Haraway (among others), also analyses how care matters, pointing to its embeddedness in situated entanglements where we are not in charge but we are involved. We are attuned to ways in which entanglements with smoke, fire and COVID-19 disturb fantasies of control and interrupt circuits of care.

Queer kinship studies can also be valuably deployed in this analysis, moving the field of queer kinship studies beyond preoccupations with queer bodies, desires and reproductive practices. Like Lauren Silver (2020: 219), we are using queer kinship 'as a way of seeing beyond the normative grain, and … to include diverse forms of family making'. It might seem odd to employ such an approach when, despite our best efforts, all of our participants identified as heterosexual (or 'normal' as some described themselves). Queer kinship studies helps us account for the ways in which care is undone and recalibrated in climate-related disasters, producing queer relations and mobilities. Clearly, queer kinship is not something only associated with bodies that purport to be queer – we are intentionally taking queer kinship elsewhere with this reading. Such accounts of kinship and climate crises also help us understand what people – in this case white middle-class Australian women – perceive as 'normative' in expectations of care. COVID-19 has meant that normative expectations about kinship and access to care networks were often unfulfilled.

While this analysis does not engage with queer, people of colour or First Nations participants, we can learn from these analytics to consider how climate crises make diverse individuals susceptible to harm. Murphy argues that unsettling sites and scales in studies of care

> requires analysis that is in solidarity with the thick and hard-won analytics created by women and queer people of color as well as anti-racist and decolonial feminisms. Beyond a simple politics of dismantling, unsettling is a politics of reckoning with a world already violated: it is a commitment to desedimenting relationships that set the political, economic, and geopolitical conditions of knowledge-making, world-making, forgetting, and world destruction. *Unsettling does not promise good affect.* (2015: 732, emphasis added)

Luciano and Chen make a similar point in their study of queer theory and the more-than-human, warning against a preoccupation with unsettling that might somehow move a focus away from normativity and its privileges. By pointing to how care is queered by climate, we are not seeking to promise good affect, but rather wondering how normative ideas relating to care, reproduction and justice might be stretched. In our study, COVID-19 is sometimes considered as an ally; protecting participants from heteronormative expectations about networks of care and newborns. How might interruptions to care experienced by those whose expectations are otherwise normative have potential benefits for parents and babies who may not harbour such expectations? Structurally, for example, the interruptions of the pandemic have seen a rise in antenatal care being delivered by TeleHealth in Australia:[1] this may enhance care for people who struggle to physically access clinics because of their remote location, lack of childcare and/or related financial constraints.

Participants talked to us about how kinship networks were disrupted and negotiated anew – in private – and in relation to public health and various governance structures that continuously evolved during both the bushfires and the pandemic. 'Families' were evoked in very particular ways by health and other governmental authorities, and by citizens, as key forms of social organization and support. 'Families' were often connected to 'homes', as if they are the same thing. New terms, such as 'care bubbles', had to be invented to acknowledge that this is often not the case, and new rules were crafted to answer questions about who was close enough (emotionally, geographically and legally) to be allowed to be physically co-present in homes they do not legally share. Many social practices of closeness and connection – such as visiting and physical touch – were severely disrupted, even legally banned. Health care was also curtailed by these restrictions during both the fires and the COVID-19 pandemic. Unsurprisingly, mental health and parenting support services in Australia have recorded a large increase in numbers of parents of newborns seeking help for depression and anxiety (Westrupp et al, 2021).

In their recollections of these events, participants reflect on how their relations with neighbourhoods and environments altered as they attempted to stay safe when the world around them seemed anything but safe. They shared pictures of animals behaving in queer ways, likely trying to find an urban haven when their environment was under threat (see Figure 5.1). Katya reflects on how the bushfires and smoke impacted on the environment, killing millions of animals and destroying complex ecosystems: "It was ridiculous, like, however many animals were lost during it, how many trees were done … I always go back to the Aboriginals, if we burnt like the Aboriginals did, this would never have happened. Houses and lives would never have been lost, and I just think that it has just been so mismanaged."

Figure 5.1: Kangaroos in Canberra in the middle of day during the bushfires, enjoying irrigated grass

Source: participant photograph

Katya evokes the Pyrocene in her assessment of the fires. In the following sections, our participants talk about fleeing from and returning to places devastated by fires; some describe having to move numerous times as a response to smoke or moving fire fronts. Katya attributes a general refusal to listen to Aboriginal Australians' knowledge of the environment – specifically cultural burning knowledge – as part of her understanding of how this devastation unfolded. There is also a dream here that if we listen and then "burnt like the Aboriginals did", we could prevent such large-scale destruction. For Katya, who does not accept the reality of climate change (see Interleave 6), there is a hope that humans can manage the environment, but only if they work alongside Aboriginal communities. The damage already done – the devastation wrought by colonization and carbonization – is not referenced here. Indeed, the relations between care and interdependent worlds and ecosystems only occasionally appeared in our transcripts.

However, like Adele Clarke (2018) in her introduction to *Making Kin Not Population*, Katya is keenly aware that what happens to one species is felt by others. For her, kinship is multispecies and the devastation of the fires is about many species and environments; a more-than-human loss. Relations between such devastation and the scale of loss cannot easily be calculated. As discussed in Chapter 1, while we agree that paying attention to First Nations' knowledge of fire is vital, it is insufficient, in our view, to address the unfolding climate

Figure 5.2: Canberra Hospital cloaked in smoke

Source: participant photograph

crisis. Fire management is only one element of addressing the increasing number and intensity of fires in the Pyrocene. How, then, did our participants act with care when faced with the realities of extreme fire events?

Care and the queering effects of smoke

Smoke queered the Canberra environment for at least 40 days and nights over the summer of 2019–2020. Sometimes it felt biblical, like the end of days. Several participants shared images of local hospitals, where they were accessing maternity care, cloaked in smoke, both inside and out (see Figure 5.2). Endocrinologist Christopher Nolan, leader of the MC2020 research team, notes that clinics for pregnant women continued to run and that women would:

> report the smoke exposure, and their concerns about it. I was surprised that, you know, it was not the majority that were actually talking about

it, even though the smoke was billowing down the corridors … at the hospital … It often took prompting to say, "How are you coping with the smoke, you know, how have the bushfires affected you?" … I can remember being surprised that they weren't out front. There were some, a smaller percentage that said, "I'm worried about this smoke and potentially what affects it could cause on my baby", but that was a smaller percentage.

Many pregnant women's failure to connect the bushfire crisis and care for newborns was notable for Chris. While our participants told us that they cared about the smoke, this was not his experience, even with smoke billowing down the corridors of the hospital. The women attending his practice had to be prompted to ask questions about the smoke's implications for their own and their foetus' health; Chris observes that their focus was on more mundane matters of care. This was a surprising finding: we might have expected his patients to echo our participants' (and our own) concerns about exposure to smoke and associated air pollution, as described in Chapter 4. This discrepancy points to something we are not seeing in our participant group: that negotiating pregnancy and parenting took priority for many, even when hospitals were almost uninhabitable in relation to pollution associated with smoke.

In Chapter 4 we wrote about the ways in which our participants tried to stop smoke from entering their homes. The majority of our participants had bachelor degrees or higher. Overall, Canberra's population is 15 per cent more likely than the rest of Australia to have tertiary qualifications, and this advantage is also reflected in home ownership and household income (Australian Bureau of Statistics, 2016). Although home ownership is increasingly out of reach for average Australians, of the 24 couples in our study, 16 owned their homes. Care for family was necessarily entangled with home ownership. There is little in the way of public policy relating to rental housing or building of new housing stock that provides protections for people who are renting in relation to bushfire smoke and air pollution. People's capacity to alter domestic environments is fundamental to how they will respond to unprecedented air pollution. According to the 2021 Census, around a third of Australians live in rental accommodation. These people need the rights, both practically and legally, to ensure that their accommodation is habitable. While political and environmental organizations demand that rental housing has adequate heating and air conditioning for extreme temperatures, as well as ventilation for mould, currently there is little public discourse about the need to protect renters from exposure to smoke and other types of air pollution. We all have to inhale climate change, but our exposure is stratified by differential access to housing that can withstand the various onslaughts associated with our changing climate.

Figure 5.3: View of smoke and hose from a balcony

Note: The clearly inadequate garden sprinkler, situated to repel ember attack in this forest setting, highlights the limits of domestic responses to the threat of megafires.

Source: participant photograph

In their discussion of environmental politics and reproduction, Lappé et al (2019) point to the challenges of taking people's anxieties about issues relating to environmental catastrophes seriously, while refusing a retreat to fantasies about normal lives, normal climates and individualized control. They remind us that care is always emplaced; care in crisis is emplaced and displaced in ways that we and our participants did not foresee.

Care is always entangled in the human and more-than-human, in privilege and in affective economies. Sometimes non-human actors, like the garden hose in Figure 5.3, provide a sense of 'being prepared' despite their clear inadequacy. The entanglements of care are always queer; in what follows, we list some of those described in participant interviews. Mundane routines like laundry became confounding: people had to stay indoors and found themselves surrounded by mounting piles of dirty linen because they couldn't use their clothes line. Without childcare or school, many families were stuck inside all together, all day, both during the smoke and fires and during parts of the pandemic. Parents tried to entertain young children when heavily pregnant and confined to one room. Naomi describes how Lego and laxatives (her toddler was struggling with toilet training) got her family "over the line". People gave themselves permission to adapt caring practices, sometimes resorting to activities that they might otherwise have avoided (such as using laxatives with their children because they couldn't bear dealing with more nappies, or licensing unlimited use of Lego) because they could see no other way to get through the day.

Libby, who lived in Canberra during the smoky summer, is very health conscious, working as a health practitioner herself. She was very concerned about the impact of the smoke and associated lack of exercise on her foetus' and her own health. As discussed in Chapter 4, she was also critical of the lack of medical knowledge relating to impacts of smoke pollution. She talks about how "everything's intensified" already when you are pregnant, but this intensification was amplified by the devastation she associated with the fires:

Libby: I think the hardest, like, you know ... the animals and the knowledge that that's going to take so long to recover and things like that. But I mean, we are human. The truth is that we empathise best with humans ... one of the hardest things was driving past and there was an old couple sitting and they had a little caravan that had clearly just been put there, and they were sitting on two deckchairs looking out, and behind them was the ruins of a burnt-down house. Just thinking, gosh, I cannot imagine, you know, what some people have had to go through.

Libby describes the devastation she observes relating to the fires and how this spread across species, though she also notes how she is most affected by the spectacle of human suffering. While scorched landscapes and dead animals were devastating to behold, she is also distressed at witnessing older people who she assumed had been left homeless by the fire.

Libby was one of the few participants to remark explicitly about how care is stratified across species. It is also possible to see here how care can be vexatious, signalling how our 'forms of attachment can work with and through the grain of hegemonic structures, rather than against them' (Murphy, 2015: 719). In the midst of climate crisis, our shared tendency to "empathise best with humans" might also be our undoing. Elsewhere, Libby is keenly aware of care's hegemonic structures regarding women who are pregnant. In Chapter 4, she rails against what she perceived as the false reassurance she was offered by clinicians. Instead, she wants information about what scientists do and do not know. She experiences being reassured, *when that assurance does not appear well founded*, not as caring but as condescending.

Sarah, who lives in Canberra, gave birth towards the end of the summer of intense smoke pollution in Canberra, when the pandemic was just starting. She had what she describes as a difficult pregnancy, managing three older children, smoke and gestational diabetes. She also lived in an older house that was severely impacted by the smoke, to the point of making it uninhabitable. Sarah and her family (three children under the age of six) ended up moving in with their in-laws for several days because of her concerns about impacts of smoke on her unborn baby and her daughter's asthma. She recognizes that the situation was stressful for all involved. Like Libby, Sarah was particularly aggrieved by people's attempts to reassure her and how she experienced this as infantilizing:

Sarah: My husband's parents. Just dreadful, dreadful. And just they would give me that "Oh, what are you worried about? In our day everyone smoked!" Okay, great. Let's never evolve. Let's do what we did before, because it was terrible. Let's just keep doing that. I think they tried to reassure you through making you feel like you're worrying about nothing. And I don't like that … just making them feel like you're being an idiot. It was like, you know, they were probably stressed having us there. And I'm worried about everyone, worried about everything, but yes, it was just that wasn't good.

… [M]y main problem is my parents – normally very sympathetic and very sensible – were overseas … I remember my dad sending me something about New Year's Eve and a little message or whatever. And I just thought, "You have no idea what we're going through. I'm inside, inside my house with a P2 mask on, I can't see the back fence. I'm so worried about my baby and what's going on and you're sort of [enjoying] New York celebrations" … They just didn't get it. And I think I was very needy at that point being pregnant and everything … I did feel – without trying to be too dramatic, but it was like the hardest time of my life in many ways.

For Sarah, the loss of control, and the ways in which this was diminished by relatives' lack of attention and care, meant that she felt like she was not heard. She felt particularly let down by her parents, who didn't grasp what she felt was the "hardest time" in her life.

Naomi recalls the challenges of connecting with family over the summer of 2019/2020:

Naomi: We were supposed to go, my family have a house in the Southern Highlands … But the fires came right up to their boundary lines, it was like a fire zone, the Hume [highway] being closed and then open and then closed and then opened … it wasn't a situation where they can have extended family come and stay and we would not be going anywhere near that. And then my mum was finding it difficult even to come down from [coastal city] because the Hume kept getting closed. And so she was just really nervous about kind of getting here and then getting stuck … So I suppose it meant that really, we didn't have time with my family for months as it came to be

... Because we didn't see them in December or January and then and or February, and then all of the COVID stuff came in March.

At first glance, Naomi's account of why she was unable to access her family appears to be climate- and COVID-19-related. A follow-up question suggests otherwise:

Rebecca: So would your mum have come down for a decent chunk of that time to give you a bit of support or ... ?

Naomi: No, not really. To be honest ... She did come down on Christmas Eve and spent the day with us, but that's pretty typical of what she would do anyway. She doesn't like to be away from home overnight. So she's not a, she's not a support mechanism for us, you know ... She's not here and [my partner's] parents live in [a nearby suburb], but they're also not particularly helpful, they're not part of our kind of regular support routine.

Naomi's mother and in-laws are never really factored into her care calculations, but they are still a presence. There's an expectation – maybe in the interview questions, maybe for Naomi – that family (especially mothers) are central to pregnancy and baby-related care. For Naomi, however, her mother and her parents-in-law come into the picture only to clarify that she does not rely on them for support. Normative expectations relating to care are entangled in the accounts, inserting themselves, even if only to point to their absence. Naomi's story reminds us to resist over-reading how relations between care and kinship might be impacted by environmental disasters. Observations about who could move, when and where were central to our participants' narratives, but the speed of mobilities differed in relation to the smoke, fires and COVID-19. In the next section we pay attention to shifting mobilities and immobilities associated with evacuations specifically relating to the risk of fire.

Fire im/mobilities, care and crisis

Adey and Bissell (2010: 2) argue that 'the study of mobilities is a key conduit for understanding the connections, assemblages, and practices that both frame and generate contemporary everyday life'. Although all of our participants were impacted by smoke, only a few were directly impacted by the bushfires. Making decisions about when and where to evacuate was challenging. In the excerpts to follow we hear from participants who decided to leave town altogether because of the stress associated with watching the fires burn the landscape around them. Others talk about shifting accommodation in their communities, trying to find appropriate places where they could care for their children, while people were necessarily crammed together in private housing and public evacuation centres. They talk about the challenges of trying to care for children and the frail elderly in communal spaces. The unfamiliarity of such situations also highlights the privilege many Australians enjoy in relation to privacy in the domestic sphere. The interviews also tell stories situated in small towns on the coast and hinterlands of south-eastern Australia. These towns' populations expand rapidly over the summer months and, quite predictably, the bushfires were in the midst of Australia's peak tourist season. The evacuation centres had to deal with a lot of people, many of whom would not have had any alternative accommodation because they were not locals. In all these situations, care and kinship were materially entangled with buildings, cars, animals, plants, fire, people and smoke.

Katya talks about deciding when to leave and the unbearable memory of watching a fireball approach her coastal community:

Katya: [O]ur unit, we look right over the bay, and where the fires are coming from in [other coastal town], I said ... "I can't watch it", like, I didn't know what to expect. I said, "I cannot see this fireball coming towards our house." I said, "I'm not staying here. I want to be over at Mum and Dad's place", who live a bit out of town. They had a really good fire plan set up and we didn't really have to watch the fires as much, but if they were coming from north to south, then they would have definitely lost their house.

Rebecca: And so did they go up to Sydney with you?

Katya: We went the next morning ... once the police came [to tell them to evacuate], we went to [coastal town], we had some friends who got us into a house because there was no accommodation, and I did not want to take [daughter's name] to the evacuation centre, because it was high stress enough, and being around people who were even more stressed and, you know, fake news and this is happening and whatnot, I didn't want to be around that. I just want to be at one place, watch the news, and just think for myself really. And then once I heard that the fires were five kilometres out of [another coastal town], I rang Mum and Dad and said, "Just get here. Just leave."

The evacuation centre was not an option that Katya considered because she associates this place with stress, fake news and misinformation about the fires. She could also make a decision to leave the area, which she eventually did, but not all of our participants had this option. Anita, also located on the south coast, started off in an evacuation centre when her family were directed by authorities to leave their house in the middle of the night:

Anita: I think one thing that would have been really helpful is at the evacuation centre, more, like, support for people with really young kids, like a parents' room or something. Like, we got there, and we were just told there's room for you. I actually had a friend staying, so she evacuated with me and the girls to help me with the girls, and of course, my girls were upset, and I just remember being forced in the backseat of the car, between the two car seats, breastfeeding one while cuddling the other one to sleep. Like, if there was just somewhere that was designated for families, so your kid could cry, and you weren't on edge ... and you weren't going to have all these people looking at you ... a lot of them ended up leaving the evacuation centre and going to the shopping mall because there was a parents' room there and there was an indoor playground ... most parents ended up having to do that if they didn't have a home. So that would have been helpful.

For Anita, the evacuation centre and later a shared house also proved challenging – having multiple generations gathered together was not ideal, but was unavoidable. The mall proved a better option, but presumably this was only open during the day.

   Like Katya, Anita also found alternative accommodation on the coast through family and friends:

Anita: [T]here were two nights when, like, the whole of the [place name] valley had to be in either [town name] or [town name], so every house was packed, and the house we were staying at had close to 20 people and there was a very elderly person, so we moved out and went to another house for those two nights with some friends, and then we move back to the original house.
Rebecca: Wow. And where was that house? Was it in [coastal town]?
Anita: Yeah, that was in [coastal town]. In town.
Rebecca: And so that place had a whole lot of bushfire refugees staying there?
Anita: Yeah, yeah, obviously by that point, we were about three or four days into ... our evacuation situation, and just when the ... there was a really elderly lady there, she was, like, 97 or something, and we just felt there was a lot of animals,

and we just didn't think a toddler and a newborn were really needed. I was really worried the toddler, my older daughter, would, like, just trip over, like, just by accident into the elderly lady or, you know, there was just a lot going on. And so that's why we went to some friends, who had kids as well. So, you know, our older daughter had a friend, and they could play and, you know, she'd been inside for a whole week in one room, so we just needed that – [the] change of scene as well helped.

I remember my little one, because obviously being five weeks old and breastfeeding, she was sort of constantly in my arms, and she'd be grizzling because she was just so hot. Like, cuddling her, she was just so hot, but we couldn't really put her down anywhere because we weren't in our own house. I remember, yeah, like, we just couldn't keep her cool.

And I remember my older daughter, just the tantrums and all those … like, her behaviour. And it's hard because how much of that was the fact she had a newborn sister and how much of that was the fact everything she had known, you know, her home and everything and her parents was stressed. So I don't know what was what but her behaviour for months after, and it really started at the fires, was just so not her. And that was tough for the months after, and I think the fires … like, I know she would have been tough anyway with a newborn sibling, but I think the fires definitely made that a lot harder.

Anita speculates on how the stress of evacuations magnifies the challenges of being a new parent and having a toddler. She recognizes it is not possible to disaggregate these entanglements, but it is apparent that being thrust into unfamiliar spaces, with strangers, animals and frail elderly people, meant that the stress of smoke and fires was incredibly acute.

The challenges of reproducing and caring amidst bushfire and smoke are no longer exceptional in Australia. Living in the Pyrocene requires better ways of adapting to the threat of smoke and fire, and including places of refuge in which people and pets, across generations, may safely come together, sometimes for days at a time. Our data suggest that currently, places of refuge cannot adequately accommodate all the people and creatures that might need them – effectively meaning that women who are pregnant and parenting are choosing other options rather than negotiate breastfeeding and childcare in what they perceive as stressful and inhospitable shelters. Some people, like Anita, might avoid shelters because they are full of animals. Others told us that the presence of animals at shelters kept their children entertained. The complexities of multispecies refuges has the potential to make fleeing from fire even more stressful for both animals and humans – an issue that is particularly concerning as fires become more frequent. Community refuges, as they are currently configured, are not fit for purpose.

Such architectures of care are further compromised when they coincide with pandemic-related lockdowns as they did in April 2020 in the South Pacific. Communities in Fiji, the Solomon Islands, Tonga and Vanuatu were negotiating Tropical Cyclone Harold and gathering people together in evacuation centres at the same time as they were trying to implement travel restrictions and lockdowns to halt the spread of COVID-19. A similar problem arose as we revised this chapter in November 2021. Communities in northern NSW were evacuated from floods during lockdowns. Evacuation centres are designed to bring together as many people as possible in a space where they can be secure against fire/smoke/wind/water, but such centres could be treacherous if they simultaneously allow airborne diseases to flourish.

Im/mobilities associated with the fires were being negotiated from November 2019 through March 2020, a few weeks prior to the onset of COVID-19 in Australia. In November schools were shut because of fire danger. Communities were put on alert for extended periods, told to have their fire plans ready so they could leave at any moment or be prepared to stay and defend their homes. Bridget talks about the process of decision making and the calculations her family was making about when to go, and where to go:

Bridget: We sort of hung around and then the 4th [of January] was the day that everyone was saying was going to go nuts. And so it was, like, if you want to go, you've got to go before the 4th, but how are you going to get home, sort of thing. And everyone was saying different stuff, like, I remember the night, the 3rd. No, it must have been the 2nd or something, people came and took one of our elderly neighbours and they were, like, banging on our door and they were, like, "You've got to go now, you've got to get out or you're going to be trapped here, like, [coastal town]'s not safe, it's going to be on fire." And we were, like … yeah, it's just, like, heaps irrational, spontaneous decision making and we're like, okay. Our elderly neighbour had lung cancer, and so we were, like, "She shouldn't be going out".

Here, the decision to leave is described as a "heaps irrational" assemblage including everyone saying different things, worries about being trapped and not being able to get home, and concerns about older neighbours with cancer who shouldn't be going anywhere. As communication blackouts took hold due to interruptions to telecommunications infrastructure, spontaneous decision making became very local. You had to decide what to do based on what everyone was saying, but when everyone is saying different things, making rational decisions is not straightforward. Caring here is about neighbours urging others to leave, looking out for the elderly in the community, and concern that leaving wasn't necessarily going to be the best form of care – especially for older people with compromised lungs. How would they fare in crowded evacuation centres? Eventually Bridget decided to leave, but this meant:

> 'going into the fire to, like, escape the fire. So you get to Cooma, and we were going to stay with a friend at [inland town], and then we got the text, because as you go through the area, they all come in and it's, like, Jindabyne, Snowy Mountains, evacuate now, fire, and we're, like, "Okay, let's not stay at [inland town]." So we got to Canberra, and my best friend lives there, so we stayed there the night and got up early the morning, came down Kangaroo Valley and back home. And then the valley shut down because the fire got to Kangaroo Valley.'

Our participants make plain the irrationalities and unpredictability associated with bushfires and associated mobilities. We see our participants asking themselves when to move, where to move and how to move – especially when safety literally involves having to go towards fire. A number of our participants moved multiple times, relying on strangers, friends and family to find places of refuge. Matilda's experience of trying to escape smoke-filled Canberra with her family, which is told in Interleave 5, exemplifies the complexities of finding refuge. After a stressful holiday inland, friends sought to provide Matilda's family with relief from the Canberra smoke, inviting them to the coast. Unfortunately, fire came close to the coastal town and everyone had to move:

Matilda: So then we got evacuated from that house to the beachfront. That was terrifying. So because I can't walk fast, being pregnant and sick and having a small child, and I couldn't drive, so I waddled down in this thick smoke with hot ash falling out of the sky and the singed gum leaves and sat on the beach for two hours, wondering what on earth was going on, and just talking to the baby inside my stomach saying, "Stay in there, stay in there, stay in there."

A darkened day, a disoriented toddler, thick smoke, sirens, people running, air pollution, poor visibility and terrifying drives through thick smoke – together these mobilities formed the assemblage this family negotiated. These assemblages continued on their return to Canberra when Matilda and her family ended up hosting the friends from the coastal town – an older couple with their own medical needs – for two weeks. They were also joined by Matilda's mother-in-law, who had come to assist because Matilda had been so unwell throughout her pregnancy. This resulted in seven people living in a three-bedroom house, which Matilda described as "utterly exhausting." Mobilities associated with the smoke and fires were chaotic, throwing friends, strangers and relatives together, sometimes for extended periods, in conditions that compromised health and wellbeing.

Challenges to human agency are further evoked in Rae's account of haphazard moves choreographed by the smoke and fires. In an irony that was not lost on Rae, she and her South American partner had decided to return to Australia specifically for her son's birth. Laughing, she told us that they "thought it would be the safest, the most relaxing place for the birth of our baby", and expected that soon after the birth they would return to South America:

Rae: We were in [coastal town] and … then we got evacuated and we were in about three different places within a week … So I think we went from here to one place to another to another. So I think we had four places in total before we found somewhere … we left, I think New Year's Day, super early and went into Canberra, but I was eight and a half months pregnant … I couldn't go to my godmother's [in coastal town] where I'd booked in [to the hospital to give birth]. So we had to … book in at Canberra [hospital] … and find somewhere to stay. 'Cause you know, my son could have arrived at any moment, so we couldn't just move around. We had to find somewhere and be like, okay.

For Rae, plans to have her baby in the coastal town – to be near her godmother – were undone by the fires. She, her partner and mother found themselves moving four times trying to find a place where they could find accommodation and care, knowing that her baby could come at any time. Eventually they found temporary accommodation at an Airbnb in Canberra.

While the bushfires sent people moving from town to town – often at short notice – and left people separated from family for days at a time, the COVID-19 pandemic set different challenges: shutting borders and placing people together in close proximity for extended periods, stretching and reformulating relationships between generations. Jo Chandler, an Australian journalist, reflects on a conversation with Lesley Head, Professor of Geography at the University of Melbourne, about how COVID-19 and climate feels for privileged white women – women like themselves and many of the participants in our study:

Teasing out some of the connective threads between the COVID and climate crises, she [Head] reflects " this precarity, this sense of being rather unmoored, is going to be with us for ages and is probably quite a precursor of how climate change will increasingly feel. " Or how it already feels, she immediately self-corrects. We glimpse ourselves in our Zoom lenses, middle aged, middle-class white women marooned in the iso-comfort of our homes. With COVID, says Head, "affluent white people are feeling what it is like to live a precarious existence for the first time." As Gorrie [First Nations] writer Melissa Lucashenko succinctly put it, "so cry me a river, bitches". (Chandler, 2021: 63)

Lucashenko is accustomed to living with the impacts of 200 years of colonization and its deracinating and devastating effects on kin and Country. For us, and maybe for our participants, the fires highlighted our precarity and the scale of climate disasters to come in powerful new ways. Such fears, we suggest, trigger denial-led hopes in more privileged people that these trials can be overcome with thoughts about utopian reproductive futures borne by the next generation. This will be the focus of the following chapter.

COVID im/mobilities: ruptures in care and fantasies of control

As Australian journalist Jo Chandler wrote in 2021: 'There's this tiny little virus that is shaping social life at the moment, and that is one of the dilemmas with the Anthropocene as well, of climate change: once things take hold in complex systems, there are limits on your ability to control it' (Chandler, 2021: 63). Australian COVID-19-related lockdowns were, at least in some Australian states and local government areas, lengthy and highly restrictive in terms of travel. By the end of 2021, people in Melbourne had spent over 200 days locked down – a length of time that has only been matched in a few cities around the globe.[2] Lockdowns also included curfews in some jurisdictions as well as limits on exercise outside the home (one to two hours per day). People were also unable to cross many state borders, let alone contemplate international travel: Australia's borders were effectively closed from February 2020 through to the end of 2021. Australian citizens trying to return home had to navigate expensive and frequently cancelled flights, as well as expensive periods of quarantine on arrival. If you were allowed to leave Australia, there was certainly no guarantee that you would be able to make it back. There were strict limits in terms of movement away from home – shopping was banned except for essential items (which included alcohol and hardware). In many locations there were bans on all social gatherings; people were unable to visit relatives in hospitals or aged care homes (some exceptions were made for birth and end of life care, but only if those events related to kin in Australia – births, deaths and marriages of relatives overseas were rarely the basis for a travel exemption).

While stratifications relating to international travel are a feature of the daily existence of many Australians, for us, and for our participants, limits and disruptions to care and kinship relating to international and domestic travel often emerged for the first time. As in the bushfires, pandemic (im)mobilities have brought precarities into focus for privileged populations. Like so many others (notably, refugees and asylum seekers who are unable to return home because of restrictions imposed by nation states), we were reckoning with not being able to cross borders to care for kin. People interpret, respond to and experience lockdown rules in myriad ways, with shifting degrees of concern, exposure, anxiety and financial cost. None of our participants talked about bearing financial costs relating to COVID-19; this may be an indication of their privilege, but we did not ask specifically about this. It is apparent that in Australia the pandemic's effects are unevenly spread, with morbidity rates much higher in local government areas where low-income workers work in jobs and households that leave them much more vulnerable to the virus itself and its economic impacts (Andrew et al, 2020).

Predictably, our participants' discussion of caring and COVID-19 often revolved around how their bubbles were negotiated. On becoming pregnant, Rae had imagined communities of support as a new parent, with pets, other travellers and family members in close proximity. Instead, these people remain dispersed – in Australia and overseas – unable to provide the intimacy she craves. The life she anticipated after the birth of her baby is out of reach:

Rae: You know, our pets and our families … we thought that we would be surrounded by people. But we're here in … a very rural spot and, you know, perfect for a pandemic, but it is very isolated. So it's like the opposite of what we thought. And like all our families are overseas … My sister's in Canberra, but she's always very busy. [Baby cries] … It's tough. So we thought we would have them, you know, my parents at least have met our son, but my partner's family hasn't met him at all.

During the pandemic, assemblages of motherhood that assume proximate bodies, pets and places were disturbed. The disruption of such expectations is felt through the body, working against expectations of motherhood and kinship. For Rae and her family, motherhood has become about a nuclear family living in a small rural community. Rae and her partner managed and lived in a hostel for travellers prior to COVID-19. Her vision of becoming a mother in community with her partner's family and people from around the globe who may visit was radically discordant with the reality in which she became entangled during the pandemic. A loss of control and unfulfilled expectations about mobilities and kinship permeate Rae's story. She and her partner's lives prior to the fires and COVID-19 were predicated on mobilities that assumed international travel and coexistence with other international travellers. They had imagined returning to that life after the birth of their baby, but these thoughts had to be put aside, at least temporarily. Uncertainty about just how much time one has to spend putting things on hold is a question that is unresolved, at least in Australia at time of writing.

Bubbles shift and unanticipated relationships form. One participant talks happily about her brother moving from Melbourne with his partner and children to become part of a family bubble in regional NSW. Two other participants moved interstate permanently because of concerns about smoke or COVID-19. Our small sample is quite mobile, which is not surprising for Canberra, a city where many people come for work and therefore have extended families that are not nearby. None of the Australian research team lives in the same town as their families; throughout this research, we have all been negotiating border closures, both state-based and international. In relation to COVID-19, we sometimes felt stuck in Canberra, experiencing anxiety about not being able to see relatives. Rebecca's family are in different parts of Australia, Aotearoa-New Zealand and Scotland. Celia has family throughout NSW and close friends in England. Mary Lou's family are in Melbourne. During the pandemic, we were all communicating via Zoom, sometimes with relatives who struggle to use the technology. We were also navigating deaths of relatives without the benefit of being able to grieve with family members.

The research team has also been working out how to negotiate bubbles during COVID-19 – a source of myriad ambivalent tensions relating to care and kinship. Mary Lou had the privilege and dilemma of making decisions about where to locate in each lockdown. Should she place herself in the same state as older relatives, even though it was unlikely she would be able to visit due to restrictions? Being in the same state offers the illusion of proximity – significant comfort at a time when state borders were, for the first time in Australian history, impermeable. As a new Head of School, Mary Lou also juggled obligations to be near work – colleagues, students and friends – even as all classes and meetings were taking place virtually. Making decisions about where to live is discombobulating. Celia, who returned to Australia in 2018 after 17 years abroad, has been unable to see friends in England. As we wrote the first draft of this chapter in October 2021, all of the research team, and our participants, were locked down in Australia and Aotearoa-New Zealand. Rebecca was unable to visit family in Aotearoa-New Zealand since 2019 and to date Louisa has been unable to visit us to collaborate on this book in person.

In Canberra, Mary Lou (and sometimes her partner) shares a house with a woman in her twenties (and sometimes her partner). When possible, the home owners (also in their fifties and sixties) also live in the house – but during the lockdowns, they were unable to travel to Canberra. This cross-generational and cross-species arrangement (a rescue dog was adopted in the first weeks of the pandemic) was sustaining; a source of joy and companionship – something that Mary Lou particularly valued, being relatively new to Canberra. COVID-19 put these arrangements under pressure, posing unforeseen stresses and risk calculations. Quickly it became apparent that, at least in this household, people in their twenties and people in their fifties and sixties negotiated different relations to bubbles, social distancing and COVID-19-related anxieties. Ultimately, this influenced Mary Lou's decision to leave Canberra – she and her partner returned to live in their own home in another state for one lockdown, and returned to Canberra for the next. They were in a privileged position – they could decide the parameters of their bubble by physically removing themselves from a potentially uncomfortable/unsafe arrangement. People we know, sometimes people we or our kin live with, would not and could not abide by the lockdown restrictions and contracted COVID-19 as a result. Fantasies of control had to be abandoned early on, ratcheting up anxiety about lockdowns and potential unexpected consequences. At the same time, all over Australia, others were unable and/or unwilling to make such decisions, finding themselves cohabitating in homes where differing relationships to risk across generations proved lethal.

The loss of control and the unanticipated consequences of COVID-19 on kinship relations is apparent in Alice's discussion of her decision to move to Melbourne because of the smoke and ultimately becoming entangled with her parents after the onset of the pandemic:

Alice: Well, Melbourne hasn't been so great with COVID [laughs]. So we were fine in the beginning ... I had a very, very tough labour, so I had five days of labour, and it was long and horrendous and fraught with all sorts of tension in my family. And because my parents had had traumatic birth experiences, so that just totally did not go down well. And that was also when Corona became quite serious. We started seeing some reports about, like, premature babies, babies born with smoker's lung, all sorts of things, and I was just so frightened and nervous and, like, suddenly I was, like, living with my parents again, which is always never good [laughs] ... it's hard living with moving back in with your parents, not everybody gets along, that's hard ... we didn't have an apartment, we didn't have anywhere to go. We were still living with my parents. Like, I knew there was no way I was ever going to see my apartment again.

Smoke, the pandemic and the trauma of birth are woven together for Alice. She is living in a different state, with her parents, which is 'always never good', and she has left behind a life in Canberra. There is a lot of uncertainty and anxiety circulating through Alice's narrative – the worry that the baby would have "smoker's lung" is compounded by her and her partner's strong concerns about smoke pollution. Murphy's theorizing of infrastructures of reproduction enables us to contemplate relations between environment, crisis and reproduction that come together in Alice's story. Reproduction for her is an assemblage of air quality data, intergenerational birth trauma, disrupted living arrangements, family conflict, COVID-19 lockdown and smoker's lung. It is not possible to make sense of Alice's story without thinking about the environment and reproduction together. It is worth comtemplating the challenges such a politics of habitability might pose for researchers and policy makers trying to understand these entanglements!

Calculations of vulnerability – older people, vulnerable children, those who had kin who were immuno-compromised – often shaped people's bubbles. In this way COVID-19 (unlike the fires where strangers were sometimes thrown together in close proximity) reinforced strict limits on who counts as close kin or part of your 'inner circle'. Restrictions on travel ultimately led Libby, for example, to leave Canberra soon after the birth of her baby so that she could be closer to her family interstate. We were all asked to prioritize particular people; inevitably this meant that many friends and family had to be excluded. Shelley, already a mother of two, shares her concerns about negotiating bubbles with friends so that she knew her son would be somewhere safe while she was giving birth:

Shelley: We spoke to close friends that live across the way and they're never as vigilant as we are about anything [laughs] but so we're like, are you actually like being careful? Like are you … And they were like, "We're going into lockdown at the same time with you … Don't worry about it. And we're working from home, we've got the kids out of daycare." That was an important one for us because we were really worried about [our son] having exposure to their kids if they were all in daycare still and, and then bringing it home and having infected the baby or me.

Such conversations are fraught; they break rules about the sorts of expectations we might have of neighbours in terms of care and responsibility. To be comfortable about the birth of her child, Shelley not only had to find people that would look after her son, but was also wanting reassurance about her neighbours' work and childcare arrangements, and any other possible ways in which their bubbles might be breached, potentially making her and her children susceptible to COVID-19 infection. The pandemic meant that such anxieties had to be distributed and anxieties about birth couldn't be privatized – care obligations were recalibrated – potentially bringing neighbours closer together as they relied on each other to undertake responsibilities that might otherwise be allocated to biological kin. In this way, COVID-19-related disruptions to care might sometimes be seen to be queering neighbourhoods.

Katya describes herself as very "family orientated." She had a traumatic time during the fires and this was compounded by the pandemic. While she wanted her family to meet her daughter, she felt unable to visit because she has a niece with cystic fibrosis:

Katya: And then they were hating on me for it because I wouldn't let her see her, but I said, "Well, I've got a priority here, who's my niece, and I have to keep her safe." And, you know, if she gets COVID, then, you know, it's just … [She's] *really* vulnerable to it. So that was a really hard thing for me. I couldn't see my parents, I couldn't get any help in that period, so that was really tough.

Katya felt unable to visit, which also meant she was unable to receive any support from her family. This was at a time when she was experiencing significant mental health difficulties associated with bushfires and her daughter's respiratory issues. The proximity of the smoke and bushfires, and her family's vulnerabilities, amplified her anxieties and social isolation.

Libby's experience of negotiating care bubbles was less fraught, but they still jarred with her expectations about what life might like with her first child:

Libby: [N]o one's even been able to see her other than on a screen … You know, we really firmly believe that, you know, children should be raised by the village, and COVID's made that very difficult … unless you are in the inner circle of someone's [care bubble] … then they're not going to come and see you because, you know, you're trying to limit your circle down to those few people. And, you know, the reality is that, you know, if you've got an elderly parent, they're your circle … you don't want to be seeing 20 people, you want to be seeing two or five.

The limits and challenges of kinship that is entirely mediated through screens came as a rude shock to many of us. Libby's ideal – it takes a village to raise a child – was certainly unsettled by COVID-19. Her expectations, like those of many of our participants, were high and could be characterized as somewhat utopian. We wonder whether our and our participants' experiences of climate/pandemic-related disasters will shift expectations about what they might expect in terms of support and kinship in the years to come. Maybe people who have been cocooned from crises are less able to assimilate what's ahead precisely because of their expectations that plans made will come to fruition? The idea that adjustments might have to continue feels unreal and highlights feelings of being out of control.

Continuous adjustments to norms relating to birth and reproduction are apparent in Renee's storying of how plans put in place for support from family and friends were undone by COVID-19 and how this compounded her feelings of postnatal depression:

Renee: I was flatter than I'd ever been after a birth, like, the world didn't care that you'd had a baby … Nobody could come to visit … So it's not that people didn't care, but, like, cards weren't sent because people didn't go to post offices. And that sounds really weird, but when you've just had a baby and … And so many people, even before I gave birth, I had people ringing up who kind of didn't get it. They're, like, "Gee, it must be so awful being pregnant now." And you're like, "Why are you saying that to someone who's 41 weeks pregnant?" And I ended up saying to them, "Oh, it's actually fine, because we're going to be in our own newborn bubble anyway", and you try to be positive because you're trying to turn it around for yourself. And then heaps of people just kept saying, "It must be so awful, it must be so traumatic." I'm like, "How about congratulations on having a baby? What's her name?"

Unanticipated inhospitable affects surrounding her pregnancy and the birth of her child pervade Renee's interview. Renee, understandably, anticipated being surrounded by excitement, cards and greetings. Because this is not her experience, Renee feels defensive – spinning a somewhat unconvincing yarn to herself about the "newborn bubble" being a positive thing as a defence against people's associations of her child's birth with trauma – presumably because she was bringing her baby into a world where things were not fine, despite her protestations. The shift we are attending to here is that affects associated with birth, at least for Renee, have become tainted. She desires a return to that place, a reconfiguration where congratulations trumps trauma, but this is not forthcoming, so she has to do this work herself.

Care arrangements, especially at the time of birth, were a particular area of focus for our interviews. Continuously shifting restrictions on travel within Australia (between our States and Territories) made it incredibly challenging to plan visits anywhere, including to support family members. Within States and Territories, there were also very strict rules on visitation in hospitals. In August 2021, at the beginning of another lockdown, the Canberra Health website advised that 'no visitors are permitted to enter Canberra Health Services facilities unless in exceptional circumstances such as end of life, birthing or for paediatric care. Visitors are strongly encouraged to keep in touch with patients at CHS facilities via phone and/or video calls'.[3] While exceptions were being made for birthing, these were also highly constrained.

Lisa planned for her mother to look after her son while she was in hospital, but she was unable to come because of travel restrictions associated with COVID-19. Instead, her partner finished work earlier than planned so that he could be home with their son, who couldn't come to the hospital. They were able to call on his step-grandmother to look after him while they were in hospital, but he was not allowed to visit after the birth:

Lisa: He [their son] couldn't visit us at all in the hospital, he
                   wasn't allowed in at all. So she met him through the glass
                   door, and there are, like, photos of us, like, me bending,
                   like, knelt down with [the baby], [our son] crying and
                   be, like, "Mummy!" because he was missing me, and it
                   was just, like … it was just really … it was really tough
                   being separated from your kids. So that was really hard.
                   And I probably left a little bit earlier than I would have
                   because I missed him, and I needed to be with him.

Despite Lisa having concerns about her daughter's low birthweight in the context of the bushfire smoke, there were no major complications after the birth, and she decided that leaving hospital early was the only solution to alleviating her family's distress at being separated. Another participant, Deborah, had to be in hospital for an extended stay because of postpartum complications. She recalls the lack of support she received in negotiating her multiple care responsibilities while in the hospital, including negotiating arrangements to continue breastfeeding her 18-month-old child – as well as having a five-year-old child who was barred from visiting:

Deborah: [A]nd they're, like, "Well, he'll just have to cope." … they
                   were very unsympathetic in it. And then they said, "Well,
                   I guess your husband can bring him in just to feed", and
                   I said, "What about my five-year-old?" and they said,
                   "No, she can't." Like, what do you want us to do with
                   her? [Laughs] And then it was, "Well, don't you have
                   anyone else that can watch her?" [and I said] "Well, you
                   just told me it's a pandemic." I just found it all very …

and it was very sort of smacked me in the face how little understanding there is of the importance of some of this stuff for our mental health and then onto physical health because, you know, women that have postpartum and then don't have access to family, that's particularly worrying.

Deborah is keenly aware of the adverse physical and mental consequences that can ensue from care arrangements designed to protect public health – constraints that sometimes split families, leaving women and newborns alone in hospitals, while partners tending to children unable to visit must also stay away. All family members can be adversely impacted when fundamental caring responsibilities are not accommodated by regulations seeking to limit broader public health risks. How can spaces that are critical to sustaining families' physical and mental wellbeing be created within institutions supporting birthing mothers and their families? If women are experiencing a stressful environment – and cannot rely on social networks or other caring arrangements they have put in place – how does this affect their wellbeing and that of the foetus/newborn and of older siblings and partners?

Silver linings

As Mary Lou has noted earlier, on her return to Canberra, after the first lockdown, the household had expanded – a boyfriend and a rescue dog were now part of the mix. Louie the dog was one of a surfeit of pets acquired during the pandemic (many people sought kinship with pets as a means to sustain them amid rolling lockdowns). Obtaining a pet, especially a dog, became almost impossible as the pandemic rolled on; correspondingly, the cost of puppies skyrocketed. Dogs provided legitimate opportunities and motivation for exercise and the chance to socialize – at a COVID-19 safe distance – with other dogs and their humans. At least for our queer share house, this was one of the silver linings of the pandemic, and we were not alone in having such experiences. The pandemic produced quite a few stories described by participants as 'silver linings' relating to kinship and care.

For some, the pandemic provided a way to rationalize and reinforce a happy distance between families, especially soon after the birth of their baby. Being COVID-19-safe meant they didn't have to entertain friends or relatives. They rejoiced in being in their own small bubble: no need to make cups of tea and wait on visitors. Before the pandemic, family visits are very difficult to resist; it's socially unacceptable to push back against people, especially family, who want to be in proximity to the new baby. While some participants lamented the absence of relatives, a significant number expressed relief at these altered kin relations. Lockdown became a space in which they could hold themselves; where partners could more often work at home, where they had intensive time together as a small family unit. Bridget, from the NSW South Coast, talks about the onset of COVID-19 coinciding with her second week postpartum:

Bridget: [I]t was perfect timing because, like, I know that's really selfish to say, but we didn't have the pressure of having to say no vaccine, no visit, sort of thing. And recovering from the C-section meant I wasn't, like, under pressure of a lot of people coming to visit, like, you know, and we could just actually really enjoy [the new baby] ... and have time to heal.

Similarly, Lily describes her birth experience as "perfect":

Lily: Like, peaceful and not rushed and I had a midwife all to myself for the whole time ... Like, there wasn't this need for, like, a hundred people to be in the room, you know, like, it was all just this, wow, like a mindfulness, lovely presence around it, it wasn't bad, because of COVID.

With her mother as backup, Lily was able to enjoy quiet time with her husband and the new baby. This was in sharp contrast to other's experience of the restrictions, which meant they were unable to see their own children in addition to imposing restrictions on the amount of time they could also see their partners (because as a couple they had no access to childcare).

Infrastructures of care in disasters

Susannah Clement and Gordon Waitt draw on Deleuze and Guattari's assemblage thinking and feminist care ethics to argue that 'entanglements with bodies and materials alongside ideas, emotions and affects shape how motherhood becomes and is felt on-the-move through "moments of care"' (Clement and Waitt, 2017: 1185). They reflect on 'the idea that becoming a mother is always "distributed" through the entanglement of bodies and materials in place' and that '"moments of care" are felt through the body, and are thought of as the coming together of material and social entities that work towards and against achieving motherhood' (Clement and Waitt, 2017: 1188–1189).

Our participants' reflections show how infrastructures of care can be queered in disasters like bushfires. Before the pandemic, Zoom was an unfamiliar technology; by the time of the interviews, it had become familiar as a way to stay connected, but this infrastructure was not available to some of the women we spoke to. Our participants were also aware that Zoom entanglements were no substitute for coming together physically. Katya lives on the south coast of NSW in a town directly impacted by the fires. She laments the absence of a mother's group in her community:

Katya: Even if you could do a Zoom, like, a mothers' group Zoom. That wasn't an option for us, and it should have been. I feel like that would have been really supportive because then also, too, if your baby is losing it, you've got that support that's, you know, a visual thing, you can see what other mums are going through as well. We couldn't go out for coffees and we couldn't go for walks together and things like that. Even through the bushfires and stuff, it would have been really good to have something like Zoom where you could talk about it and at least see each other and your baby seeing other babies rather than just being in complete isolation … I don't think Zoom came out until, like, a bit later on in the year. I just feel for those mums who didn't have that, who were struggling with, you know, babies who had to be, you know, fed in different positions, they had no physical support whatsoever.

While we heard about mothers' groups shifting to Zoom in Canberra during the pandemic, some participants also said they were unable to access a group. Gina, who is Canberra-based, talked about the stress of not having access to a mother's group:

Gina: [A]ll the maternal health clinics and things like that, they have, like, drop-in sessions that you can go to, they have little groups, they have classes that you can go to. All of that stopped. So we don't have those resources … The sad part is that we can't see families that are interstate, we can't go to mothers' groups, we can't do any of the classes or anything like that … Yeah, we're really confined to our own houses and our own family that live here.

The loss of ritual and affective communities, with other new mothers, and with families, compounded people's feelings of isolation. It's difficult to comprehend why these groups either weren't running (at least online) or why women found them hard to access if they were running. One participant in Canberra talked about a mothers' group being made available to her, but that it ran in the evening, after dinner. The passionate ways in which our participants felt the absence of these groups speaks to the sociality of motherhood. For some, as Clement and Waitt suggest, achieving motherhood involves a coming together of material and social entities. While some women struggled to find such entities, others had contrasting experiences. Helen, also based in Canberra, reflects on the importance of a postnatal yoga group she had been attending with her baby before COVID-19:

Helen: And then when COVID started, [the instructor] moved it online and we would Zoom in every Wednesday morning instead of going. And she would still do the sharing circle. So yeah, that was a lifesaver. It was like my one thing that I had every week that I had to do, and my partner would look after the baby so I could get my hour of yoga in, and then sharing circle. That meant that that group could catch up every week ... When you're not seeing other people, you don't have a chance to be like, "So my baby does this, is that normal? Is this weird?" Um, but in that sharing circle we could talk about all that, sleep troubles that you're having and ask those questions. So it was good.

For Helen, the space created by this instructor was "a lifesaver". The rituals associated with this yoga group, like the sharing circle, meant that women could take time for themselves, ask questions and communicate worries. Some of the websites associated with these courses constitute new mothers as needing 'special nurturing to make the best of that "sacred window of time" after having her baby. Rest, massage and the correct nourishment at this time can reset her body health and vitality like at no other time of her life'.[4] If our participants shared visions of this 'sacred window of time', they were undone by the pandemic.

Both Helen and Katya emphasize the importance of being able to see and talk to other mothers in order to better understand themselves and their baby's development. Visual connection was something they valued; being able to see one another helped the women to work out what's 'normal' and what's 'weird'. Anita found her mother's group, located in another fire-affected community on the NSW South Coast, to be highly supportive:

Anita: But the only playgroup that was run this year was the mothers' group, and I'm so grateful the nurses prioritized that one ... it's a fluid group ... the ones that I sort of got to know, we all had babies in the bushfires, we all had COVID, you know, like, we all went through a similar [experience] ... they're probably the only people that have been through that experience. And, you know, there's mums from [towns ravaged by the fires], there's people who were really lost ... I don't think anyone lost their house, but a lot of people lost land and things ... My mothers' group was probably the biggest support network for me, because they were the only

people that got it ... I felt like people from outside of this
area didn't really get it ... there's a [community health] nurse
at every single one and so not just the mothers' group, but
the support of the community health nurses, and they really
prioritize mothers' group. They've been incredible.

Anita stresses the value of being able to share the experience of loss and
devastation within this support network, to participate in an affective
community of people that understood the enormity of the experience. For
her, this was something that couldn't be communicated to those who didn't
live through it. The contrast between Helen and Katya's experience, in
communities that were not far apart geographically, speaks to the complex
nature of infrastructures of care. Why were some communities making
such groups a priority, while others offered no infrastructure, not even a
Zoom meeting?

Matilda's focus was on the provision of spaces that were safe to take your
child in relation to air quality (a concern that echoed during COVID-19,
but with quite different technical and architectural issues involved). She
would have loved access to

an indoor space that was filtered where you could have rationed a play
space with proper air that you could take your child for an hour and
then, okay, you have to clear out for the next 30 families to come in.
Some sort of family-friendly spot that has clean air to allow a child
to be a child, instead of a factory hen. That would have been great.

Rae, who moved numerous times during the summer because of smoke and
the risk of bushfires, and to access maternal care, ended up in Canberra. For
her, a principal concern was affordable accommodation:

Rae: Suddenly right before my son was born, [I] had to start paying
for accommodation ... there's like bushfire support for people
who have their homes damaged and, or property damaged or
destroyed – of course – but I guess there wasn't really much
support for someone like me who had to suddenly pay for
accommodation, you know? ... people don't necessarily think
about pregnant women in that situation. I know when I booked
into the hospital in Canberra you know, like a few weeks before
my baby was born, they were like, "Oh yeah, you're the second
or third person who's been evacuated and come in" ... it would
have been good if there was some government assistance ...
If you're evacuated, you just have to figure it out and then go
back when it's safe, but not everybody could.

A fundamental of care, a place to stay, is something that doesn't appear to have been factored into government assistance. Evacuation is often represented as something short-term, when lives and property are at risk. And if property is destroyed, then contingencies are put in place. However, if you can't access your house because of smoke and risk of fire *and* you need to be near a hospital, you can slip between the cracks.

Conclusion: response-abilities and making bushfire babies

In the Coda to *Matters of Care*, Puig de la Bellacasa attends to the tensions that emerge in decentring humanist ethics at the centre of thinking about care. This is a move away from 'our bodies, our *selves* and our environment … without discharging humans from specific and situated ethico-political response-abilities' (Puig de la Bellacasa, 2017: 217; emphasis in original). We have tried to get to grips with the ways in which kinship, care and climate crises come together in entanglements that queer normative understandings of all these things and the ways in which they hang together. As Fergie at al note in their discussion of breath and convergent crises in Australia, 'shared air and the breath of intimacy have become recognisable markers of our mutuality of being' (2020: 58). We have noticed how care, kinship and intimacy are being continuously reconfigured through converging crises. These crises queer many of us, if we think of queer as something that helps us question normativities, often forcing us into experiences where expectations about intimacy and care are askew or out of joint. We also recognize that care and intimacy are not something over which we humans always have ready control. This was true prior to our discussion of the crises that have drawn our attention in this book. If climate crises are cumulative and likely to accelerate in their intensity and frequency, then finding ways of learning how to be together and care for one another is critical. We need to think about kinship in ways that foreground sustaining more-than-family, more-than-neighbour and more-than-human relations.

Unsettling normative understandings of care is not easy: the Pyrocenic legacies of colonialism and associated environmental degradation have been layered over many centuries; generations of kin are woven into the converging crises we are attempting to understand. These inheritances also shape the ways we think about, react to and imagine what response-ability is in the midst and wake of such crises. We have shown how kinship, care and climate are distributed in ways that are uneven, ambivalent, and imbued with colonial and anthropocentric histories. Many of our participants, understandably, have been affected by these crises, but maybe less so than those living in Australia and elsewhere with precarities that mean that they are regularly exposed to the threats of colonialism and associated environmental degradation. During the pandemic, the Australian government famously rolled out welfare policies that were unprecedented in terms of the ways in which they provided housing for people who were homeless and social benefits for those in various forms of precarious employment. At the same time, they 'also ignored the 2.17m people presently in Australia on a temporary visa (visitor visa holders, international student visa holders, temporary skilled visa holders and working holiday visa holders), who do not have access to unconditional work rights and government payments' (Andrew et al, 2020: 764). International students in Australia were instructed by our Prime Minister to go home when many of them were unable to get home. As a result, many experienced extreme levels of financial precarity and associated vulnerabilities (Coffey et al, 2021).

It feels hopelessly utopian to suggest that kinship and care have to be imagined in ways that are capacious enough to embrace human and nonhuman, citizens and noncitizens. Will we care more or better if we are better able to apprehend the interdependencies we share, for good and for ill? In the next chapter we look at how what we are terming Pyro-reproductive futures produce particular types of logics (population and regeneration) and affects (escape, ambivalence and solastalgia) among our participants.

Interleave 6

Eucalyptus trees have evolved to survive fire through high flammability. The potential loss of particularly rare trees was a feature of news media stories during the fires. In the Blue Mountains National Park to the west of Sydney, for example, citizens risked their lives to protect a group of nationally significant Wollemi Pines (the so-called 'dinosaur trees').

Talking about climate change: conflicting views (two interview transcripts)

Rebecca: One aspect of this is that people have talked about climate change and, you know, you have some young environmental activists who pledge not to have children because they feel like that's what they can do in terms of protesting, you know, inaction on climate change. What do you think about those kinds of debates?

Katya: Oh, look, I think they're extremists. I think, again, I think that there's underlying issues there for those people where perhaps they don't want to tell their truth, and they look for an excuse. Here's my theory on climate change. The earth is over 150 million years old. We know that because of the dinosaurs and things like that. Our records go back a hundred years. That's all we go off, and that's why they're like, "Well, in the last hundred years, this is what happened in climate change." We've had two Ice Ages since then, you look at how the world used to be and how it's changed, you know, we've got all these different islands and countries and things like that because of how the world's changed. So how can you say that we actually have an impact on climate change in such a short period of time when you look at it from the whole perspective of the universe and how long it's been around for? Do I think that from the revolution of the industries where, you know, factories and stuff started happening and use of coal, has that impacted? Yes, but I don't think it's at a degree where we can actually say it's due to climate change. That's my personal opinion on it.

Rebecca: Yeah, so you don't think you can make that direct connection between things like industry and climate change based on the evidence?

Interleave Figure 6.1: Bush burning 700 metres from a participant's house in rural NSW

Source: participant photograph

Katya: Yeah, on the evidence. But I think we can do more. I mean, sure, there's, you know, what's happening in the Amazon and deforestation, that can definitely be monitored a lot more. We are losing a lot more forests than what we should be, things like selective logging and that can help out, and you should be. And this is where I'm saying, yes, there should be X amount of national parks in the area, but they need to be monitored and not just left.

Rebecca: Yeah, yeah, managed.

Katya: Managed. Yeah, absolutely. On a global scale, like, not just in Australia, but especially looking at the Amazon. I really think that there needs to be … yeah, a global management of forests and things like that.

Rae: I really respect people who want to not have children for the environment. And I think that we need people like that so that, you know, the world can hopefully become less populated. So I think that's really important and then at the same time, I guess I feel personally very strongly that I want children and that I do want to raise them environmentally. And I think it's great that we're not all on the programme of needing to have children, you know, like it was maybe a hundred years ago everyone had kids, you know, without really thinking about if they wanted to or not. So, you know, I totally think that's so great. And, maybe a part of me wishes I was stronger to be like that too, but, you know, I do believe in following your heart as well. And I think that my real strong intuition tells me to have children. I've always been open to adoption as well, which, you know, I think people who don't maybe have their own biological children for the environment often are open to.

         It's interesting actually, my godmother, she had a friend and when they were younger, she decided to adopt for that same reason that she didn't want to overpopulate the earth. And … the daughter she adopted ended up having seven children of her own. So her, my godmother's friend, now just laughs like "I should have my own child!" Like "I've adopted this girl who's had seven children!" Totally the opposite of what she wanted to happen ... I think it's really good that people are aware of, you know, the environmental impacts that having children can have and try to kind of steer children to be little environmental warriors for the future. And then if they feel like they don't want their own children, then there's no pressure.

6

Pyro-reproductive Futures

In a forum on *Making Kin Not Population* (Clarke and Haraway, 2018), anthropologist Marilyn Strathern writes: 'Population and reproduction are cunningly entangled; increasingly they are also entangled with climate. The cunning of the concept [population] is that it can be exposed where it hurts: try not thinking of babies when you think of population' (Strathern et al, 2019: 160). In our study, we talked to people about how they make decisions about having children and we saw how this was entangled with their imaginings of, and relations to, population and climate crisis. Participants were not only speculating about their own reproductive futures, but were also observing those around them discussing and making reproductive decisions in relation to concerns about the environment, and, specifically, overpopulation.

In order to explore these connections, we asked participants in this study: "How do you feel about the idea of people having children in general, in the context of climate change?" Answering this question when you have recently had a baby might be tricky. Answering this question when you've just had a baby and are living through the start of a frightening global pandemic that has followed quickly on the heels of devastating bushfires is, as one of our participants said, "confronting". Actually, we hesitated to ask. Although we really wanted to know what our participants think about wider issues relating to reproduction and climate, we did not want to evoke guilt or shame or to add to their already considerable list of worries. So, we posed the question at the end of the interviews, after a rapport had been built, and tried to keep it rather light in tone.

In this chapter we analyse participants' responses as articulating the logics and affects of Pyro-reproduction as they unfold in their worlds. We explore the conceptual and material threads participants drew upon – perhaps consciously, perhaps not – to formulate their answers and to explain to us what they felt the connections between having a child and climate change might be. Sometimes their responses felt like a justification or a defence, at other times more like perplexity, but in almost all cases our question provoked disconcertment and even embarrassed laughter. Thinking about babies and population together, no matter how 'natural' the connection seems, exposes us where it hurts.

Pyro-reproductive logics

Overpopulation

In her essay 'Against population', Michelle Murphy (2018) makes a plea for thinking about population beyond the politics of personal choice and reproduction. Her work is part of a growing body of feminist/ecofeminist literature exploring climate and population. The majority of this work critiques a trend towards 'neo-Malthusianism' in debates about population control and climate change, which bases its argument that increasing population will lead to economic and/or environmental disaster on the idea that the earth has a 'carrying-capacity'. Critics argue that neo-Malthusian thought – derived from the theories of the 18th-century writer Thomas Malthus – is a reductionist and alarmist ideology that has profound implications for the gendered politics of reproduction. Hendrixson et al (2020: 308) argue that population control has often been framed as 'an urgent response to the challenges of climate change' that responsibilizes individual women. For Murphy, the very concept of 'population' is inextricably entwined with sexist and racist accounts of 'the good life' and with genocidal histories of reproductive violence in the name of economic development and prosperity. 'The histories of the use of "population" are ignored at our peril', she insists (Murphy, 2018: 103). Focusing on fears of overpopulation, she adds, 'is also a distraction' (Murphy, 2018: 106): 'It deflects from the crucial fact that it is the structures of industrial accumulation, militarism, and consumption – justified by the goal of improving macroeconomic measures – that have overwhelmingly produced the material violence of climate change, extensive planetary pollution, and death-making terraforming' (Murphy, 2018: 106).

This theme is elaborated upon in Jade Sasser's book *On Infertile Ground: Population Control and Women's Rights in the Era of Climate Change* (2018). Sasser critiques discourses relating to population control framed through the neoliberal lens of 'reproductive choice' and 'women's empowerment'. She notes that 'much of the population discourse that circulates in the environmental realm is about blame, and that the blame has been misplaced' (Sasser, 2018: 149). She also emphasizes that 'direct environmental impacts driven by human numbers are nearly impossible to tease out because they are not, and never have been, simply biological – they are the result of biological, and political, and economic, and technological, and cultural processes and practices' (Sasser, 2018: 150).

Similarly, Ojeda et al argue that environmental narratives on population and climate 'conflate the environmental impacts of human activity with the impacts of human numbers' and 'human bodies with rapacious resource use and the destruction of the environment' (Ojeda et al, 2020: 317).

In our interviews, different strands of thinking on population and climate change shape our participants' thinking about reproduction. These entanglements are the focus of the first section of this chapter, in which we describe strong repetitive patterns or logics posing ideas of goodness, care and conscious or intentional reproduction against their 'opposites'. These Pyro-reproductive logics draw on historical and contemporary ideas that circulate in many cultural arenas: governmental policy, scientific articles, environmentalist campaigns and school curricula. These are the histories of population in action, and we ignore them at our peril.

Our participants were often highly educated and sometimes critically assessed their own feelings and statements as they made them. In response to our difficult question "How do you feel about the idea of people having children in general, in the context of climate change?", Alison, a public servant living in Canberra, for example, examines her assumptions about population and reproduction and how they shifted as a result of her spending time in India with her partner:

Alison: [L]iving in India, my conception, [or my] preconception [was that everyone would have] enormous families. And this was probably just a cultural class type issue ... so these were all Indian military families that we hung out with, but it was extremely uncommon for any of them to have more than one child. Like, it was pretty much if they had any, it was, like, "one and done" ... So I have thought about all those things, but yes, I can't say they've influenced my thinking ... I guess there's the kind of micros as in Australia, micro and macro. Like, Australia has an ageing population, all that kind of thing, so for the country, it's probably beneficial for me to have more children. But globally, probably not ... Japan seems like they're in a pretty bad way. So, you know, obviously, some countries have bigger issues than others on that front.

Although Alison recognizes that some of her own thinking about population and family size has been based on misconceptions – observing that while India has many citizens, this does not mean that all people in India are likely to have many children – she states that this realization has not affected her decision making about having children herself. The spectre of overpopulation surfaces as Alison tries to imagine how thinking about population size globally might be relevant to her own calculations about reproduction, but is then dismissed.

Alison's statement articulates common entanglements of ideas and feelings about population, climate and reproduction, and draws upon sociological and demographic language. As well as sharing preconceptions about the "enormous" size of families in India, she raises the prospect of ageing populations in Japan and Australia coinciding with population decline as a solid rationale for having children in these countries. Imaginings of population and reproduction are sometimes bounded by the borders of the nation, but here, as in much scientific and policy 'population talk', comparisons between countries surface in people's minds as part of the technology of population in which they are entangled.

Tania, an emergency nurse, clearly has concerns about overpopulation on her mind when imagining relations between climate and reproduction. Her views are quite strong – she makes a determined argument against the possible implication of our question that not having children might be environmentally sound. Here again, comparisons with other countries and demographic 'facts' and terminology play a key role in the argument:

Tania: Just by not having children doesn't mean you are contributing to the fight around climate change. Climate change is about education and you know, there's a direct correlation between education and how many babies women have. So actually what you need to do is encourage women to be educated. And it's not necessarily in Australia because our birth rate is actually declining … Same as Japan. America is the same. Canada's the same, these big educated Western countries … that have a good solid education and encourage women to be educated. Their birth rate is dropping. In … Third World countries where … women are not encouraged to educate themselves, the birth rate is still incredibly high and that's why it is, you know … My thing is the greatest invention of the 20th century was contraception empowered women. And that's what it needs to be. It needs to be about grassroots level of educating women and educating men too, because I'm sure there are men out there who don't want to have a family of 10 or 20 kids. You know?

Tania's reflections on climate change and population are infused with narratives of education as the answer to too many children – a narrative that is powerfully reproduced in numerous campaigns to empower non-Western girls. Murphy illustrates how the 'economization of life' has become attached to the figure of uneducated, poor non-Western girls (Murphy, 2018: 114) – an attachment grasped by economists, liberal feminists and many of our participants. In this calculus, Western women are empowered and will have fewer children, and those children will lead better lives (though, as we will see subsequently, what constitutes good parenting in relation to climate change is also inflected with narratives relating to class and education within the nation state). While contraception, education and empowerment are climate-friendly, non-Western men and women who may produce (too) many children – because they are deprived of access to education and contraception – are, implicitly, contributing to climate crisis. Our participants understand that debates about reproduction and climate change are linked to anxieties about population size, and that imagined divisions between the West and the rest are connected to contraception and women's and girls' empowerment.

Sarah, a manager from Canberra who works in information technology, entangles vegans, overpopulation, education, youth and contraception when contemplating relations between climate and reproduction. Here she discusses activists who refuse to have children until the environmental situation improves:

Sarah: And I worry that these kids, they're so young, I don't know what it's going to feel like down the track, when I think, hang on, I want to revisit that decision … It's like a vegan who wants to have a sausage, you know! It's like, if you say "that's it", people go, "Oooh, you said it!" You're too young to know. And I don't think depriving yourself of such a wonderful thing is necessarily going to do that. I understand the thinking, like I understand overpopulation of the world, but from everything I've read, we're much better off educating women in the developing world and giving them available, you know contraception and things like that rather than just saying ["I won't have children"].

Here again the relationship between climate change and overpopulation is entangled with debates about education of women in the developing world. The repetition of this narrative underscores the ways in which debates about climate, population and reproduction are racialized and embedded in familiar liberal feminist aspirations. Throughout the data we see two imaginable reproductive futures related to climate and reproduction. On the one side we have the empowered, educated reproductive mother who is making decisions about reproduction in a context where contraception is available and desirable. On the other side is the woman from the developing world who requires education in order not to contribute to the problem of overpopulation. Capitalism, colonialism and existing structural inequalities are generally not in participants' sights – the focus is rather on individual men and women being given the capacity to control their reproductive lives. Focusing on individual responsibility is, it appears, more common among our participants than an interrogation of how racism or capitalism runs deep in Australian discussions about population.[1] Murphy asks: 'How is it possible to feel the future in other ways?' We will return to this question later in the chapter.

Sarah also evokes the image of young women ("kids") as being child-like when they announce a decision not to have children because of climate crises. She is concerned that decisions about reproduction will have consequences that young women cannot fathom – presumably because they are too young to really comprehend what not having a child might mean. There is little research that can apprehend relations between age, reproduction and climate, but Sarah's remarks may offend young women, especially those who are vegans! Infantilizing (Mayhew-Bergman, 2021) such weighty decisions closes down conversations between generations about climate and reproduction. This isn't to say that conversations are straightforward: we share Sarah's concerns about the increasing responsibilization of women to link reproduction decision making to climate change, but also repudiate the logics of conversations about having children that end up with white women calling for the education of black and brown women in non-Western countries so that they are empowered to use contraception, rather than critiquing the forms of colonialist high-consumption capitalism that wreak environmental havoc, often most adversely impacting people in the Global South.

Regeneration, reassurance and reparative parenting

Our participants' responses to the question "What do you think more generally about having children and climate change?" also produced logics founded on fantasies of what we call reparative parenting. In these logics, participants draw on reassuring cultural discourses, common in Australian accounts of bushfires, about the power of nature to regenerate itself. Alison, for example, expresses concern about bushfire's impact on animal habitats and vegetation; in fact, she is one of the few participants to make such concerns explicit. Although she is optimistic about the prospects of regeneration – feeling "sure it [habitat impacted by the fires] will regenerate as it always does" – she affirms "it's still a huge loss of the koalas". (As mentioned in Chapter 1, the fires devastated many important koala habitats, causing grave concern for the survival of this already highly endangered species.) In this section, we explore how participants mobilize faith in the power of the Earth to repair itself and their sense of themselves as good, environmentally conscious people. This works to reassure themselves about the capacity of their children to address the damage caused by our own and previous generations.

In response to our question about climate change, Lily, a medical specialist living on the south coast of NSW, stated she wasn't planning to have more children: 'No, we're happy now ... once I'd had my second child, and she was a girl, I was, like, I'm complete now.'

For Lily, a nuclear family, specifically one that involves a boy and a girl, is associated with feeling complete. This contentment with the status quo is also reflected in her response to the fires: she echoes what we refer to in Chapter 1 as the 'nothing to see here approach' that normalizes fire in Australia. Lily moved around several family properties while pregnant in order to escape the fires and smoke, and was more directly impacted by this extreme fire season than many of our participants. Certainly her experience was more proximate than that of many Australians. Maybe this proximity makes it harder for Lily to perceive these fires as exceptional. For Lily, fire continues to be constituted as something very Australian:

Lily: I think the bushfires didn't ... it feels like, you know, I still go back to the philosophical approach that Australian bush needs it, and it's a regenerative thing. And we still take precautions but nature's nature and it's going to happen and, you know, we manage risk when we're ready. You know, like, we'll be resilient when it happens, you know, like, not as if we were directly traumatized by it. No.

Lily's storying of bushfire is familiar in the Australian context. In the 'nothing to see here' narrative, fires, even at the massive scale of 2019–2020, are constituted as natural, manageable and, ultimately, regenerative. In contrast, while many fire experts, including Indigenous scholar Victor Steffensen, do argue for the 'naturalness' and necessity of fire – indeed, this is the basis of the Pyrocene concept – all agree that the 2019–2020 fires vastly exceeded a regenerative or safe intensity or extent of fire (Pyne, 2019b; Steffensen, 2020; Bowman et al, 2021; Gammage and Pascoe, 2021). Lily has gotten the wrong end of the stick here, and her account sweeps aside devastating losses of habitat, plants and animals and associated human and nonhuman animal suffering, including her own, in the name of "resilience". In such storying, losses and potential extinctions associated with habitat, plants and animals are invisibilized, constituted as a part of nature and therefore insignificant. The looping temporalities of bushfires, in other words, are trivialized in these stories of regeneration. The connection between Lily's account of the fires as natural and her contentment with her 'one boy, one girl' family remain unspoken, but it seems to us that particular attachments to the status quo animate both.

Critical/queer geographers Clark and Yusoff propose a different reading of the regenerative capacity of fire in a piece written prior to the summer of 2019–2020. They 'see fire as one of the most vital and effusive ways through which the generative potential of the organic and the inorganic meet and join forces, a pre-eminent means by which living things 'contact and cross-fertilize the earth' (Grosz, cited in Clark and Yusoff, 2018: 13).

This account of fire as vital and effusive, and as ultimately regenerative, is linked to their understanding of kinship – which is a kinship not only with creatures but with ' "anorganic" and incorporeal forces of earth and cosmos' (Clark and Yusoff, 2018: 22). In this reading, although the generative force of fire might mean extinctions, it does not necessarily spell the end of kinship, because for Clark and Yusoff kinship is not human-centred. Clark and Yusoff's storying of fire and regeneration is very different from the mainstream narrative (articulated here by Lily) that centres humans' resilience in relation to fires and their capacity to manage risk.

Our continuing investments in particular carbon and reproductive futures are linked to a faith in regeneration. People want to believe that the status quo is just that, something that will continue. One of the most challenging elements of the Pyrocene, as described by Pyne and others, is that fire is intensifying as the climate crisis compounds and Aboriginal land practices are rendered impossible or forgotten. In December 2021 Mary Lou hiked through mountain landscapes in the alpine areas of NSW. Parts of this country were still clearly adversely impacted by the fires. Because the heat of the fires was so intense, significant parts of the landscape had barely any green shoots almost two years later. Indigenous and other scholars argue that although new habitats will eventually emerge, those that have been lost will not regenerate for hundreds or thousands of years, if at all, as time unfolds.

Ideas of regeneration and hope also inform contemporary accounts of parenting. Lily talked about localized parenting as something she wants to focus on. For holidays, she said, "a caravan park halfway home from Nana's house is totally all they need at two. You don't need to be going to Hamilton Island on a plane, you know". Lily's motivation behind this localized parenting is not entirely clear. One reading could be that Lily's concern for the environment shapes her commitment to staying in her locality rather than flying interstate for holidays. Lily, who does not appear to believe in the climate change discourse of bushfires, is committed to localized parenting. Relationships between doing things for the environment and environmentalism aren't narrated in predictable ways.

Anita, a teacher from the NSW South Coast, expresses her hope that children in her community will be well conceived, in every sense. She's sad about the number of people she perceives as not making intentional decisions to reproduce:

Anita: [L]iving in a country town, there's a lot of people that are young and have kids, because they don't really have any other ... don't feel they have any other options, and I think that's really sad. But I think if you really want a kid and you really care about the environment, you can make it work and you can, I guess, view it as raising the next generation of little wildlife warriors. [Laughs] I think ... and I say this, as a teacher, you know, someone who's so interested in child development and everything, I think that it would be ... the best thing you can do is just have the kids you want and love them and raise them to be really nice people, I think is better than not having kids that you don't really want and kind of resenting that.

Clark and Yusoff suggest that 'heteronormativities and filial modes of inheritance [are] prevalent in contemporary "green" thought' (2018: 13). Our data show that these strands are tightly woven together for some of our participants. For Anita, "the best thing" is no longer *just* about being a good parent; stewardship of the environment also goes hand in hand with good parenting, itself predicated on conscientious decision making about reproduction (only have the children you 'really want'). In this account, logics of choice (Mol, 2008) are extended beyond the belief that good parents can somehow guarantee that they will have good children, to the idea that environmental values can also be passed on – just like goodness.

Anita's observations about the value of having children intentionally are not a new sentiment. The Australian middle class have long chided people who don't reproduce for the right reasons. Social censure related to not having children intentionally was the basis of much family planning education in Australia as far back as the 19th century (Bashford and Strange, 2004). A number of our participants express the hope that their children will be decidedly good for the environment – the next generation of wildlife warriors. Is the reverse side of these environmental futures inhabited by children who weren't planned and who weren't raised to fight for the environment? Within this reproductive calculus, will they contribute to – rather than ameliorate – the environmental challenges associated with the Pyrocene? Are the middle class becoming more censorious of those who fail to plan their families intentionally because of worries associated with climate crisis and generalized concerns about overpopulation and Earth's carrying capacity?

Our participants identify themselves as being involved in conversations about what it means to have more children on a potentially overpopulated planet. But they also imagine themselves as the type of people who should be reproducing, precisely because of their focus on environmental issues. Delilah, a senior public servant from Canberra, is confident of her capacity to raise children "in a very crowded world":

Delilah: It sounds a bit conceited to say this, but I think my
             conclusion comes down to, well, I think that the kind of
             person that we would raise, and kind of throw into the world
             would be a positive contribution. I think the values that my
             family and I have, and the expectations that we would kind
             of instil in our children would be a positive thing. And there
             are a lot of shit people out there [laughs] producing some
             pretty unpleasant contributions to the world. And in some
             ways, it's a positive thing to contribute a good person.

Similarly, for Alice and Nathan, a public servant and environmental activist
from Canberra, being environmentally conscious is something they want to
prioritize above all other issues, and they perceive this orientation as part of
what makes them desirable parents:

Alice: But I think both of us ultimately feel like we can only...
             there should be more people like us. [Laughs] So for us,
             it's a good thing to have more kids.
Nathan: We [have more reason?] to be very environmentally
             conscious. It's definitely in the forefront of her mind. You
             know, when I voted in the US, I'd just vote with whoever's
             best for the environment, because I think people tend not
             to look at the long-term, and you have to. So whoever
             I think is … in my mind, it's like almost the only issue, and
             not because all the other ones aren't important, but, like,
             none of the other ones matter if we don't have a planet left
             for us to do … what does it matter if there's no planet to
             have a war on, or whatever it is.

Notions of overpopulation entangle with Pyro-reproductive futures
manifesting in a responsibility (and perceived capacity) to produce "good
people": people who will vote according to environmental consciousness
and commit good deeds like purchasing solar panels. Our participants feel
accountable, likely to us as researchers and members of their community,
but also to their children for their environmental actions – not doing
anything is no longer an option. Their felt capacity to produce good
people ameliorates a palpable frustration at the Australian government's
inaction on climate:

Delilah: And I think it [the fires] did make us do things like, you
             know, we've had solar panels put on the house since then.
             Like, there is that real sense of, like, well, if the fucking
             government's not going do it, individually, there must be

some things that we can do because it's, you know, it can't just be left the way it is.

What is unsettling in such accounts is the strong entanglement of personal attributes with action on climate change; such accounts not only provide a picture of those who might make positive contributions, but are also strongly suggestive of those perceived to be compounding problems through producing people who will not contribute in a way that they feel assured their own children will.

Tania, a nurse living in Canberra, describes the bushfires as "the forerunner of an environmental disaster that, you know, if we think very negatively about it could be the start of the sixth mass extinction ... Yeah, I do worry about the environmental impact of having kids". For Tania, reproduction and environmental crisis are clearly interwoven, but this is not a deterrent to having more children: she already has three children and would be happy to have one more. For Tania, having kids is offset by her attention to minimizing the environmental impact in her day-to-day life, and by raising children who, she assumes, will care similarly about the environment, by virtue of her example:

Tania: I do worry about the environmental impact of having kids. I worry about ... my justification for having children ... I'm doing everything I can every single day to reduce my impact on the environment, which means I'm increasing the amount of people who are going to be doing that every day as well. So if I figured out that my children will think like that, and then, you know, that's not a bad thing.

The reproduction of values associated with care for the environment is a strong thread through our participants' stories. Alice spoke of the number of children an environmentally conscious person might have in a different way:

Alice: I don't think ... the climate issues would cause us to limit the number of children we had, that would be based on health. I tend to think that one of the best positive things you can do in the world is to raise children in a way where they can contribute to change, because one person can only do so much, and if you make three more people, they can do more. As long as they're taught and, you know, empowered to do their own sets of good.

Our participants worked to produce themselves as responsible parents by demonstrating that they were being intentional about having children, as well as by raising children who would in turn be responsible for the environment. Tania even suggested through having children, you can pass on an environmental inheritance by encouraging them to care for the environment:

Tania: And the other thing too, I find about simplifying it is, you know, when you pass away, you pass away and your thoughts on processes of environmental love and environmental care and all that kind of stuff passes with you. But if you have kids, you encourage it.

In this scenario, those who don't have children extinguish their love and care for the environment when they die. Here, the only way to ensure environmental futures is by having children. Other ways in which people who don't have children themselves might care for the environment (educating other people's children, caring for the land, supporting environmental organizations and parties in their communities, to name but a few) are subtly diminished in such imaginings of what care for the environment might look like in future generations.

The inheritance of care, through the production of progeny who will care for the environment, was a key element of our participants' answers to our question about climate change. These imaginings of responsible regeneration in the Pyrocene also evoke imaginings of '"wasteful" bodies – maybe those who aren't environmentally aware – expanding uncontrollably in space' (Ahuja, 2015: 369), potentially crowding out the reproductive futures (Ahuja, 2015: 369) of those empowered to do good. Murphy and other ecofeminists reject narratives about human density as 'too many' that aren't also calling for a reordering of capitalism and heteropatriarchy. For them, individualized accounts of reproductive choice and responsibility are insufficient, as they cannot account for the entanglements of reproductive inequalities and environmental violence. In alignment with critical Australian narratives, like those expressed in Steffenson (2020) and Gammage and Pascoe (2021), Murphy suggests a 'reparative' path that starts by recognizing the historical entanglements of environmental damage and infrastructures of dispossession.

Pyro-reproductive feelings

Neel Ahuja, writing about queer theory and the extinctions associated with climate crisis, talks about how 'any vision of freedom in the global North – including visions of freedom *both* staked on the reproduction of the nuclear family and on the refusal of it – are imbricated in racialized forms of carbon privilege that disperse social and biological precarity' (Ahuja, 2015: 367).

Australian ecofeminist Jennifer Hamilton, too, recognizes the immanence of extinction, but doesn't imagine we can easily reject our attachments to reproductive futures. Instead, she asks us to multitask – to 'posit new kinds of communal formations and also reckon with the difficult work of reforming the current structures within which we live at the same time' (Hamilton, 2019: 475).

In their responses to our difficult question, we see our participants surfing some of these tensions; they recognize the challenges presented by their own and other's attachment to existing heteronormative formations of kinship while trying to pay attention to climate change. Many complex feelings arise: some participants imagine geographical and communal formations where they could seek refuge from environmental disasters, for themselves and future generations; others profess profound ambivalence about reproduction; and many express solastagia – the loss of capacity to gain comfort from one's environment. This section explores this range of feelings.

Escape

Hamilton's analysis highlights the challenges of breaking away from existing formations of kinship: 'Everyone is so (understandably) eager to walk towards new kinship formations, they are not thinking about the possible difficulties involved in walking away from the current ones. It is as if breaking up with the extractivist, capitalist, colonial patriarchy is easy' (Hamilton, 2019: 471).

While breaking up with climate crisis is hard to do, some of our participants, and their partners, had put significant effort into thinking about when to leave, where they might go and what resources they might need to make their escape from the fires. Participants' plans for their own Pyro-reproductive futures were sometimes hastily put together during extreme events. Alison recalls her partner's fantasies of escape with some amusement:

Alison: [A]s I said, my partner is an army officer, so he was, like, "Oh, you know, we need to plan, like, maybe if he's born and the fires are bad we'll just get on a plane and go to Queensland." So he'd already looked up, like, what age babies can fly, you know, all the different airlines, policies, he pretty much said, "Why don't we just book flights now?" I'm, like, "I am, like, 40 weeks pregnant, I cannot even think about packing up, flying to Queensland with a newborn and no fucking idea what we're doing." [Laughs]

Rebecca: That's interesting, because some people said that that was the possibility, right, that the only alternative was to leave if you were pregnant. But as you say, that's such a big ask. Especially when you're about to give birth. Just impossible.

Alison: Yeah, and you're like, you have no idea what's going to happen with the birth, what if you need a Caesarean, then you're going to be in hospital for days and you can't fly anyway, you know, all these things. So I was just going, "No, no, come on." But yeah, he would probably have just got on the plane if I'd agreed.

The prospect of escape in the heat of the moment, when one is almost due to deliver, felt unrealistic to Alison.

Shelley, a public servant from Canberra, had worked on issues related to climate change before her pregnancy. Her partner works for an NGO as an environmental activist. This professional and personal focus on the environment was shared by many of their friends and work colleagues. Shelley said that she had regularly discussed the ethics of having children, specifically in relation to environmental issues. Like many of the participants, she was also focused on how to live in a way that aligns with her environmentalist values. During the fires, her concerns about bringing up children became entangled with thoughts about where she and her family should reside. Here, she thinks about possibly seeking to migrate because of what she perceives as increasing vulnerabilities associated with climate change in Australia:

Shelley: I know that we're in a position of privilege, but I think what the bushfires did was like, they took, they really showed how Australia is vulnerable, despite having many, many advantages. So we looked at, we usually look at ourselves as a place where refugees would flee to, and then all of a sudden it was looking like we wanted to flee from it. And we were looking at where we live internationally, is Canada good? We've got family there. And yeah, it kind of turned people's thinking about that kind of refugee issue, climate refugee.

Rebecca: And so that was a discussion that came up, around the potential of actually moving away from Australia over that period?

Shelley: Where in Australia would you move? … Maybe actually we should leave Australia because you can't tell which spot in Australia, like all of it is potentially vulnerable.

For Shelley and her family, carbon privilege doesn't assuage feelings of vulnerability. At the time, Shelley's imagining of all of Australia as potentially vulnerable was common currency in reporting on this topic. In 2021, in response to the release of the Intergovernmental Panel on Climate Change

(IPCC) report, newspaper articles appeared with titles such as 'Australia's extreme climate leaves it vulnerable to global warming' (Ludlow, 2021). Such articles drew on Australian experts on climate to reinforce perceptions and feelings of vulnerability in the face of climate change:[2] 'Andrew Pittman, director of the ARC Centre of Excellence for Climate System Science at the University of NSW, says climate change will exacerbate the current extremes of Australia's weather. "We're a bloody big continent. There's lots of space to be hit by extremes", Professor Pittman says.'[3]

In 2022, after a series of catastrophic floods in northern NSW and southern Queensland, media sources reported studies claiming that approximately one quarter of Australia's housing stock has become uninsurable because of the risks posed by climate change and associated extreme weather events (Hutley et al, 2022). People are unable to afford insurance because their homes are considered to be high risk, and the evening news frequently depicts communities experiencing displacement because of flood or fire. Underinsurance means that some people are more likely to become homeless, and those living in areas most exposed to environmental disaster – on the river flats of regional towns or the urban fringes of cities, for example – are more likely to be financially vulnerable. It is also worth noting that most housing in Australia is privately owned; at the last census in 2021 only 3.8 per cent of Australians lived in public housing. Under such housing stress, many families consider moving, although many express a strong desire to stay where they have always been. Whether staying or going, most people are making this decision in the absence of any option to access government supported housing.

During the 2019–2020 summer, Nathan and Alice moved to escape the Canberra smoke. This move came just before the pandemic hit, which was not something they could have foreseen. They moved to Melbourne, the Australian city that ended up having one of the longest experiences of lockdown anywhere in the world. Due to this move, they ended up living with extended family for a long time, a situation they described as quite stressful. Interviewed together, this couple articulated a conviction that it is possible to find a haven from climate risk, if only one is willing to do the research and find the 'right' location. This conviction doesn't appear to have been shaken by the lack of control they lived through in relation to the smoke and COVID-19:

Nathan: [G]iven what we know about the climate and all the modelling, *where will be the best place to live? You know, the place that's most insulated from the various extremes* ... I am actively looking to figure out, like, is there some place maybe inland that's more stable or insulated by geographic features like mountains and, you know, and how do you balance that with community?

… So whatever area has the most buffers built in, right, either bodies of water, certain mountain regions, I think that might be the safest, and I am looking for it. We probably won't make any move like that for several years, at least but it's definitely in my consciousness. And I imagine such places will start to have a much higher attraction. So you ideally want to get in before the land, the property values go up.

Alice and Nathan are actively engaged in finding a place that can literally and figuratively buffer them from future extremes relating to climate crisis; they have already moved away from Canberra because of the smoke associated with the bushfires. In their imagining of reproductive futures, finding a physical place of refuge is prioritized above bonds with family and people in their community. They recognize that finding such a place is likely an expensive prospect and therefore exclusive. Theirs is a vision of distributed reproduction only open to a few: those with plenty of resources and foresight, and who are willing and able to leave existing connections.

Ambivalence

For a minority of our participants, our question "How do you feel about the idea of people having children in general, in the context of climate change?" evoked expressions of deep personal ambivalence about reproduction. Feelings of ambivalence were also projected onto the bodies of participating expectant mothers and new parents by people they encountered. This ambivalence, we suggest, resonates with, and is fostered by, prevalent and contradictory cultural stories about reproduction that frame 'having kids' as environmentally destructive consumerism, while simultaneously bemoaning (some) women's lack of appropriate attention to issues of in/fertility *and* extravagantly celebrating babies and motherhood. In many public stories, overpopulation, reproduction and climate change are woven together: 'ideas of livable worlds are changing with increasingly catastrophic narratives of environmental change, impacting the sense of responsibility individuals may feel to future humans – but there is no guarantee of shared agreement about what that responsibility is or what forms it should take' (Lappé et al, 2019: 142).

Our question about people "having children in general" was often answered personally. Lisa, for example, was clear that after the bushfires, there would be no more children for her:

Rebecca: Did the bushfires or anything else this year impact at all
             on your thoughts about having kids in general?
Lisa: That's a good question. You know what, I think it might
             have. I hadn't really thought about it in that way. Before
             we had her, we'd always sort of said, like, "Oh, two or
             three", kind of thing. After this, like, I don't know if it
             was just the external, like, environmental stuff, or if it
             was also miscarriages or the health issues, or whatever
             but we're both just, like, "No, we're done. Two in, two
             out, net zero." … Climate change and the world actually
             becoming sick and not being sustainable, so are you going
             to put children into it? Like, maybe that's a selfish thing
             to do.

For Lisa, having two children is environmentally responsible – she and her
partner revised their earlier plans to have more children, partly in relation
to climate change, wondering if having more than two might be selfish. It is
interesting to see the infiltration of policy language into this discussion: the
term 'net zero' is synonymous with a response to climate crisis that 'helps
to perpetuate a belief in technological salvation and diminishes the sense of
urgency surrounding the need to curb emissions now' (Dyke et al, 2021: np).
Environmental scientists Dyke et al (2021) characterize net zero approaches to
climate crisis as 'licensing a recklessly cavalier "burn now, pay later" approach
which has seen carbon emissions continue to soar'. Lisa's use may also be
connected to population-related ideas of 'replacement reproduction' – that
is, 'two children replace two parents', an idea central to popular articulations
of neo-Malthusianism.

    While Lisa sees a 'net zero' approach to having children as sustainable,
some environmental researchers and activists have been critical of
such thinking in relation to reproduction and climate, urging people
to have fewer or no children in order to fight climate change. The
graphic in Figure 6.1 is taken from an article in *The Guardian* with an
emphatic title: 'Want to fight climate change? Have fewer children'
(Carrington, 2017).

    The graphic shows how much CO_2 can be saved through a range of
different actions. Kimberly Nicholas, who coauthored the paper on which
the graphic is based (Wynes and Nicholas, 2017), is quoted talking about
reproduction as 'deeply personal', but also as something that needs to be
curbed. In this rhetoric, the lives of new humans are compared to the carbon
impacts of nonhuman actors, and reproduction is literally measured against
other consumption-related activities such as buying cars or light bulbs. All
of these entities and actions are collapsed into 'lifestyles' that can and should
be consciously constrained to reduce carbon emissions:

But we can't ignore the climate effect our lifestyle actually has ... It is our job as scientists to honestly report the data. Like a doctor who sees the patient is in poor health and might not like the message 'smoking is bad for you', we are forced to confront the fact that current emission levels are really bad for the planet and human society. (Carrington, 2017)

Like our participants, scientists and journalists are making diverse connections between having children, reproduction and climate. In this way of communicating about reproduction and climate change, emissions are all equal and equally bad for the planet, but having children is particularly egregious in terms of scale. As Kristina Rukaite notes in her thesis

Figure 6.1: 'Have Fewer Children' graphic from *The Guardian* newspaper (Carrington, 2017)

Tonnes of CO2-equivalent per year for one person undertaking each action

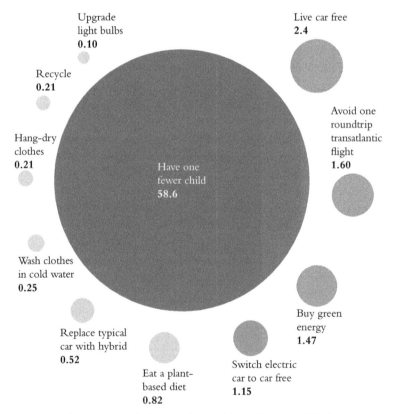

Note: The graphic shows how much CO2 can be saved through a range of different actions.

Source: *The Guardian*, Wynes & Nicholas, Environmental Research Letters, reproduced with permission

'Reproduction in the (m)Anthropocene: exploring the roots and implications of environmentally friendly restrain from childbearing',

> quantifying an unborn child in emissions savings and suggesting [people restrain from having children] ... must be understood in the socio-political and historical context which drives the individualization of climate causes and solutions; gives authority to "value-neutral" science to produce and naturalize reproductive recommendations; and ignores the patriarchal history of reproduction within capitalism. (Rukaite, 2020: 2)

Unsurprisingly, the problem of reproduction and emissions is on the minds of our participants – they are making connections between having children and the need to live sustainably. In 2020, such concerns were particularly highlighted in news reports about the UK's BirthStrike movement, described as a place for people who had decided to forgo children because of concerns about climate. Ambivalence was rife here: within a year, the founders closed its website because the movement was perceived as being aligned with the 'overpopulation' topic and thus as anti-women.

Participants in our study have a range of responses to the call to reproduce less. Libby, a paediatric osteopath, is ambivalent about how to respond to different injunctions about having children:

Libby: If we were environmentally, ethically, financially conscious, none of us would have children. [Laughs] The race probably needs to die out, let's be ... you know, and from both a personal and a sociological context, we should probably stop breeding. There are too many humans ... but I guess, you know, biology is a really strong driver, because here I am with a baby, despite that. ... people who love and care for the environment and ... wanting to raise a child who is, you know, emotionally connected and engaged in the world, you know, we need those people. So if all of the people who are raising those sorts of kids aren't having kids because ethically, we probably shouldn't, I think the human race is actually more fucked, not less – excuse my language – because then we have a whole pile of people who maybe aren't aware or engaged or, you know, and that's a problem, because you're not going to stop everyone.

Libby indexes a shared ambivalence among our participants about having children. Maybe the question we asked participants – "How do you feel about the idea of people having children in general, in the context of climate change?" – invites ambivalence. When our participants were asked to put reproduction and climate together, they perceived a problem – having too many children – and, as parents, they often situated themselves as part of the 'problem'. Once having children is perceived as a problem (and we have demonstrated that this is a common understanding among our participants), the question of who should be having children quickly surfaces. One of the outcomes of this study might be a concerted effort to interrupt such patterns of thought because they often appear to result in speculations about who should and should not be having children in the Pyrocene.

Solastalgia

Solastalgia, a concept developed by Australian philosopher Glenn Albrecht (Albrecht et al, 2007: S95), describes 'the distress that is produced by environmental change impacting on people while they are directly connected to their home environment'. Participants shared experiences of being questioned by others about their decision to reproduce in the midst of an environmental disaster, and the reactions and feelings this produced for them. Solastalgia specifically refers to feelings of desolation and the associated incapacity to feel solace because of the loss associated with environmental degradation, in this case caused by smoke and bushfire (Albrecht et al, 2007: s96). In relation to having children, these feelings were often compared to participants' sense of their own relatively safe childhoods.

Sarah, an IT manager from Canberra, had a difficult pregnancy that was compounded by gestational diabetes and the smoke. Because she lives in an older house, the smoke from the bushfires penetrated her home, so she decided to cohabit with her in-laws for a period of time in order to protect the family from the smoke. Sarah was very worried about how the smoke might impact her unborn child. When we asked her about the relationship between having children and climate change, she told us about her own childhood:

Sarah: [A] lovely pleasant childhood of summers that would have a few hot days, but actually be lovely. And at night, I grew up in Tasmania and you could open a window and you would always be cool at night. Is that something they're not going to experience? That's just talking about enjoyment, but their food security, their health, and worry about all those things I really do, but it would never be worth – it would never mean that I wouldn't have them because I think people who are educated in care, they will be the people who would change the world.

Sarah's memories of growing up in an environment which she remembers as pleasant are intermingled with anxieties about what her own children might experience. However, her feelings of concern about how climate change might impact her own children don't appear to run too deep: they are quickly allayed by her faith in the capacity of "people who are educated … who would change the world". Sarah's faith in the capacity of her children to create positive change works against feelings that she might need to deny her desire to reproduce. Here, solastalgia and ambivalence fuel the problematic logics of Pyro-reproduction we described earlier.

Delilah, a senior public servant, described how she felt immediately after giving birth in Canberra in early January, in the midst of concerns about bushfires and ongoing smoke inundation:

Delilah: I had this off feeling, and probably even in the couple of weeks before too of … like, it kind of felt like the world was ending at that time, or that we were … we, the human race, have lived as long as we can on this planet and here's the beginning of the end. Like, it had a real doomsday feeling and bringing a baby into the world and feeling like it's this terrible thing to have done. Like, it didn't feel like a world that you could celebrate … so it did have a strange feeling about it. Yeah. I mean, that kind of went away when the bushfires went away really, but it was … yeah, it was odd.

Emotional flatness accompanying the birth of her first child stands out in Delilah's story, but her "doomsday feelings" didn't persist beyond the fires. In our study, people's relationships to climate and reproduction had moments of intensity in 2019–2020, but generally these feelings did not persist (in part because of weather patterns involving significant rain, but also because of the overwhelming impact of the ensuing pandemic). The bushfires, while wreaking havoc in Canberra because of the associated smoke, also felt distant to Delilah: "I think a lot of people have that feeling of, like, it's not even *our bushfire*, you know, it's just kind of, like, smoke coming from somewhere else." As we discussed in Chapter 4, the smoke associated with fires that you can't see has a different emotional valence to fires experienced first hand.

Feelings of solastalgia also extended to the environments in which people were located. Bridget, a teacher from the South Coast of NSW, remembers feeling very sad about the local fauna and flora. For her, these fires were quite distinct from other experiences of bushfires she had experienced growing up in a regional location:

Bridget: It's pretty devastating … it's just sad … after the fires came through here and we went down to Mum's, I think, the week after they came through, and there was, like, she was just letting the rosellas eat all the fruit on her fig tree because

she's, like, "There's no food." There were people paddling
up the lake to feed the kangaroos, hand-feed them.

It's, like, you can't really put your finger on it, but you don't
realize how much love you have for your local area until it's
burnt and destroyed ... I don't think we'll ever get over it.
And I grew up with fires, like, as a kid, you know, bushfires
are a part of living in a regional area. Yeah. I wouldn't want
to go through it again. Or see the area go through it again.

Although Delilah described the fires as belonging to other people, Canberra
did experience a massive local fire. On 27 January 2020, the Orroral Valley fire
burnt about 80 per cent of Namadgi National Park (82,700 hectares) and 22 per
cent of Tidbinbilla Nature Reserve (1,444 hectares) and 3,350 hectares of rural
land. Namadgi and Tidbinbilla are Canberra's closest wilderness areas: Namadgi
comprises 46 per cent of the total land area of the ACT, where Canberra is
located. Unbearably, this fire was accidentally started by a Defence helicopter on
a reconnaissance mission to identify landing zones that could be used to insert
and extract remote area firefighting teams. Lisa talked about the emotional toll
of these fires and how she processed their impact on the local area:

Lisa: I think there was an emotional toll there, like, Canberra's
really special to both of us, we both were both born
here, both of our families lived or live here. Most of
our lives and, you know, part of the special thing about
Canberra is really the environment and the nature. It's
not just around but, like, through every single suburb.
Yeah, I mean, it was really sad. We watched the news a
lot and saw places that we've spent a lot of time growing
up had been affected by it, and it just felt like another
really visceral reminder of, like, climate change being
really, like, apparent now, you know, the effects of it.

I think up until this year, you know, it was talked
about a lot and people were aware that we were seeing,
you know, more of the effects, but I think, like, having
it sort of thrust into your lap in two different, like,
really different ways in one year is, like, pretty scary ...
Canberra always just felt kind of untouchable. Like, it's
such a pretty, you know, what's the word, mild, but, like,
you know, not a lot happens here that's really scary, like,
didn't used to happen like that.

And I think, you know, they talk about the Canberra
bubble in terms of, like, the socio-demographics as well
and it's a pretty affluent sort of little community, and

we all just kind of … we used to be able to do what we wanted really, you know, go to work, go to the cafe, do whatever. Yeah, I think it's just a bit of a wake-up call about … there's real effects being seen already.

And, you know, I still feel like I'm young, I've got a lot of life to live, and then I look at my kids and I'm like, "God, how are you going to have to manage? Like, what are you going to have to deal with in your lifetime if this is already happening now?" Yeah, that's scary.

Participants' descriptions of feelings about the places in which they experienced the fires were another way in which we came to know how reproduction and climate have become entangled. Lisa talks about how feelings of loss resonated for her as a visceral reminder of climate change, in a place which she describes as feeling "untouchable". She grew up in a suburb of Canberra that had been directly impacted by bushfires in 2003, resulting in four people's deaths and significant destruction of property and bushland. But still, for her, Canberra has felt like a safe bubble because of its affluence. By their own accounts, our participants on the NSW South Coast and in Canberra are imbricated in the carbon privilege that Ahuja (2015) references. While feelings of physical precarity were exacerbated by the fires of 2019 and 2020 and the accompanying smoke, folded into COVID-19, mostly our participants expressed optimism about their futures and about the capacity of their children to create better futures. They did, however, also worry about how climate disasters might accelerate and adversely impact future generations. As Murphy (2018) argues, the idea that apocalyptic futures are yet to come is itself a strong indicator of privilege.

Our project did not incorporate people who do not yet have children, so those who explicitly choose to care about the climate by deciding not to have children are excluded from this particular discussion of kinship, care and climate. Ahuja (2015) does not distinguish these two groups and reminds us that there is no sovereign place from which 'we' in the Global North can assess reproductive processes from the outside. The fantasies about neoliberal freedoms to reproduce good children that surface in our research are, we argue, perhaps as embedded in privilege as the fantasies of queer publics that resist reproduction altogether or, alternatively, rely on reproductive technologies to make babies, as Ahuja describes.

When asked about whether COVID-19 and the bushfires influenced her thoughts about having children in the future, Gina, an office manager in Canberra, recalled that her partner

'said if we hadn't had a baby yet, he said he would have stopped trying at this point. Yeah, I was very surprised, to be honest. And I was like,

"What?? Are you serious?" and he was, like, "Yeah, I don't want to …
I would not have wanted to bring a baby into this at this point." And
I was like, "Okay, wow, that's pretty … that's a pretty big statement.'"

Gina's partner's ambivalence about having children is, as she points out "a
pretty big statement", perhaps especially so because this was their first child.
Gina's partner was more immediately impacted by the smoke because he
works outdoors. During the bushfires, he was admitted to hospital after
being adversely affected by smoke. He finds it hard to articulate to Gina just
how he arrived at this feeling. Feeling inarticulate and questioning thoughts
about reproduction under such duress is, in retrospect, pretty understandable.
Gina is also ambivalent about the era in which she finds herself, but not
about the decision to reproduce – for her, these things can be kept distinct:

Gina: [F]or me personally, I think it's an awful time. It is, like, it's
                not what I imagined it would be. But for me personally,
                it wouldn't have stopped me trying to have babies. I think
                we're all going to go through crappy times in our lives,
                like, there's not always going to be, you know, severe
                bushfires and global pandemics, hopefully, but for me
                personally, like, I've always wanted a family. So I don't
                think it really would have put a stop to it … It is, yeah,
                like, a pretty crappy time to be pregnant and, you know,
                try and raise a newborn with everything that's going on.
                But yeah, it wouldn't stop me, but I kind of need my
                husband to be on board, too. [Laughs]

Gina's husband's reluctance about having children taps into broader
community concerns about what it means to have children now. Matilda
reported being interrogated about having children while she sheltered from
fires on the beach on the NSW South Coast, a visibly very pregnant woman.
Her response to such questioning was understandably restrained: "'What do
you think about bringing a child into this world?" is what they were saying
to me as we could see a glowing red horizon in [seaside town]. "What
do you think about it?" I'm, like, "Yeah, yeah, it is kind of confronting,
you're right.'"

Conclusion: bushfires, babies and population troubles

In her essay 'Against population, towards alterlife', Murphy (2018) rejects
population frameworks, or the 'figures of massified life', for their fetishization
of human density as 'too many' without demanding the reordering of
capitalism and heteropatriarchy. She argues individualized accounts of

reproductive choice are not sufficient either, as they cannot account for the entanglements of reproduction with environmental violence. In our research we see participants struggling with these concepts, shifting in their answers to our difficult question "What do you think in general about having children in climate change?" between the vast scales of global population, through the complexities of local towns, cities and forests, to the intricacies of 'personal' choices which turn out to be neither individual nor private. Parents of newborn babies are unlikely to express regret about their children's existence and are increasingly likely to have had to come up with some forms of justification for having gone ahead and had a child, despite the associated carbon emissions! What we heard in our discussions with our participants was a rather narrow and contradictory set of stories about 'good' people: parents who do everything they can to protect the planet, including reproducing with conscious intention; and children who will grow up to be just like them. Such stories, sometimes explicitly and sometimes not, also had more shady characters: those who reproduce without wanting to; who won't educate their children properly in the ways of eco-responsible citizens; and whose children may well be planetary burdens. These stories, as we have argued, have worrying resonance with earlier accounts of population troubles.

It would be easy to point fingers at our participants, to chide them for their assumptions and to condemn their naive hopes of their offspring. It might be more helpful, we suggest, to instead think about where these stories come from, to explore how they circulate (particularly in times of life-threatening crisis) and how we might help to generate alternatives. What kind of stories could we tell about reproduction and climate that both refuse population thinking and complexify individualized responsibility without pointing to such equally huge edifices as heteropatriarchy, racism and capitalism? What can people do to pay attention to climate *and* its relation to reproduction without sliding into guilt or shame and associated denial and fantasy? We will pick up these threads in our final chapter.

Interleave 7

Finally seeing clear sky: Rebecca's story

I started looking at our garden as a possible fire risk and started googling 'fire resistant' plants. The gum trees we love across the road leading from the nature reserve became less attractive. My husband put socks full of sand in the gutters in case we had to fill them with water. The air at this time felt so dry I almost imagined it crackling. For several days, sleep was constantly disrupted by checking in on the radio and apps. I burst into tears at one point and suggested to him that we leave and stay with friends in town (he was much calmer than me). He decided he was okay to stay at the house and use the hoses to hose down the garden and roof if necessary, but would leave when advised to. I was okay with this – at one level I was aware 'rationally' that the fires were not likely to reach us, but I was still pretty on edge and felt vulnerable knowing they were relatively close, and that an 'ember attack' (which sounded very dramatic and militarized) was within the realms of possibility if the wind changed. I was finding it stressful staying home (exacerbated by the disrupted sleeping), so my daughter and I spent the weekend with friends in Bungendore and Civic (central Canberra).

On several days we found burnt gum leaves blowing on the deck and fine ash on the cars. The gum leaves I found particularly disturbing; it seemed to bring home/make intimate the loss of wildlife and trees and plants in Namadgi [a National Park south of Canberra]. Again, as significant places and walks in Namadgi were burnt, we felt really upset, knowing how stunningly beautiful and full of wildlife those places had been and that we'd recently been walking in them with family from the UK. On another occasion I remember driving home from work as the fires were near Tidbinbilla reserve (a favourite walking and picnic place

Interleave Figure 7.1: Participant's hand-drawn care map showing how her social world was reduced during the COVID-19 lockdown

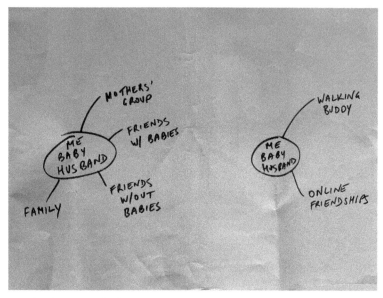

Note: The drawing on the left indicates what she expected to happen; the drawing on the right indicates the reduction of connections.

Source: participant drawing

Interleave Figure 7.2: Ash on the car, Canberra

Source: Rebecca's photograph

that we regularly visit) and parking up near the Arboretum to watch. I felt upset because I could see how close the fires were and assumed that the areas that we knew so well had been/would be destroyed, or at least transformed beyond recognition (thankfully it wasn't, only back sections of the reserve were burnt, although 80 per cent of Namadgi National Park was burnt).

I remember how happy we were to see clear, blue sky. I remember my daughter being suspicious of billowing clouds or low cloud for months after, asking if it was smoke. It was such a relief and felt deeply restorative to see rain fall in February.

7

Making Bushfire Babies

Donna Haraway's exhortation to 'Make kin, not babies' has accompanied us throughout this text. The slogan is used in Haraway's speculative fiction experiment, 'The Camille Stories', and elsewhere in her book *Staying with the Trouble* (2016). It derives from Haraway's belief that there are too many humans in the world and that privileged people should focus on building kin relations beyond those predicated on producing more human individuals[1] (Haraway is clear that some marginalized and oppressed people do not have enough children and should be helped to have more) (Haraway, 2018: 69–74).

In conversation with Haraway, and working within the frame of ecofeminism and environmental humanities, Australian feminist Jennifer Mae Hamilton draws our attention to the hard work of mothering. Like us, Hamilton is interested in caring, particularly 'the sweaty work implied by the notion of making kin' during extreme bushfires. Hamilton pushes back against Haraway's injunction to 'Make kin, not babies', arguing Haraway romanticizes the work of kin making and asking:

> What does it take to make kin and not babies? Perhaps it takes the strength of a mother breast-feeding in an apocalyptic heatwave, in a house poorly designed for the climate, oriented badly on the subdivided and fragmented stolen land? Perhaps the caregiver is dripping in sweat trying to keep this other being alive. Breathing is hard. Caring is hard. In other words, the kinds of embodied, sweaty work implied by the notion of making kin ... is probably going to be eerily like the more undesirable and mundane kinds of housework involved in making babies. (Hamilton, 2019: 486)

We agree that Haraway's emphasis on kin making in 'The Camille Stories' could be characterized as optimistic, even romantic. The dream that each human or symbiont[2] child should have three (or more parents), for example (Haraway, 2016: 138; Haraway 2018: 96), both underestimates the number of parents many children have already (thus affirming heteronormative, settler models of one- or two-parent families) (see also Benjamin, 2018; Tallbear, 2018) and assumes that more parents means better parenting and a more positive experience of growing up. Of course, having three not-so-great parents could be worse than having only one or two of them! 'The Camille Stories' also skip over what might be involved in 'discouraging' people from having babies even while 'actively cherishing' reproductive freedoms and rejecting coercion (Haraway, 2016: 139).

The slogan 'Make kin, not babies' also formed the basis for the excellent collection, *Making Kin Not Population: Reconceiving Generations* (2018), edited by Haraway and Clarke, which we have cited numerous times throughout this book. The shift from 'babies' to 'population' in the book's title is an important one. As we have discussed in Chapter 6, the term 'population' has increasingly come under critical scrutiny within feminist studies of reproduction. Its connection with babies is strong and highly contested; as readers may remember, Strathern (2019: 160) challenges us to: 'Try not thinking of babies when you think of population.' Unlike much ecofeminist writing, in this book, we have been engaging with babies – and their parents – as well as grappling with ideas of population. Our argument is directly informed by stories about pregnancy, birth and parenting newborns during two back-to-back biosocial-ecological disasters, understood by many as the outcome of the long-term, accelerating environmental destruction constituting colonization and industrialization that is only partially captured by the term 'climate crisis'. Our focus has been directly on the experiences of people 'making babies', hence the title of our book!

Although fully cognizant of the racist, sexist and disablist histories of the concept of 'population' (see, for example, Haraway, 2016: 208–210), Haraway is concerned with numbers of humans, and at least part of her motivation for exhorting us to make kin is to reduce these: 'babies should be rare and precious', she argues in several places (Haraway, 2016: 138; Clarke, 2018: 4). Each child having three parents is one proposed strategy and, despite our criticisms noted earlier, we certainly agree with Haraway that it would be great if adults could be involved in parenting without having to 'make babies'. We are also on board with her goals to expand humans' thinking about who or what counts as kin and therefore, as discussed in Chapter 6, what counts as care. This approach has strong resonance with Louisa and Mary Lou's goals, for example, to trouble sexuality education's prophylactic focus on prevention (whether it be prevention of babies, sexual assault or gender- and sexuality-based harassment) and instead to explore pleasure, though we also recognize that is a not unproblematic exhortation (Allen et al, 2014). We agree that 'making kin' opens up possibilities for relationality beyond the biological and beyond the human. Like Hamilton, however, we see making kin and making babies as forms of embodied labour that are closely connected, that are usefully thought together as 'reproduction' or, more specifically here, 'Pyro-reproduction'. While we all have ethical obligations relating to making kin and making babies, our respons-ability doesn't begin or end with the human. Throughout this text we have tried to attend to ways in which our and our participants' attention was drawn to the obliteration of plants, animals and ecosystems during the bushfires. The tendency to focus on the human and to neglect the nonhuman other is part of the reckoning of reproduction in the Pyrocene we are trying to process.

Our participants have helped us understand the complexity of Pyro-reproduction (making kin and making babies in the Pyrocene) in so many ways. The stories they have shared help us understand the profound absurdity of mum–guilt in smoke disasters – where mothers berate themselves and apologize to their foetuses for being unable to breathe in a way that protects them from possible harm. This has prompted our exploration of an ecofeminist politics of breathing that can conceptualize how things like smoke and viruses shape human subjectivity and action, and simultaneously elude human control. Breath configures who we are and shapes our relationships with human–nonhuman others at the level of being. But as we see throughout the interviews, the desire to protect a foetus or newborn baby is deeply felt and sometimes overwhelming, and letting go of guilt is hard work. A wishful belief in the sovereignty of the human to control entities like population, breath, and exposure to viruses, fire and smoke permeates our interviews.

We have shown how reproductive life in the bushfires was marked by environmental and body monitoring, and the collective community pooling of relevant data about air quality. Like exposure to fire and smoke, this worry about air quality was not evenly distributed. Some participants sought access to more information in an effort to protect themselves and their families, and took preventative actions in the home, taping up gaps, purchasing air purifiers and regularly monitoring air quality so they knew when they might safely exit the home or give permission for children to play outside. Others decidedly turned away from such monitoring, refusing the burden of the information offered by various experts, 'weird' and otherwise.

Many of our participants keenly felt a gap in knowledge about how smoke might impact themselves and, concomitantly, the health of their children. Indeed, experts seemed to have little information they could impart, which is part of what prompted this study to be undertaken in the first place. Somewhat worryingly, funding for the biomedical component of the study proved elusive, further contributing to the lacunae in knowledge about how prolonged exposure to bushfire smoke impacts mothers and children. In addition to producing more biomedical knowledge about smoke and reproduction, we want experts to take seriously the activities and experience of citizens that materialize public health injunctions to 'follow information'. What is the value of governments and clinicians telling people they need to worry about smoke when they cannot escape it? What types of advice are helpful in the Pyrocene and what types of advice compound fear and guilt? Should mothers, babies and pregnant women comply with directives to evacuate to emergency shelters or smoky beaches? How are the authorities that are designing and designating places of refuge making space for people they are designating as vulnerable?

We have seen that reproduction in the Pyrocene can be unpredictable and scary: exposure to fire and smoke are widely but unevenly distributed, tracking familiar lines of gendered, classed and racialized privilege. Trying to make sense of their own desires and experiences of having a baby during and across ecological disasters, our participants often evoked ideas of 'responsible reproduction'. Like Haraway in 'The Camille Stories', they produced narratives of good parenting and of childhoods that contribute to making 'a habitable, flourishing world' (Haraway, 2016: 168) rather than 'that immense irreversible destruction that is really in train' (Haraway, 2016: 102). In their valorization of 'intention', such narratives, we have argued, are themselves articulations of privilege. Symbionts and collective decision making aside, our participants' lives were also already very similar to those imagined in 'The Camille Stories': during the fires and the pandemic, they were all trying to support their families and friends, to teach their children how to live, and to learn how to live better in their damaged surroundings.

Learning from wombats and orchids

> One way to live and die well as mortal critters in the Chthulucene is to join forces to reconstitute refuges, to make possible partial and robust biological-cultural-political-technological recuperation and recomposition, which must include mourning irreversible losses. (Haraway, 2016: 101)

In this book we have used participant photographs to convey elements of the experience of living through bushfires that are beyond words. For us, looking through these photographs evokes embodied memories of the smell of smoke, the panic of evacuating and the boredom of being sealed in our homes. We have had two wet and cool summers: the grass is long and the trees and birds look healthy, there is plentiful water in the lakes and rivers throughout the ACT and NSW. We have written part of this book next to Lake George, or Weereewa as it is known to the local Indigenous community, just north of Canberra. During the bushfires, the lake was dry and had been so for many years, dry enough to schedule regular artistic performances in the basin. Now kangaroos and swans have returned to the lake as it fills with water. The abundance of the present moment, along with the passing of time (three years), and the intensity of COVID-19 (Canberra is experiencing around 1,000 new infections a day at time of drafting this chapter in June 2022) mean that, not unsurprisingly, the fires have started to feel quite distant.

Although our universities continue to insist on mask wearing and many meetings take place on Zoom, in the wider community many COVID-related restrictions have now been lifted, both in Australia and Aotearoa-New Zealand. International travel is tentatively restarting. As we completed this book, Rebecca flew to visit family in the UK (navigating a chaotic international travel industry and, somewhat ironically, succumbing to flu picked up en route), but we had still not met up physically with Louisa. Privileged assumptions of seamless travel and dreams of embodied reconnection after so much immobility and social distancing are still halting and fraught for many. It has been a challenge to cowrite a book at such a distance.

Our participants' photographs are often eerily empty. We specifically asked them to give us images without people, but animals and birds are often also missing. These absences speak to unimaginable losses: as we noted in Chapter 1, three billion animals, insects and birds died in the fires. The loss of iconic species – koalas in particular – quickly became a linchpin in environmentalist accounts of the fires, and campaigning for alternative forms of forest management often focuses on restoring and protecting habitat for these creatures. Searching for new stories in the awful repetitiveness of fires everywhere, journalists and writers looked to scientific and lay stories about animal experiences of fires. For example, feminist philosopher Danielle Celermajer's story of her rescue pig's survival became a bestseller (Celermajer, 2021).

Another story that circulated widely, and has stuck in our minds throughout writing this book, stars wombats. Wombats are large marsupials that have up to 12 burrows in a home range, with three to four main burrows that include multiple entrances and sleeping quarters (McKenna et al, nd). Covered in dense fur, wombats have strong digging claws and small eyes and ears. They are nocturnal and only venture into the outside world at dusk. In Canberra, and many places in Australia, they also frequently suffer from mange – volunteers track animals with notable skin and fur problems so they can be treated. During the fires, people reported seeing wombats ushering other animals and birds into their burrows to escape the fires. On social media, these wombats were hailed as 'heroes' who were doing better than the federal government to provide much-needed refuge.

In an article in *The Conversation*, animal ecologist Dale Nimmo (2020) discredits the heroic tropes of these stories – wombats, he argues, did not act altruistically in the face of fire. Other animals, however, did benefit from wombats' tunnelling labours and, indeed, always do. Wombats, Nimmo tells us, do not live in 'a home', but produce multiple networks of tunnels, moving between these frequently, leaving most of them 'empty' much of the time. Video-based research has shown that native and non-native species – koalas, rabbits, birds, wallabies, skinks, even penguins! – frequently enter these tunnels in search of food and/or safety. During the fires, then, the tunnels provided important places of refuge from the heat, smoke and flames: temperatures underground can be 20 degrees lower than those outside.

This story highlights many themes of our book. First, the significance of multispecies relationships, not only to humans but also to other animals. Wombats, koalas, rabbits and penguins live together and try to find ways of going on, even in times of intense crisis. It makes little sense to analyse environmental disasters without taking account of complex relationalities or kinships. Second, the story highlights the importance of places of refuge, and the challenges and opportunities of sharing these (see also van Dooren and Rose, 2012). For the families in our study who had to evacuate from fire, the public places of refuge were sometimes difficult because they were not planned with babies or pregnant women in mind: in one memorable story, there was not enough water to make up baby formula.

The participants in our study sometimes avoided evacuation centres because they could not imagine being there with newborn babies and small children. During the extreme smoke events in Canberra, pregnant women longed for public places of respite with clean air, where they could take their toddlers to play or just breathe more easily for a while. Staying at home, sealed in, did not always feel like a positive refuge experience. Like wombats and many other animals, then, humans need a range of 'home-like' spaces in order to sustain themselves – sometimes alone, sometimes with close kin and other times with strangers. As the climate emergency unfolds, we will need innovative architectures of refuge that can be shared with many others (see also Lopes et al, 2018). Finally, the story also highlights – idealistically, Nimmo argues – the importance of care during disasters. Perhaps the wombats were not shepherding or hosting others, but we humans were heartened by tales of their actions, which we could easily read as caring. Like many disasters, the fires and the pandemic inspired millions of acts of care, affirming amid the fear and devastation that care builds connection and acknowledges relationality.

In the end of his critical account of the wombat story, Nimmo insists that we shouldn't forget the plight of wombats and the other creatures hiding in the tunnels after the fires have passed. When they finally venture outside, their worlds are immensely changed – smouldering, black and relatively empty. How can they find food and water now? For some, these changes also bring new predators – feral cats, for example, have been shown to move towards smoke and fire to catch exposed rodents and tiny marsupials such as dunnarts. The sobering message here, Nimmo writes, is that immediate survival on its own is not enough; re-establishing habitats and homes and supporting animals and people while that happens is equally important. In Australia, this work continues as we write: three years later, many people are still without a permanent home[3] and much bushland, as we noted in Chapter 5, remains charred and quiet. These are the looping and intergenerational temporalities of bushfires.

In a 2022 podcast interview, First Nations fire and agriculture expert Bruce Pascoe tells the story of 'Black Duck', his property in rural northeast Victoria (just south of where some of our study participants live on the NSW South Coast).[4] Increasingly well known due to Pascoe's important books educating the wider Australian public about Aboriginal firestick farming and other care-taking practices, this property showcases the possibilities of farming native grasses for food and the positive effects of First Nations' forest and grassland management practices. Although Pascoe's house was saved the property was otherwise entirely burnt during the 2019–2020 fires. In the podcast, Pascoe describes the emotional devastation of this loss and his surprise that he was not as resilient as he thought he would be, despite his personal and cultural history. What kept him going, he says, was the collective of young people working alongside him, who encouraged him to get up each day and get back out to observe and care for the land. What they witnessed, he says, was stunning: amid the regrowth came species of native orchid Pascoe had never before seen. Seeds that had lain dormant for decades now had space to spring into life. Alongside irreparable loss and intense mourning, here is something more than survival: a kind of new flourishing, partial and robust, that we might also name Pyro-reproduction.

Notes

Chapter 1

[1] https://interaktiv.morgenpost.de/australia-area-burned-interactive-comparison/

[2] https://www.abc.net.au/news/2019-12-28/thirsty-koala-fed-by-cyclist-in-adelaide/11830276

[3] See Wilson (2019) for an analysis of the complex cultural politics of these debates in Australia prior to the 2019–2020 fires.

[4] See Haraway et al (2015) for a discussion of the Anthropocene, Capitalocene and other alternatives.

[5] In their book *Country: Future Fire, Future Farming* (2021), Gammage and Pascoe state that: '"Country" is an English word Aboriginal people have transformed. Country is physical, communal and spiritual – land, water, sky, habitats, sites, places, totems and relationships, a world of the mind, a way of believing and behaving. Creator ancestors made Country in the Dreaming, and they still oversee it. Not only obvious features that newcomers name, but every pebble and ripple disclosed both the ecological logic of its existence and the Dreaming's presence' (Gammage and Pascoe, 2021: 81–82). It should be noted that while Gammage and Pascoe use a capital C (which we will follow in this book to convey the specific Aboriginal transformation of the word), other authors do not.

[6] Shelley Pacholok's book *Into the Fire: Disaster and the Remaking of Gender* (2013) is a detailed analysis of the ways in which gender was remade among firefighters during an extreme wildfire event in Canada.

Chapter 2

[1] https://www.stuff.co.nz/national/117314221/why-the-smoke-from-bushfires-makes-the-sunrise-and-sunset-so-colourful

Chapter 4

[1] The associated website clarifies that: 'For pregnant women most will not experience problems due to smoke. For a small proportion, exposure to smoke over several weeks during pregnancy may slightly reduce the weight of their babies. This slight reduction is unlikely to have a long-term effect on the health of the babies' (https://nceph.anu.edu.au/phxchange/communicating-science/how-protect-yourself-and-others-bushfire-smoke).

[2] See also https://www.theguardian.com/lifeandstyle/2021/jan/11/air-grievances-silence-swirls-around-the-toll-of-bushfire-smoke-during-pregnancy

[3] Marc Böhlen's research into water quality monitoring in New York similarly found that citizens' judgements, based on smell, do not tend to correlate with scientific measurements of contamination levels in water at public beaches (Böhlen, 2016).

Chapter 5

[1] https://www.aihw.gov.au/reports/mothers-babies/antenatal-care-during-covid-19/contents/did-access-to-antenatal-care-change-during-the-covid-19-pandemic

[2] See https://en.wikipedia.org/wiki/COVID-19_lockdowns for a table of lengths of lockdown across different jurisdictions

[3] https://www.health.act.gov.au/news/visitor-restrictions

[4] https://www.yoganatal.com.au/nurturing-mums-after-birth.html

Chapter 6

[1] The Immigration Restriction Bill, which enacted the White Australia policy, was one of the first substantive pieces of legislation to be introduced to the new Commonwealth Parliament in 1901 (Kendall, 2008).

[2] Objectively, countries that are already experiencing disadvantage are more likely to be worse off. This is apparent in the Global Climate Risk Index produced by Germanwatch, a German NGO that measures North-South Equity and sustainability (see https://www.germanwatch.org/en/19777). According to this index, Australia's climate risk is not extreme, while its overall performance on climate change mitigation is very low. This ranking was awarded by another German NGO, the NewClimate Institute for Climate Policy and Global Sustainability (see https://newclimate.org/2021/11/09/the-climate-change-performance-index-2022/).

[3] See https://www.afr.com/politics/australia-cops-the-brunt-of-global-warming-20210809-p58h6n

Chapter 7

[1] The question as to whether or not there are too many animal individuals is not addressed in this book, but see Haraway (2008; 2018).

[2] 'All new human members of the group who are born in the context of community decision making come into being as symbionts with critters of actively threatened species' (Haraway, 2016: 139–140). Only those born 'through individual reproductive choice' (that is, outside the community's decision-making arrangements) are fully human genetically.

[3] See Schlunke (2016) for a queer, feminist account of the immediate aftermath of losing one's house to bushfire.

[4] https://open.spotify.com/show/6xYiLlNKuOFoU1p99IZRYy

References

ABC News (2020) 'Australia's bushfire smoke spreads to NZ as Canberra's air quality goes off the scale'. Available at: https://www.abc.net.au/news/2020-01-01/smoke-shrouds-australia-as-nsw-bushfires-continue/11835734

Abdo, M., Ward, I., O'Dell, K., Ford, B., Pierce, J.R., Fischer, E.V., and Crooks, J.L. (2019) 'Impact of wildfire smoke on adverse pregnancy outcomes in Colorado, 2007–2015', *International Journal of Environmental Research and Public Health*, 16(19): 2–16.

Adey, P. and Bissell, D. (2010) 'Mobilities, meetings, and futures: an interview with John Urry', *Environment and Planning D: Society and Space*, 28(1): 1–16.

Ahmed, S. (2010) *The Promise of Happiness*. Durham, NC: Duke University Press.

Ahuja, N. (2015) 'Intimate atmospheres: queer theory in a time of extinctions', *GLQ: A Journal of Lesbian and Gay Studies*, 21(2–3): 365–385.

Albrecht, G., Sartore, G.M., Connor, L., Higginbotham, N., Freeman, S. and Kelly, B., et al (2007) 'Solastalgia: the distress caused by environmental change', *Australasian Psychiatry*, 15(S1): S95–S98.

Allen, I.K. (2020) 'Thinking with a feminist political ecology of air-and-breathing-bodies', *Body & Society*, 26(2): 79–105.

Allen, L. (2020) 'Breathing life into sexuality education: becoming sexual subjects', *Philosophical Inquiry in Education*, 27(1): 1–13.

Allen, L., Rasmussen, M.L. and Quinlivan, K. (2014) *The Politics of Pleasure in Sexuality Education*. Abingdon: Routledge.

Allen, L., Roberts, C., Williamson, R. and Rasmussen, M. (in preparation) 'Mothers' agency and responsibility in the Australian bushfires: a new materialist account'.

Allen, P. and Sachs, C. (2012) 'Women and food chains: the gendered politics of food', in P. Williams Forson and C. Counihan (eds) *Taking Food Public: Redefining Foodways in a Changing World*. Abingdon: Routledge, pp 23–40.

Andrew, J., Baker, M., Guthrie, J. and Martin-Sardesai, A. (2020) 'Australia's COVID-19 public budgeting response: the straitjacket of neoliberalism', *Journal of Public Budgeting, Accounting & Financial Management*, 32(5): 759–770.

Anthony, T. (2020) '"I can't breathe!" Australia must look in the mirror to see our own deaths in custody', *The Conversation*, 2 June. Available at: https://theconversation.com/i-cant-breathe-australia-must-look-in-the-mirror-to-see-our-own-deaths-in-custody-139848

Aoki, P.M., Honicky, R.J., Mainwaring, A., Myers, C., Paulos, E., Subramanian, S. and Woodruff, A. (2008) 'Common sense: Mobile environmental sensing platforms to support community action and citizen science', in *Adjunct Proceedings of the Tenth International Conference on Ubiquitous Computing*: pp 59–60.

Australian Bureau of Statistics (2016) *Australian Bureau of Statistics (ABS). (2016) 2016 Census QuickStats*. Canberra: Australian Bureau of Statistics. Available at https://www.abs.gov.au/statistics

Australian Institute of Health and Welfare (AIHW) (2020) *Australian Bushfires 2019–2020: Exploring the Short-Term Health Impacts*. Cat. no. PHE 276. Canberra: AIHW. Available at: https://www.aihw.gov.au/getmedia/a14c3 205-784c-4d81-ab49-a33ed4d3d813/aihw-phe-27 6.pdf.aspx?inline=true

Australian Medical Association (2020) 'New health threats from escalating bushfire crisis'. Press release, 3 January. Available at: ama.com.au/media/new-health-threats-escalating-bushfire-crisis

Avakian, A.V. and Haber, B. (2005) 'Feminist food studies: a brief history', in A.V. Avakian and B. Haber (eds) *From Betty Crocker to Feminist Food Studies: Critical Perspectives on Women and Food*. Amherst: University of Massachusetts Press, pp 1–28.

Basilio, E., Chen, R., Fernandez, A.C., Padula, A.M., Robinson, J.F. and Gaw, S.L. (2022) 'Wildfire smoke exposure during pregnancy: a review of potential mechanisms of placental toxicity, impact on obstetric outcomes, and strategies to reduce exposure', *International Journal of Environmental Research and Public Health*, 19(21): 1-29.

Barad, K. (2003) 'Posthumanist performativity: toward an understanding of how matter comes to matter', *Signs: Journal of Women in Culture and Society*, 28(3): 801–831.

Barad, K. (2007) *Meeting the Universe Halfway: Quantum Physics and the Entanglement of Matter and Meaning*. Durham, NC: Duke University Press.

Bashford, A. and Strange, C. (2004) 'Public pedagogy: sex education and mass communication in the mid-twentieth century', *Journal of the History of Sexuality*, 13(1): 71–99.

Beck, U. (1992) 'Modern society as a risk society', in N. Stehr and R.V. Ericson (eds) *The Culture and Power of Knowledge: Inquiries into Contemporary Societies*. New York: De Gruyter, pp 199–214.

Beck, U. (1996) 'Risk society and the provident state', in S. Lash, B. Szerszynski and B. Wynne (eds) *Risk, Environment and Modernity: Towards a New Ecology*. London: Sage Publications, pp 29–43.

Benjamin, R. (2018) 'Black afterlives matter: Cultivating kinfulness as reproductive justice', in A.E. Clarke and D. Haraway (eds) *Making Kin Not Population*, Chicago: Prickly Paradigm Press, pp 41–65.

Black, C. et al (2017) 'Wildfire smoke exposure and human health: significant gaps in research for a growing public health issue', *Environmental Toxicology and Pharmacology*, 55: 186–195.

Böhlen, M. (2016) 'Field notes in contamination studies', in D. Nafus (ed) *Quantified: Biosensing Technologies in Everyday Life*. Cambridge, MA: MIT Press, pp 169–188.

Bowman, D.M., Williamson, G.J., Gibson, R.K., Bradstock, R.A. and Keenan, R.J. (2021) 'The severity and extent of the Australia 2019–20 Eucalyptus forest fires are not the legacy of forest management', *Nature Ecology & Evolution*, 5: 1003–1010.

Braidotti, R. (2013) *The Posthuman*. Cambridge: Polity Press.

Braschler, B. (2009) 'Successfully implementing a citizen-scientist approach to insect monitoring in a resource-poor country', *BioScience*, 59(2): 103–104.

Brown, A. (2020) 'Canberra air quality: more than a third of all summer days had hazardous air quality', *Canberra Times*, 6 March. Available at: https://www.canberratimes.com.au/story/6665438/just-how-bad-was-the-air-quality-in-canberra-this-summer/

Calvillo, N. (2018) 'Political airs: from monitoring to attuned sensing air pollution', *Social Studies of Science*, 48(3): 372–388.

Calvillo, N. and Garnett, E. (2019) 'Data intimacies: building infrastructures for intensified embodied encounters with air pollution', *Sociological Review*, 67(2): 340–356.

Carrington, D. (2017) 'Want to fight climate change? Have fewer children', *The Guardian*, 12 July. Available at: https://www.theguardian.com/environment/2017/jul/12/want-to-fight-climate-change-have-fewer-children

Carskadon, M.A. and Herz, R.S. (2004) 'Minimal olfactory perception during sleep: why odor alarms will not work for humans', *Sleep*, 27(3): 402–405.

Celermajer, D. (2021) *Summertime: Reflections on a Vanishing Future*. Sydney: Penguin.

Chandler, J. (2021) 'Tales from the frontline: the emotional impact of climate change', *Griffith Review*, 71: 51–71.

Chenery, S. and Cheshire, B. (2020) 'Fighting fire with fire', *ABC Australian Story*, 13 April. Available at: https://www.abc.net.au/news/2020-04-13/how-victor-steffensen-is-fighting-fire-with-fire/1 1866478?nw=0

Choy, T. (2012) 'Air's substantiations', in K.S. Rajan (ed) *Lively Capital*. Durham, NC: Duke University Press, pp 121–152.

Choy, T. (2018) 'Tending to suspension: abstraction and apparatuses of atmospheric attunement in Matsutake worlds', *Social Analysis*, 62(4): 54–77.

Choy, T. (2020) 'A commentary: breathing together now', *Engaging Science, Technology, and Society*, 6: 586–590.

Clare, S. (2019) 'Reimagining biological relatedness: epigenetics and queer kin', *Signs: Journal of Women in Culture and Society*, 45(1): 51–73.

Clark, N. and Yusoff, K. (2018) 'Queer fire: ecology, combustion and pyrosexual desire', *Feminist Review*, 118(1): 7–24.

Clarke, A.E. (2018) 'Introducing *Making Kin Not Population*', in D. Haraway and A.E. Clarke (eds) *Making Kin Not Population*. Chicago: Prickly Paradigm Press, pp 1–39.

Clarke, A.E. and Haraway, D.J. (eds). (2018) *Making Kin Not Population*. Chicago: Prickly Paradigm Press.

Clement, S. and Waitt, G. (2017) 'Walking, mothering and care: a sensory ethnography of journeying on-foot with children in Wollongong, Australia', *Gender, Place & Culture*, 24(8): 1185–1203.

Clifford, H.D., Pearson, G., Franklin, P., Walker, R. and Zosky, G.R. (2015) 'Environmental health challenges in remote Aboriginal Australian communities: clean air, clean water and safe housing', *Australian Indigenous Health Bulletin*, 15(2): unpaginated.

Coffey, J., Cook, J., Farrugia, D., Threadgold, S. and Burke, P.J. (2021) 'Intersecting marginalities: international students' struggles for "survival" in COVID-19', *Gender, Work & Organization*, 28(4): 1337–1351.

Colebrook, C. and Weinstein, J. (2015) 'Introduction: Anthropocene feminisms: rethinking the unthinkable', *Philosophia*, 5(2): 167–178.

Colen, S. (2009) 'Stratified reproduction and West Indian childcare workers and employers in New York', in E. Lewin (ed) *Feminist Anthropology: A Reader*. Malden, MA and Oxford: Blackwell Publishing, pp 380–396.

Convery, I. and Bailey, C. (2008) 'After the flood: the health and social consequences of the 2005 Carlisle flood event', *Journal of Flood Risk Management*, 1(2): 100–109.

Crighton, E.J., Brown, C., Baxter, J., Lemyre, L., Masuda, J.R. and Ursitti, F. (2013) 'Perceptions and experiences of environmental health risks among new mothers: a qualitative study in Ontario, Canada', *Health, Risk & Society*, 15(4): 295–312.

Dahl, U. and Gunnarsson Payne, J. (2014) 'Introduction: (re)thinking queer kinship and reproduction', *Lambda Nordica: Tidskrift om homosexualitet*, 3–4: 11–27.

De la Bellacasa, M.P. (2017) *Matters of Care: Speculative Ethics in More Than Human Worlds*. Minneapolis: University of Minnesota Press.

Dennis, S. (2015) 'Explicating the air: the new smokefree (and beyond)', *Australian Journal of Anthropology*, 26(2): 196–210.

Dennis, S. (2018) 'Becoming enwinded: a new materialist take on smoking pleasure', *International Journal of Drug Policy*, 51: 69–74.

Dennis, S. and Musharbash, Y. (2018) 'Anthropology and smoke: editors' introduction to the Smoke Special Issue', *Anthropological Forum*, 28(2): 107–115.

Dow, K. (2016) *Making a Good Life: An Ethnography of Nature, Ethics, and Reproduction*. Princeton: Princeton University Press.

Downey, L. (2005) 'Single mother families and industrial pollution in metropolitan America', *Sociological Spectrum*, 25(6): 651–675.

Duden, B. (1993) *Disembodying Women: Perspectives on Pregnancy and the Unborn*. Cambridge, MA: Harvard University Press.

Dyke, J., Watson, R. and Knorr, W. (2021) 'Climate scientists: concept of net zero is a dangerous trap', *The Conversation*, 22 April. Available at: https://theconversation.com/climate-scientists-concept-of-net-zero-is-a-dangerous-trap-157368

Eng, D.L. (2010) *The Feeling of Kinship: Queer Liberalism and the Racialization of Intimacy*. Durham NC: Duke University Press.

Eriksen, C. (2013a) *Gender and Wildfire: Landscapes of Uncertainty*. Abingdon: Routledge.

Eriksen, C. (2013b) 'Gendered dimensions of Aboriginal Australian and California Indian fire knowledge retention and revival', *Current Conversation*, 7(1): 22–26.

Eriksen, C., Gill, N. and Head, L. (2010) 'The gendered dimensions of bushfire in changing rural landscapes in Australia', *Journal of Rural Studies*, 26(4): 332–342.

Eriksen, C. and Hankins, D.L. (2015) 'Colonisation and fire: gendered dimensions of indigenous fire knowledge retention and revival', in A. Coles, L. Gray and J. Momsen (eds) *The Routledge Handbook of Gender and Development*. Abingdon: Routledge, pp 129–137.

Erikson, K. (1994) *A New Species of Trouble: The Human Experience of Modern Disasters*. New York: Norton.

Fergie, D., Lucas, R. and Harrington, M. (2020) 'Take my breath away: transformations in the practices of relatedness and intimacy through Australia's 2019–2020 convergent crises', *Anthropology in Action*, 27(2): 49–62.

Fong, K. (2018) 'Free divers have long defied science – and we still don't really understand how they go so deep', *The Conversation*, 17 March. Available at: https://theconversation.com/free-divers-have-long-defied-science-and-we-still-dont-really-understand-how-they-go-so-deep-92690

Foucault, M. (2000 [1970]) *The Order of Things: An Archeology of the Human Sciences*. New York: Routledge.

Gabrys, J, Pritchard, H. and Houston, L. (2019) 'Sensors and sensing practices', Special Issue of *Science, Technology and Human Values*, 44(5).

Gammage, B. (2011) 'Fire in 1788: the closest ally', *Australian Historical Studies*, 42(2): 277–288.

Gammage, B. and Pascoe, B. (2021) *Country: Future Fire, Future Farming*. Port Melbourne: Thames & Hudson Australia.

Garnett, E. (2020) 'Breathing spaces: modelling exposure in air pollution science', *Body & Society*, 26(2): 55–78.

Godfree, R.C., Knerr, N., Encinas-Viso, F., Albrecht, D., Bush, D., and Cargill, C., et al (2021) 'Implications of the 2019–20 megafires for the biogeography and conservation of Australian vegetation', *Nature Communications*, 12(1): 1–13.

Górska, M. (2016) *Breathing Matters: Feminist Intersectional Politics of Vulnerability*. Linköping University, Sweden: Linköping Studies in Arts and Science, No. 683.

Górska, M. (2018) 'Feminist politics of breathing', in L. Škof and P. Berndtson (eds) *Atmospheres of Breathing*. Albany: SUNY Press, pp 247–259.

Graham, S. (2015) 'Life support: the political ecology of urban air', *City*, 19(2–3): 192–215.

Griffiths, T. (2020) 'Born in the ice age, humankind now faces the age of fire – and Australia is on the frontline', *The Guardian Australia*, 1 November. Available at: https://www.theguardian.com/austra lia-news/2020/nov/01/born-in-the-ice-age-humankind -now-faces-the-age-of-fire-and-australia-is-on-the-frontline

Hamilton, J.M. (2019) 'The future of housework: the similarities and differences between making kin and making babies', *Australian Feminist Studies*, 34(102): 468–489.

Haraway, D.J. (1988) 'Situated knowledges: the science question in feminism and the privilege of partial perspective', *Feminist Studies*, 14(3): 575–599.

Haraway, D.J., Ishikawa, N., Gilbert, S.F., Olwig, K., Tsing, A.L. and Bubandt, N. (2015) 'Anthropologists are talking – about the Anthropocene', *Ethnos*, 81(3): 535–564.

Haraway, D.J. (2003) *The Companion Species Manifesto: Dogs, People, and Significant Otherness*. Chicago: Prickly Paradigm Press.

Haraway, D.J. (2008) *When Species Meet*. Minneapolis: University of Minnesota.

Haraway, D.J. (2016) *Staying with the Trouble: Making Kin in the Chthulucene*. Durham, NC: Duke University Press.

Haraway, D.J. (2017) 'The biopolitics of postmodern bodies: determinations of self in immune system discourse', in J. Price and M. Shildrick (eds) *Feminist Theory and the Body*. New York: Routledge, pp 203–214.

Haraway, D.J. (2018) 'Making kin in the Chthulucene: reproducing multispecies justice', in A.E. Clarke and D. Haraway (eds) *Making Kin Not Population*. Chicago: Prickly Paradigm Press, pp 67–99.

Harms, A. (2020) 'Fortifying breath in this moment of spray: face masks beyond COVID-19', *Social Anthropology*, 28(2): 277–278.

Hendrixson, A., Ojeda, D., Sasser, J.S., Nadimpally, S., Foley, E.E. and Bhatia, R. (2020) 'Confronting populationism: feminist challenges to population control in an era of climate change', *Gender, Place & Culture*, 27(3): 307–315.

Hester, H. (2018) *Xenofeminism*. Cambridge: Polity Press.

Hitch, G. (2020) 'Bushfire royal commission hears that Black Summer smoke killed nearly 450 people', *ABC News*. Available at: www.abc.net. au/news/2020-05-26/bushfire-royal-commission-hearings-smoke-killed-445-people/12286094

Holstius, D.M., Reid, C.E., Jesdale, B.M. and Morello-Frosch, R. (2012) 'Birth weight following pregnancy during the 2003 Southern California wildfires', *Environmental Health Perspectives*, 120(9): 1340–1345.

Howlett, M. (2022) 'Looking at the "field" through a Zoom lens: methodological reflections on conducting online research during a global pandemic', *Qualitative Research*, 22(3): 387–402.

Hunt, E. (2019) 'BirthStrikers: meet the women who refuse to have children until climate change ends', *The Guardian*. 12 March. Available at: https://www.theguardian.com/lifeandstyle/2019/mar/12/birthstrikers-meet-the-women-who-refuse-to-have-children-until-climate-change-ends

Hutley, N., Dean, A., Hart, N. and Daley, J. (2022). *Uninsurable Nation: Australia's Most Climate-Vulnerable Places*. Sydney: The Climate Council.

Irigaray, L. (2004) *The Age of Breath*. New York: Continuum.

Jones, R. (1969) 'Fire stick farming', *Australian Natural History*, 16: 224–228.

Kendall, T. (2008) *Within China's Orbit: China through the Eyes of the Australian Parliament*. Canberra: Australian Department of Parliamentary Services.

King, S. (2019) 'Cultural burning boasts range of benefits for Indigenous Rangers, families and communities', *National Indigenous Times*, 20 December. Available at: https://nit.com.au/20-12-2019/898/cultural-burning-boasts-range-of-benefits-for-indigenous-rangers-families-and-communities/

Klepac, P., Locatelli, I., Korošec, S., Künzli, N. and Kukec, A. (2018) 'Ambient air pollution and pregnancy outcomes: a comprehensive review and identification of environmental public health challenges', *Environmental Research*, 167: 144–159.

Knowles, S.G. (2021) 'First person: Stephen J. Pyne. Fire management in an age of contagion', *American Scientist*, 109(1): 11–13.

Lal, A., Patel, M., Hunter, A. and Phillips, C. (2021) 'Towards resilient health systems for a more extreme climate: insights from the 2019/20 Australian bushfire season', *International Journal of Wildland Fire*, 30: 1–5.

Lamoreaux, J. (2016) 'What if the environment is a person? Lineages of epigenetic science in a toxic China', *Cultural Anthropology*, 31(2): 188–214.

Landecker, H. (2011) 'Food as exposure: nutritional epigenetics and the new metabolism', *BioSocieties*, 6(2): 167–194.

Lappé, M., Hein, R.J. and Landecker, H. (2019) 'Environmental politics of reproduction', *Annual Review of Anthropology*, 48: 133–150.

Law, J. (2008) 'On sociology and STS', *Sociological Review*, 56(4): 623–649.

Lewis, S. (2019) *Full Surrogacy Now: Feminism Against Family*. London: Verso.

Liboiron, M., Tironi, M. and Calvillo, N. (2018) 'Toxic politics: acting in a permanently polluted world', *Social Studies of Science*, 48(3): 331–349.

Lindén, L. and Lydahl, D. (2021) 'Care in STS', *Nordic Journal of Science and Technology Studies*, 9(1): 3–12.

Liu, X. (2017) 'Air quality index as the stuff of the political', *Australian Feminist Studies*, 32(94): 445–460.

Lopes, A.M., Healy, S., Power, E., Crabtree, L. and Gibson, K. (2018) 'Infrastructures of care: opening up "home" as commons in a hot city', *Human Ecology Review*, 24(2): 41–59.

Luciano, D. and Chen, M.Y. (2015) 'Introduction: Has the queer ever been human?', *GLQ: A Journal of Lesbian and Gay Studies*, 21(2): 183–207.

Ludlow, M. (2021) 'Australia's extreme climate leaves it vulnerable to global warming', *Financial Review*, 10 August. Available at: https://www.afr.com/policy/energy-and-climate/australia-s-extreme-climate-leaves-it-vulnerable-to-global-warming-20210810-p58hir

Lupton, D. (1999) 'Risk and the ontology of pregnant embodiment', in D. Lupton (ed) *Risk and Sociocultural Theory: New Directions and Perspectives*. Cambridge: Cambridge University Press, pp 59–85.

Lupton, D. (2009) '"You feel so responsible": Australian mothers' concepts and experiences related to promoting the health and development of their young children', in H. Zoller and M.J. Dutta (eds) *Emerging Perspectives in Health Communication*. New York: Routledge, pp 123–138.

Lupton, D. (2011) '"The best thing for the baby": mothers' concepts and experiences related to promoting their infants' health and development', *Health, Risk & Society*, 13(7–8): 637–651.

Lupton, D. (2012a) 'Configuring maternal, preborn and infant embodiment', *Sydney Health & Society Group Working Paper* [Preprint]. Available at https://ses.library.usyd.edu.au/handle/2123/8363.

Lupton, D. (2012b) ' "Precious cargo": foetal subjects, risk and reproductive citizenship', *Critical Public Health*, 22(3): 329–340.

Mackendrick, N. (2014) 'More work for mother: chemical body burdens as a maternal responsibility', *Gender & Society*, 28(5): 705–728.

Malpass, A., Dodd, J., Feder, G., Macnaughton, J., Rose, A. and Walker, O., et al (2019) 'Disrupted breath, songlines of breathlessness: an interdisciplinary response', *Medical Humanities*, 45(3): 294–303.

Mamo, L. (2007) *Queering Reproduction*. Durham, NC: Duke University Press.

Mansfield, B. (2017) 'Folded futurity: epigenetic plasticity, temporality, and new thresholds of fetal life', *Science as Culture*, 26(3): 355–379.

Mariana, M., Fletcher, M.-S. and Connor, S. (2022) 'World-first research confirms Australia's forests became catastrophic fire risk after British invasion', *The Conversation*, 15 February. Available at: https://theconversation.com/world-first-research-confirms-australias-forests-became-catastrophic-fire-risk-after-british-invasion-176563

Mariel, P., Khan, M.A. and Meyerhoff, J. (2022) 'Valuing individuals' preferences for air quality improvement: evidence from a discrete choice experiment in South Delhi', *Economic Analysis and Policy*, 74(1–2): 432–447.

Martin, A., Myers, N. and Viseu, A. (2015) 'The politics of care in technoscience', *Social Studies of Science*, 45(5): 625–641.

Mayhew-Bergman, M. (2021) 'Should I have children? Weighing parenthood amid the climate crisis', *The Guardian*, 13 November. Available at: https://www.theguardian.com/lifeandstyle/2021/nov/13/children-parenthood-climate-crisis

Mbembe, A. and Shread, C. (2021) 'The universal right to breathe', *Critical Inquiry*, 47(S2): S58–S62.

McAdam, A. (2019) 'Finding hope in the end: an ecocritical analysis of the voluntary human extinction movement', presented at *Waterlines: Confluence and Hope through Environmental Communication: The Conference on Communication and Environment*, Vancouver. Available at: https://theieca.org/sites/default/files/conference-papers/COCE%202019%20Vancouver/mcadam_angie-finding_hope_in_the_end-1158989417.pdf

McKenna, K., Gould, L. and Lovett, S. (nd) 'Riparian real estate for wildlife guide: Wombat behaviour, burrows and being neighbours', *Rivers of Carbon.org*. Available at: https://riversofcarbon.org.au/wombat-behaviour-burrows-and-being-neighbours

McLean, K.J. (2019) 'Nose-first: practices of smellwalking and smellscape mapping', PhD thesis, Royal College of Art, London.

Mello, S. (2015) 'Media coverage of toxic risks: a content analysis of pediatric environmental health information available to new and expecting mothers', *Health Communication*, 30(12): 1245–1255.

Mills, C. (2017) *Biopolitics*. New York: Routledge.

Minister's Department of Health (2020) 'Number of P2 masks provided for bushfires almost 3.5 million'. Available at: health.gov.au/ministers/the-hon-greg-hunt-mp/media/number-of-p2-masks-provided-for-bushfires-almost-35-million

Mol, A. (2008) *The Logic of Care: Health and the Problem of Patient Choice*. Routledge: New York and London.

Mol, A., Moser, I. and Pols, J. (2010) 'Care: putting practice into theory', in A. Mol, I. Moser and J. Pols (eds) *Care in Practice: On Tinkering in Clinics, Homes and Farms*. Bielefeld: Transcript, pp 7–25.

Moore, J.W. (2017) 'The Capitalocene, Part I: on the nature and origins of our ecological crisis', *Journal of Peasant Studies*, 44(3): 594–630.

Morrison, J. (2020) 'How First Australians' ancient knowledge can help us survive the bushfires of the future', *The Guardian*, 11 January. Available at: https://www.theguardian.com/commentisfree/2020/jan/11/how-first-australians-ancient-knowledge-can-help-us-survive-the-bushfires-of-the-future

Mort, M., Rodriguez-Giralt, I. and Deliciado, A. (eds) (2020) *Children and Young People's Participation in Disaster: Agency and Resilience.* Bristol: Policy Press.

Murphy, M. (2013) 'Distributed reproduction, chemical violence, and latency', *Scholar and Feminist Online*, 11(3): 1–7.

Murphy, M. (2015) 'Unsettling care: troubling transnational itineraries of care in feminist health practices', *Social Studies of Science*, 45(5): 717–737.

Murphy, M. (2016) 'Alterlife in the ongoing aftermaths of chemical exposure'. Available at: https://michellemurphy.net/technoscience-meets-biopolitics/

Murphy, M. (2017) *The Economization of Life.* Durham, NC: Duke University Press.

Murphy, M. (2018) 'Against population, towards alterlife', in D.J. Haraway and A. Clarke (eds) *Making Kin Not Population.* Chicago: Prickly Paradigm Press, pp 101–124.

Murris, K. and Bozalek, V. (2019) 'Diffraction and response-able reading of texts: the relational ontologies of Barad and Deleuze', *International Journal of Qualitative Studies in Education*, 32(7): 872–886.

Nafus, D. (2016) *Quantified: Biosensing Technologies in Everyday Life.* Cambridge, MA: MIT Press.

Nimmo, D.G. (2020) 'Tales of wombat "heroes" have gone viral. Unfortunately, they're not true', *The Conversation*, 15 May. Available at: https://theconversation.com/tales-of-wombat-heroes-have-gone-viral-unfortunately-theyre-not-true-129891

Nowroozi, I. and Alvaro, A. (2020) 'Is breathing smoky air really the same as smoking several cigarettes a week?', *ABC News*, 9 January. Available at: https://www.abc.net.au/news/2020-01-09/is-breathing-in-smoky-air-really-the-same-as-smoking-cigarettes/11853188

O'Donnell, M. (2017) 'Effects of bushfire exposure on prenatal and early life development in humans: a life history perspective', PhD thesis, Australian National University. Available at: https://openresearch-repository.anu.edu.au/bitstream/1885/132117/1/O'Donnell%20Thesis%202017.pdf

O'Donnell, M. and Behie, A. (2013) 'Effects of bushfire stress on birth outcomes: a cohort study of the 2009 Victorian Black Saturday bushfires', *International Journal of Disaster Risk Reduction*, 5: 98–106.

O'Donnell, M.H. and Behie, A.M. (2015) 'Effects of wildfire disaster exposure on male birth weight in an Australian population', *Evolution, Medicine, and Public Health*, 2015(1): 344–354.

Oderberg, I. (2021) 'Air grievances: silence swirls around the toll of bushfire smoke during pregnancy', *The Guardian*, 11 January. Available at: https://www.theguardian.com/lifeandstyle/2021/jan/11/air-grievances-silence-swirls-aroun d-the-toll-of-bushfire-smoke-during-pregnancy

Ojeda, D., Sasser, J. and Lunstrum, E. (2020) 'Malthus's specter and the Anthropocene', *Gender, Place and Culture*, 27(3): 316–332.

Olsen, I. (2019) 'Hundreds join student's climate-change pledge: no kids until Canada takes action', *CBC News*, 17 September. Available at: https://www.cbc.ca/news/canada/montreal/no-future-no-children-pledge-1.5286721

Ottinger, G. (2010) 'Buckets of resistance: standards and the effectiveness of citizen science', *Science, Technology, & Human Values*, 35(2): 244–270.

Ottinger, G. (2016) 'Social movement-based citizen science', in E.B. Kennedy (ed) *The Rightful Place of Science: Citizen Science*. Arizona: Consortium for Science, Policy & Outcomes, Arizona State University, pp 89–103.

Ottinger, G. and Sarantschin, E. (2017) 'Exposing infrastructure: how activists and experts connect ambient air monitoring and environmental health', *Environmental Sociology*, 3(2): 155–165.

Oxley, R. and Russell, A. (2020) 'Interdisciplinary perspectives on breath, body and world', *Body & Society*, 26(2): 3–29.

Pacholok, S. (2013) *Into the Fire: Disaster and the Remaking of Gender*. Toronto: University of Toronto Press.

Parkinson, D. (2019) 'Investigating the increase in domestic violence post disaster: an Australian case study', *Journal of Interpersonal Violence*, 34(11): 2333–2362.

Possamai-Inesedy, A. (2006) 'Confining risk: choice and responsibility in childbirth in a risk society', *Health Sociology Review*, 15(4): 406–414.

Poursafa, P. and Kelishadi, R. (2011) 'What health professionals should know about the health effects of air pollution and climate change on children and pregnant mothers', *Iranian Journal of Nursing and Midwifery Research*, 16(3): 257–264.

Pritchard, H., Gabrys, J. and Houston, L. (2019) 'Breakdown in the smart city: exploring workarounds with urban-sensing practices and technologies', *Science, Technology, and Human Values*, 44(5): 843–870.

Puar, J. K. (2007) *Terrorist Assemblages: Homonationalism in Queer Times*. Durham NC: Duke University Press.

Puig de la Bellacasa, M. (2017) *Matters of Care: Speculative Ethics in More Than Human Worlds*. Minneapolis: University of Minnesota Press.

Pyne, S.J. (1998) 'Forged in fire: history, land, and anthropogenic fire', in W.L. Balée (ed) *Advances in Historical Ecology*, New York: Columbia University Press, pp 64–103.

Pyne, S.J. (2019a) *Fire: A Brief History*. Seattle: University of Washington Press.

Pyne, S.J. (2019b) 'California wildfires signal the arrival of a planetary fire age', *The Conversation*, 2 November. Available at: https://theconversation.com/california-wildfires-signal-the-arrival-of-a-planetary-fire-age-125972

Quince, A. and Phillips, K. (2020) 'The story of fire in the Australian landscape', *ABC RN: Rear Vision*. Available at: https://www.abc.net.au/radionational/programs/rearvision/the-story-of-fire-in-the-australian-

Rabeharisoa, V., Moreira, T. and Akrich, M. (2014) 'Evidence-based activism: patients', users' and activists' groups in knowledge society', *BioSocieties*, 9(2): 111–128.

Rapp, R. (2004) *Testing Women, Testing the Fetus: The Social Impact of Amniocentesis in America*. New York: Routledge.

Richards, J., Atkinson, S. and Macnaughton, J. (2016) 'Breathing and breathlessness in clinic and culture: using critical medical humanities to bridge an epistemic gap', in A. Whitehead and A. Woods (eds) *The Edinburgh Companion to the Critical Medical Humanities*. Edinburgh: Edinburgh University Press, pp 294–309.

Richards, L., Brew, N. and Smith, L. (2020) *20 Australian Bushfires – Frequently Asked Questions: A Quick Guide*. Canberra: Parliament of Australia.

Riggs, D.W., Pfeffer, C.A., Pearce, R., Hines, S. and White, F.R. (2020) 'Men, trans/masculine, and non-binary people negotiating conception: normative resistance and inventive pragmatism', *International Journal of Transgender Health*, 22(1–2): 6–17.

Roberts, C. and Waldby, C. (2021) 'Incipient infertility: tracking eggs and ovulation across the life course', *Catalyst: Feminism, Theory, Technoscience*, 7(1): 1–25.

Roberts, C., Mackenzie, A. and Mort, M. (2019) *Living Data: Making Sense of Health Biosensing*. Bristol: Bristol University Press.

Roberts, C.M. (2007) *Messengers of Sex: Hormones, Biomedicine and Feminism*. Cambridge: Cambridge University Press.

Rose, D.B. (2011) *Wild Dog Dreaming: Love and Extinction*. Charlottesville: University of Virginia Press.

Rosen, R. (2002) *The Yoga of Breath: A Step-by-Step Guide to Pranayama*. Boulder: Shambhala Publications Inc.

Ross, M. and Quince, A. (2020) 'The history of fire in Australia – and how it can help us face the bushfires of the future', *ABC Radio National*. Available at: https://www.abc.net.au/news/2020-02-10/fires-bushfires-in-australia-history-lessons-for-future/11937652

Rowland, M. (ed) (2021) *Black Summer: Stories of Loss, Courage and Community from the 2019–2020 Bushfires*. Sydney: HarperCollins.

Ruhl, L. (1999) 'Liberal governance and prenatal care: risk and regulation in pregnancy', *Economy and Society*, 28(1): 95–117.

Rukaite, K. (2020) 'Reproduction in the (m) Anthropocene: exploring the roots and implications of environmentally friendly restrain from childbearing', unpublished MA thesis, Lund University. Available at https://lup.lub.lu.se/luur/download?func=downloadFile&recordOId=9026329&fileOId=9026331

Salleh, A. (2021) 'COVID-19 is a good reason to fix our bad indoor air quality - but how do we do that?', *ABC News*. 25 November. Available at https://www.abc.net.au/news/health/2021-11-25/covid-indoor-air-vent ilation-air-conditioning-mould-coronavirus/100630782

Salmon, A. (2004) '"It takes a community": constructing Aboriginal mothers and children with FAS/FAE as objects of moral panic in/through a FAS/FAE prevention', *Journal of the Association for Research on Mothering*, 6(1): 112–123.

Salmon, A. (2011) 'Aboriginal mothering, FASD prevention and the contestations of neoliberal citizenship', *Critical Public Health*, 21(2): 165–178.

Sänger, E. (2015) 'Obstetrical care as a matter of time: ultrasound screening, temporality and prevention', *History and Philosophy of the Life Sciences*, 37(1): 105–120.

Sasser, J.S. (2018) *On Infertile Ground: Population Control and Women's Rights in the Era of Climate Change*. New York: New York University Press.

Schlunke, K. (2016) 'Burnt houses and the haunted home: reconfiguring the ruin in Australia', in N. Cook, A. Davison and L. Crabtree (eds) *Housing and Home Unbound: Intersections in Economics, Politics and Environment in Australia*. New York: Routledge, pp 232–245.

Searle, J. (1996) 'Fearing the worst: why do pregnant women feel "at risk"?', *Australian and New Zealand Journal of Obstetrics and Gynaecology*, 36(3): 279–286.

She, J., Liu, L. and Liu, W. (2020) 'COVID-19 epidemic: disease characteristics in children', *Journal of Medical Virology*, 92(7): 747–754.

Silver, L.J. (2020) 'Queering reproductive justice: memories, mistakes, and motivations to transform kinship', *Feminist Anthropology*, 1(2): 217–230.

Sloterdijk, P. (2009) *Terror from the Air*. Cambridge MA: Semiotext.

Smethurst, S. (2020) 'Meet the all-female Indigenous fire crew protecting community, family and sacred land', *Australian Women's Weekly*, 7 January. Available at: https://www.nowtolove.com.au/news/local-news/indigen ous-all-female-fire-crew-australia-62022

Smith, B. (2020) 'Meet the scientist behind CanberraAir.com', *HerCanberra*, 31 January. Available at: https://hercanberra.com.au/life/meet-the-scient ist-behind-canberraair-com/

Steffensen, V. (2020) *Fire Country: How Indigenous Fire Management Could Help Save Australia*. Melbourne: Hardie Grant Travel.

Stephen, M.J. (2021) *Breath Taking: The Power, Fragility, and Future of Our Extraordinary Lungs*. Washington DC: Atlantic Monthly Press.

Strathern, M., Sasser, J.S., Clarke, A., Benjamin, R., Tallbear, K. and Murphy, M., et al (2019) 'Forum on making kin not population: reconceiving generations', *Feminist Studies*, 45(1): 159–172.

Tallbear, K. (2018) 'Making love and relations beyond settler sex and family', in A.E. Clarke and D. Haraway (eds) *Making Kin Not Population*. Chicago: Prickly Paradigm Press, pp 145–164.

Tironi, M. (2018) 'Hypo-interventions: intimate activism in toxic environments', *Social Studies of Science*, 48(3): 438–455.

Tironi, M. and Rodríguez-Giralt, I. (2017) 'Healing, knowing, enduring: care and politics in damaged worlds', *Sociological Review*, 65(S2): 89–109.

Todd, S. (2017) 'Breathing Life into Education: Re-sensing the Educational Subject'. Keynote presented at the PESA Conference: 'Birth, Death and Rebirth: Does Philosophy of Education Need a New Subject?', 1–5 December, Newcastle, Australia.

Tomevska, S. (2021) 'SA cancels elective surgeries, scraps testing for interstate travel, as state records 1,472 new COVID-19 cases', *ABC News*, 29 December. Available at: https://www.abc.net.au/news/2021-12-29/sa-records-1471-new-covid-19-cases/100729810

Tyler, M. and Fairbrother, P. (2018) 'Gender, households, and decision-making for wildfire safety', *Disasters*, 42(4): 697–718.

Unmüßig, J. (2021) 'Ponderings with breathing/breathing with ponderings', *Choreographic Practices*, 12(2): 165–176.

Van Dooren, T. and Rose, D.B. (2012) 'Storied-places in a multispecies city', *Humanimalia*, 3(2): 1–27.

Vannini, P. (ed) (2015) *Non-representational Methodologies: Re-envisioning Research*. New York: Routledge.

Waggoner, M.R. (2013) 'Motherhood preconceived: the emergence of the preconception health and health care initiative', *Journal of Health Politics, Policy and Law*, 38(2): 345–371.

Waggoner, M.R. (2015) 'Cultivating the maternal future: public health and the prepregnant self', *Signs: Journal of Women in Culture and Society*, 40(4): 939–962.

Wainwright, M. (2017) 'Sensing the airs: the cultural context for breathing and breathlessness in Uruguay', *Medical Anthropology*, 36(4): 332–347.

Weir, J.K., Sutton, S. and Catt, G. (2020) 'The theory/practice of disaster justice: learning from indigenous peoples' fire management', in A. Lukasiewicz and C. Baldwin (eds) *Natural Hazards and Disaster Justice*. Singapore: Springer, pp 299–317.

Weir, L. (1996) 'Recent developments in the government of pregnancy', *International Journal of Human Resource Management*, 25(3): 373–392.

Westrupp, E.M., Bennett, C., Berkowitz, T., Youssef, G.J., Toumbourou, J.W., et al (2021) 'Child, parent, and family mental health and functioning in Australia during COVID-19: comparison to pre-pandemic data', *European Child & Adolescent Psychiatry*, 21 August: 1–14.

Whittaker, J., Eriksen, C. and Haynes, K. (2016) 'Gendered responses to the 2009 Black Saturday bushfires in Victoria, Australia', *Geographical Research*, 54(2): 203–215.

Whittle, R., Walker, M., Medd, W. and Mort, M. (2012) 'Flood of emotions: emotional work and long-term disaster recovery', *Emotion, Space and Society*, 5(1): 60–69.

Wigginton, B. and Lee, C. (2013) 'Stigma and hostility towards pregnant smokers: does individuating information reduce the effect?', *Psychology & Health*, 28(8): 862–873.

Williamson, B., Markham, F. and Weir, J. (2020) *Aboriginal Peoples and the Response to the 2019–2020 Bushfires*. Working Paper 134. Canberra: Centre for Aboriginal Economic Policy Research, Australian National University.

Williamson, R., Banwell, C., Calear, A.L., LaBond, C., Leach, L.S. and Olsen, A., et al (2022) '"I didn't feel safe inside": navigating public health advice, housing and living with bushfire smoke', *Critical Public Health*: 1–11.

Wilson, A.N., Sweet, L., Vasilevski, V., Hauck, Y., Wynter, K. and Kuliukas, L., et al (2022) 'Australian women's experiences of receiving maternity care during the COVID-19 pandemic: a cross-sectional national survey', *Birth*, 49(1): 30–39.

Wilson, K. (2019) 'The fire cult', *Overland*, 234: np. Available at: https://overland.org.au/previous-issues/issue-234/featurethe-fire-cult/

World Health Organization (2020) 'Q&A: how is COVID-19 transmitted?' Available at: www.who.int/emergencies/diseases/novel-coronavirus-2019/question-and-answers-hub/q-a-detail/q-a-how-is-covid-19-transmitted?gclid=CjwKCAjwsO_

World Wide Fund for Nature Australia (2020) 'WWF: 3 billion animals impacted by Australia's bushfire crisis'. Available at: https://wwf.panda.org/wwf_news/?364738/3-billion-animals-impacted-by-Australias-bushfi re-crisis

Wynes, S. and Nicholas, K.A. (2017) 'The climate mitigation gap: education and government recommendations miss the most effective individual actions', *Environmental Research Letters*, 12(7): 110.

Index

References to figures and photographs appear in *italic* type; those in **bold** type refer to tables. References to endnotes show both the page number and the note number (188n5).